D0087724

WAR AND THE GOSPEL

WAR AND
THE GOSPEL

by

JEAN LASSERRE

Translated by Oliver Coburn

Foreword by
Very Rev. George F. Macleod,
M.A., D.D.

JAMES CLARKE & CO. LIMITED
33 STORE STREET
LONDON, W.C.1

This translation first published 1962
© James Clarke & Co. Ltd.

Printed in Great Britain by
The Camelot Press Ltd., London and Southampton

PREFACE

THERE is a resistance movement by the clergy.

Asked about Polaris, a minister replied that he had not given it much thought as he was not mechanically minded! A Scottish Presbytery of forty-five ministers had an official conference to hear the non-pacifist case and twenty ministers turned up. At a subsequent official conference to hear the pacifist case nine turned up.

In an English town stamped addressed envelopes went to forty-five full-time religionists, from the Vicar to the Salvation Army Captain, for a reply to an offer that competent exponents on the moral issues of the Bomb would come to speak to Vestry, Woman's Guild or Youth Group. Three envelopes were returned: two requesting a speaker, the third averring that repentance should precede disarmament. The Bishop of the Diocese and the Archbishop of the Province were equally approached. Neither even acknowledged the communication.

There is a resistance movement by the clergy.

In a measure it is meritorious. The clergy are trained to take a world view of issues. They see, more clearly than some young enthusiast for nuclear disarmament, the very grave consequences were the Church to adopt a pacifist position: consequences, in the relation of Church and State, unparalleled for at least twelve hundred years. Men must be sure of their ground who would commit the Church to oppose the State at the point of its greatest expenditure.

But in a measure this resistance movement is meretricious. It appears attractive to 'stand by the ship of State'. No one in a crisis wants to rock the boat. Yet what if the ship founders for lack of the Word from the only institution that can declare it? What if the paralysis be one of mutual international fears? What if the only cure is faith so strong that only the Church's Word is its adequate repository?

The German autocracy was the ultimate cause of Eichmann's unbelievable act; resulting in the death of five million men, women and children in three years. What if our democracy is judged in years to come as the ultimate cause of a more unbelievable act: the death, by one Polaris, of ten million men, women and children in fifteen minutes? What if the Church, from which the democratic ideal seeded, is then recorded to have been silent? Faith alone can now save the State. Faith in non-violence when, short of it, violence may destroy all. 'Crown Him with many crowns, the Lamb upon the Throne': we still sing it regularly. With equal certainty we do not believe it.

Thus is the Church muddled. When one attempts to sort out the muddle, central in the fog one stumbles on a doubt about the nature of progress. Scores of clergy chant: 'I was a pacifist once.' They belonged, that is, to the idealist school that flourished too luxuriant in the days when men spoke of the 'evangelization of the world in our time'. No wonder they reply to no circular when the destruction of the world in our time has become the sober possibility.

It is a cardinal value of this book by Jean Lasserre that it discards either the evangelization or the destruction of our world. The book is biblical throughout. He has felt on his pulses all the shattering dilemmas of our time. In wartime France he knew the attractions of the Resistance, the bankruptcies of the collaborators, and the tragedy of a great nation defeated. But he also knew His Bible, the sure Sovereignty of God and, in it, the Majesty of the Crucified.

Not since G. J. Heering's *The Fall of Christianity* has there appeared, in similar compass, so compendious a statement of the issues involved in accepting the non-violent interpretation of the gospel.

The reformation of John Knox stemmed in part from his courageous condemnation of the 'monstrous regiment of women'. The central moral issue of our time is the 'monstrous regiment of the bomb'. The new reformation for which the whole reformed world waits will stem in major part from a recovery of the doctrine of non-violence as central to the message of the Cross.

A sufficient declaration of its principles is contained in this short but pungent work.

GEORGE F. MACLEOD

CONTENTS

INTRODUCTION: THE QUESTION AT STAKE

NEVER, it seems, has human life been held so cheap as today: abortions, euthanasia, elimination of mental defectives, genocide, gas chambers, and the whole concentration-camp world with its massacres, tortures, inquisitions, liquidation of traitors, A-bombs and H-bombs—and so on indefinitely.

A plane will be sent out, it is true, to save a single person who is dangerously ill; but one plane also kills a hundred thousand people in a single second. Modern science can save, but it also kills at a faster and more frantic rate. Swept along helplessly by uncontrolled technical progress, present-day man is often driven to boast of his own abdication before the murderous forces unleashed in our age, and to justify these forces. Almost all current philosophies and political ideologies have a common denominator: they set little store by the existence, either physical or spiritual, of human beings.[1]

The more clear-sighted among our non-Christian contemporaries declare that man is in danger, and they demand 'respect for the human personality.' But although their emphasis on personality is sincere, their philosophy both the sanest and the nearest to Christianity, most of them on a mere decree from their government are resolved (or resigned?) to surrender completely to the inhumanities of military discipline, and will give themselves up body and soul to the blasphemous massacre of God's creatures.

The Decalogue, in its age-old wisdom, has set out what is involved in loving your neighbour or (if you prefer) in respect for human personality. Modern man is mad indeed if he thinks he can build a civilised world while maintaining his light-hearted attitude to the sixth commandment. I believe the future of humanity turns precisely on whether he takes this commandment seriously or not. If there is one question of life or death, it is our attitude to 'Thou shalt not kill.' The planet's fate depends on this; the Church's fate also.

For it is this question above all by which modern man will finally judge the Church and its witness. Where is its vaunted Good News if it takes part in the slaughter and howls with the wolves? What real significance can Jesus Christ have, if His disciples join in collective hatred and violence so readily, if they too gamble with human life? How can the Church bring a message of hope to men oppressed by their murderous factions, if it seems to sanction these factions and murders with its moral authority? When atheists wax sarcastic against religion, they are basically betraying their contempt for the Christians who preach love and do not practise it. In the past millions of men have left the Church for good because of religious wars and the Inquisition; and today tens of millions are obviously disgusted with Christianity because of the wars which Christians wage. Today more than ever, owing to the horror of modern methods of mass-extermination, the Church's witness turns on the truly crucial question of the sixth commandment.

But alas, instead of letting the Good News be heard as a clarion call amidst a world ravaged by terrors, despairs, hatreds, and violent convulsions, the Church's preaching has a sad and uncertain sound. Before the agonising challenge of 'Thou shalt not kill,' it seems hesitant and equivocating; it drifts on in impotence and resignation. Little wonder, then, if people turn away from it in disillusionment and despair.

Despite all appearances, the masses are longing for a hope which will bring them release; the Church cannot go on disappointing them any longer. Nor can it let its own children be racked by terrible problems of conscience without speaking to them clearly. More than ever Christians are torn between their obedience as children of God, who have received forgiveness and are called on to forgive others, and their obedience as citizens called on to maintain order and justice in this sinful world. From the darkness of this deep inner conflict, they are confronted by a dilemma which seems insoluble: they must deny Christ by taking part in the general slaughter or else deny Him by evading their military duty. Has the Church really nothing to say to them?

There can surely be few tasks of greater importance and urgency than to study this problem of respect for human life, under the inspiration and direction of the Holy Spirit, in the fraternal communion of all those who invoke the name of Jesus Christ and are tormented by the tragic dilemma of whether a Christian should take part in war. In other words, if Christ is preached by a Church which submits to military laws, is He still the Christ of the Scriptures? The pages which follow are intended as a modest contribution to the common search for a true faithfulness to God.[2]

PART I

PRELIMINARIES

TOWARDS A CORRECT STATEMENT OF THE PROBLEM

THE problem under discussion is formidable indeed, and extremely hard to approach with the necessary clarity. It is all too easy to bring in a host of more or less unconscious ideas, emotions, and reactions which have nothing to do with the basic question but may well invalidate all our reasoning from the outset. So it is vital to define the problem in as exact terms as possible. Now, a study of the Bible is the essential basis for any answer to our agonising question; but before entering on such a study, we must eliminate certain non-biblical considerations which are often introduced. Christian theology should start from the Scriptures, not from preconceived ideas.

1. The Question of 'Values'

First of all, then, we must ask whether on the level of human civilisation there are any values to be protected and maintained at all costs because they have an absolute worth in the eyes of God; so that the need to 'defend' them outweighs every other consideration, including the concern to be faithful to God Himself in the methods we use. Could there, in fact, be values more important for Christians to preserve than their humble obedience and faithful witness to the Gospel?

Christianity does, of course, allow us to recognise certain values as true and good. But it must be added at once that they always contain an element of sinfulness; they are never entirely true or absolutely good, because they share the universal corruption of the human race. They are in no way divine hypostases nor post-Christian revelations, but simply stages in human development which can be spoken of before man's Maker without too great shame. For us Christians the concern to respect God's will in our actual conduct, and to bear witness to our Saviour, is obviously of greater importance than the consideration of any values which may deserve defending. As G. Gusdorf puts it,[3] 'to prefer a value, even a genuine one, to the person of Christ, is to be guilty of grave lack of faith; for values are worthless except in the context of Christian obedience.' In other words all immoderate love of human values betrays a latent idolatry. As the Bible reveals to us, they are also terribly relative, and we relapse into sheer paganism if we exalt them into a system or try to use them as a premise for resolving a problem in Christian ethics. To a Christian, human values can only be of secondary importance.

In any case, I do not believe that the history of human society shows certain catastrophic situations where Christians could legitimately consider the Gospel's moral demands as temporarily suspended and virtually unfulfillable during the time of the so-called crisis—so that they would thereby be released from the obligation to conform to such demands in their daily conduct. On the contrary, I believe that the only true crisis began with the Cross, and that this crisis will end only with the Lord's return; that till this time Christians are called to a faithful witness. They could never be absolved from obedience to their Master by any national catastrophe or even the collapse of a civilisation, nor would such things justify their being content with a cheapened version of Christianity. Quite the reverse: it is just at such moments that their love should not 'wax cold.' It is then that each Christian must 'endure unto the end' (Matt. 24:12-13; Luke 12:35-40).

2. Is Mars Dead?

I am always surprised to see how readily most Christians assume the permanent disappearance of certain forms of paganism, as personified by the ancient pagan deities. A glance through Christian literature may discover plentiful references to Mammon, but there is hardly anything about no less formidable gods, such as Bacchus and Venus, Moloch and Mars. Yet these relics of paganism are far from dead, and the mystique of Mars in particular, with its glorification of warrior virtues and exaltation of the hero (brought to its peak by Adolf Hitler), persists today as strongly as ever. Such a mystique is surely not to be found in the Gospel, however; witness the way Jesus, and later Paul, were ready to flee in order to escape from those who wished to kill them.

The terrifying thing here is that our crucial decisions are often dictated by deep-seated and largely unconscious motives, and that we then seek to justify them on a different level and by quite different arguments. It is natural for man to assess his own dignity by his capacity for fighting; he is proud of his combativeness and very ready to see it as the chief sign of his manhood. In itself this powerful instinct is neutral from the Gospel's point of view, because it is a manifestation of the flesh. But obedience to the Gospel certainly does not mean that a man is bound to yield to the combative instinct which will so readily seize, exalt, and galvanise his flesh.

Like all the other pagan deities, Mars strives to enslave men to the deepest inclinations of their flesh, and the war-god's whole art lies in honouring the combative spirit by decking it out in pomp and finery, seducing men's hearts with all manner of tricks and deceptions. For instance, throughout the ages soldiers' uniform and equipment has had a triple function. In the soldiers themselves it induces a mixture of arrogant boldness, instinctive fear, and a collective fatalism which will destroy their individuality. In their neighbours it induces a 'healthy respect' (as it is often called), which leads to ready submission. Thirdly, it induces an admiration among women which can only heighten the soldier's own conviction that he is a hero. Thus does Mars succeed, with his glittering panoply, in drawing men into his vile work.

Oh, yes, he is a cunning god, who can charm his victims the better to capture them. He dulls their wits by his solemn processions, but sharpens their emotions and their griefs by rekindling in them the flame of memory. He makes men drunk, sets them shuddering with mystical dread and ecstasy; they are literally possessed by him. Within a few seconds his clarion call snatches them out of their family traditions, their personal opinions, their religious or political faiths, fusing them together in a common fever of mass exaltation which first galvanises them, then leaves them breathless and fuddled. This pagan god has suddenly transported them into another world, has made them thrill with a new life, wild and glorious, which they will remember nostalgically. Like Venus, Bacchus, Mammon, and all the other pagan powers, Mars makes men lose themselves in something greater than themselves; and to this overwhelming force they will remain in more or less willing bondage.

This is presumably why men are so pleased to dwell on their memories of the services and wartime adventures—except for the very grimmest of these. Such memories are by no means always unpleasant; there is the pleasure of emancipation from traditional moral obligations, the strange amoral freedom Mars offers to the men and women who (by merely being 'called up') have come into his power. All the profiteers, from armament manufacturers to looters of corpses, are secretly glad of the good business which is promised them. No, Mars is a deity with a wide appeal.

But that is not the full extent of his cunning. By honouring holocausts in the name of freedom, by a mystique of shedding blood on battlefields for noble causes, he even persuades men that they are profoundly right to indulge their combative instinct. He makes them proud of their bondage to the flesh, and actually find in it their self-justification. Bacchus, Venus, Mammon do just the same; and this too is a common basis for all such aspects of paganism. Indeed Mars not only mobilises whole populations and carries them with him in his whirlwind progress; but those three other gods ride ever in his train. Everything must feed his consuming fire, and there is nothing he cannot use to heighten his triumph: courage and cowardice, loyalty and treachery, the joys of conquest and the pangs of terror, the purest love and the basest prostitution, splendid self-sacrifice and sordid private interests, truth and lies, pity and hatred, religion and atheism. In his irresistible wake he sweeps along the whole of humanity, leaving no one unscathed; no one except Jesus Christ.

For, like all the others, this pagan deity is overcome by the Crucified, whose resurrection gives the lie to fatalistic despair. Jesus quietly says no to Mars.

But the war-god is not at a loss. He hides for a while, puts on a skilful disguise, and penetrates into the Church of Christ. Christians go on chanting their Saviour's praises and victory without realising that their hearts have already been delivered up unresisting to the domination of omnipotent Mars. They sincerely love Christ, but in their churches and cathedrals stand the names of those who have given their lives for their country. They glorify Christ, but are flattered when their sanctuaries are adorned with ex-servicemen's flags. They preach Christ, but exalt the greatness of their country and the nobility of its heroic defenders. They teach love of one's neighbour, but enjoin military service. They say you cannot serve God and Mammon, but they themselves serve God and Mars. Mars laughs quietly, sure of his triumph—from which Mammon too will emerge not without profit. Mars knows he can rely on Christians' passive obedience when D-Day comes, and he despises the puny sovereignty of Christ, knowing that Christ's so-called disciples have already bowed the knee before him, Mars.

Can the pagan war-god, in whose world all is fatalism, really be reconciled with Jesus, who challenges all forms of fatalism? 'The most unanswerable charge which can be made against the military system,' writes Henri Roser,[4] 'is not that it may some day bring you to kill your fellow-men, terrible though that is; but that it introduces you into the closed circle of a completely pagan world, a world impervious to grace because it has first declared such grace inoperative or even non-existent.'

When Christians approach the problem of war, they must surely examine themselves loyally and thoroughly, to see they do not take for God's word what is only a suggestion from Mars—highly suspect because highly pagan. For 'the flesh lusteth against the Spirit, and the Spirit against the flesh: and these are contrary the one to the other' (Gal. 5:17).

3. The Cult of the City

There is another virus which has penetrated quite as deeply into the body of the Church, and that is the Roman conception of the City. The whole philosophy of ancient Rome, its religious beliefs and its marvellous system of law, were based on the fundamental principle that the City must be served first, that all other allegiance men owed should be subordinated to the service of what today we call 'our country'. The grandeur of such a conception is undeniable, and many of its fruits have had an enduring nobility.

This religion of the City—the State—is generally the common denominator among a country's inhabitants, ground on which they will unite solidly despite their differences of race, religion, education, wealth, and power. Mars understands that very well, and brandishes this idol on high; he sees everybody prostrate themselves before it, then tames it to his own advantage. But an idol it remains: for if the City's good becomes the criterion of good and evil, if the City is the supreme reality to which men must sacrifice themselves entirely, then it has taken the place of God.

Alas, from the time of Constantine, this aspect of paganism has also found its way into the Christian religion. Christianity's intoxication was so complete that even the Reformers did not succeed in shaking it off, and today only the theologians round Karl Barth try to use the Christian revelation for an assessment of the juridical order; the attempt is still in its infancy. But the oecumenical Church recognises that 'our essential fault is that we have failed in absolute obedience and self-consecration to God; this has been due, and still is, to the insidious influence of individual and collective selfishness, which makes us confuse our own will with God's, and profane

Christ's name by invoking His authority on behalf of prejudices and plans which are only too human.'[5]

4. Ends and Means

Before tackling so delicate a problem as that of war, it is essential to consider the fundamental question of ends and means.

There is an article by Roland de Pury with some masterly pages on this subject: 'If Jesus truly rose from the dead . . . and if the Crucified and the Resurrected are one and the same . . . that signifies that the End is one and the same as the means. The End is only the product of the means, the harvest of the means sown. What a man sows, says Paul, that shall he reap. Far from bad means being justified by their ends, it is they which corrupt the ends. For the end is formed by the means, as a lake is formed by the rivers flowing into it. Poisoned rivers make a poisoned lake. Evil flows on its infernal course, and there is no possible branch stream on the way, nor can evil ever be put to the service of good. Injustice will never issue in justice, nor falsehood in truth.'[6]

'Identity of the end and the means,' he declares further on, 'such is the foundation of our attitude in this world.' And he pronounces the terrible judgment: 'If during its history the Church has claimed to be following God's end by Satan's means, then without any possible doubt it was no longer at that moment the Church of Christ but had denied its Lord.'

So far, I agree entirely with the content of the article; and I cannot help thinking that de Pury's own words must almost have driven him to an outright condemnation of war. Certainly he has been careful to avoid using the word 'violence', and he does not say: 'War will never issue in peace, nor violence in justice.' Yet he has apparently sensed that his thought implied this, and that anyone who followed his reasoning would be bound to conclude: 'Therefore, a Christian cannot fight.'

But de Pury rejects such a conclusion; and in the last three pages of his article, to avoid so dangerous a plunge, he does a real 'Christiania turn', tersely declaring: 'God's means do not consist in our all letting ourselves be slaughtered.'

This seems somewhat lacking in respect towards Christian martyrs, and he is also too ready to ridicule Tolstoy, however right he is that Tolstoy should not be confused with the Gospel. Nevertheless, to use his own metaphor, his thought seems to have branched off abruptly and inexplicably into quite a different stream. Till this point he has opposed means which fit their ends to means which do not; but now he slips into an altogether different antinomy, suddenly opposing justice and mercy—as if the sole difficulty were in reconciling the claims of these two. Astonishingly, he fails to see that in exercising mercy *and* in exercising justice there is always the separate problem of means and ends. 'Sometimes the means of justice demand the use of force . . . and a certain element of violence . . . with all the obligations which that implies.' When our friend makes such an assertion, he is missing the core of the problem, which is whether murderous violence can really lead to justice and peace: he has retreated before the logical issue to his argument.

But let us hold to his affirmation in this notable article that for a Christian the end never justifies the means. Charles Westphal has written that the Church must recall this fact uncompromisingly, and that 'such a refusal to compromise is perhaps the most distinctive and irreplaceable function of the Christian in political life.'[7] But should the Christian recall it in his words alone, or by his acts as well?

5. *The Criterion of Effectiveness*

There is another important question, akin to the preceding one: can effectiveness be an ethical criterion?

Most people, when discussing the rightness or otherwise of war, at once take their stand on the terrain of effectiveness, even before they have decided on the rightness of the end to be pursued or the means to be employed. They instinctively reject any solution they do not think effective; but effective to what end? They believe they know this, but would be in difficulties if asked to justify clearly and cogently both the end and the means they have adopted. That is why arguments about war are so often confused and disheartening.

The trouble comes precisely from considering effectiveness before fidelity to the Gospel. If we were studying problems of sexual morality or financial honesty, and tried to resolve them from the standpoint of effectiveness before thinking about being faithful to God, the results would plainly be disastrous. Why should things be any different with the problem of war?

To me it seems indisputable that questions of effectiveness are secondary and should be considered wholly within the framework of faithfulness to our Saviour. 'I always try to see first what is lawful,' declared Galvin, 'and only after that what is possible.'[8] The concern for effectiveness can, of course, and even should, influence the form of our obedience; but it cannot on its own be the determining motive in our decision, nor can it ever give an ethical content to our action. We must first see clearly what end is to be attained, then try to discover what means will allow us to reach it—and means, let me repeat, which must be in harmony with the end. Only then shall we choose among these means the ones which appear to us most effective.

'But the Christian shouldn't be a yogi.' I would reply to such an objection that he certainly shouldn't be a commissar; and that when we look at yogis or at Gandhi, we can see by contrast how much our 'Christian civilisation' is saturated with this religion of effectiveness, which has absolutely nothing in common with the Gospel. In fact neither the prophets, nor Christ, nor the apostles knew anything about the reign of effectiveness.[9]

Not a single one of their moral exhortations is founded on regard for effectiveness *as a moral criterion*. Quite the reverse: the whole of the Gospel denies this Western dogma. If the men of the Bible were to return to earth now, they would be completely stupefied at the idea that an act can be *ethically founded* on such a preoccupation, that a Christian can take an important decision with this as his sole concern. They would doubtless fail to understand why we persist in giving the name 'Christian' to a civilisation for which the essential criteria are utility and efficiency.[10]   At any rate our era is really the era of pragmatism, with all the inhumanity that can imply.

Perhaps I shall be accused of having widened the area of discussion. But it is surely obvious that the way we consider the problem of war depends entirely on the attitude we take towards this corruption of Christianity by the cult of effectiveness.

Let us now listen to the Word.

PART II

THE COMMANDMENT OF LOVE

Anyone who takes his stand on the New Testament will find there a most urgent call to firm kindness, to compassion without weakness, to forgiveness: in a word, to love. The Gospel makes no qualifications on this subject: Christ calls us to love our neighbour as ourselves, as He has loved us, unconditionally. 'Whatsoever ye would that men should do to you, do ye even so to them' (Matt. 7:12). It would seem obvious that this love excludes the murder of one's neighbour, whether it is a question of individual murder or the general killing represented by war. Let us start then by examining this first proposition.

THE TEACHING OF CHRIST AND THE APOSTLES

FIRST of all, why do I take up my position on the ground of the New Testament? Has the Old Testament nothing to tell us on the love of our neighbour? Certainly it has. But it cannot be disputed that Jesus came to inaugurate a new system relative to the old Covenant. He summed up the law of the Kingdom of God 'which is come nigh unto you' (Luke 10:9) in the summary of the Law (Matt. 12:36-40), which is certainly taken from the Old Testament; but he gave these two precepts a meaning and scope which were completely new (Matt. 5:17): it is in Him that the believer will now be able to love God with all his heart, because 'the Son of Man is come to seek and to save that which was lost' (Luke 19:10), because He 'came not to be ministered unto but to minister, and to give His life a ransom for many' (Mark 10:45), and because His blood, the blood of the new Covenant, has been poured out (Luke 22:20) for the reconciliation of men with their heavenly Father (I Cor. 1:30). Love of one's neighbour, on the other hand, which is the law and witness of the redeemed of Christ (John 13:35), takes on a new value through His person, because we cannot love except in so far as we are united to Jesus by a living faith (John 15). This is why He can declare so strongly: 'A new commandment I give unto you, that ye love one another' (John 13:34), why He can proclaim with authority: 'Ye have heard that it was said to them of old time, thou shalt not kill . . . but I say unto you, that whosoever is angry with his brother . . .' (Matt. 5:21); 'Ye have heard that it was said, Thou shalt love thy neighbour and hate thine enemy; but I say unto you, Love your enemies . . .' (Matt. 5:43). So it is certainly in the light of the New Testament ethic that we must seek an answer to our question.[11]

The Old Testament can illuminate the New, it cannot contradict it or challenge it. 'Moses,' wrote Luther, 'has no longer either value or authority in the New Testament.' The Old Testament is normative for us Christians only in so far as it supports a Christological interpretation; it cannot be normative directly, without intermediary of the Gospel of the Cross. For it speaks to us of Jesus Christ, not of morality. So we must begin by looking for answers in the New Testament.

1. Loving Your Neighbour

What does it mean to love your neighbour? Jesus has explicitly replied to this question in the parable of the Good Samaritan (Luke 10:29). To love my neighbour is to come to his aid, to give him what he may have need of, to forgive him for what he is and what he has done; it is to put myself at his service (John 13:15; Gal. 5:13). It is to be really there for him, to bear his burdens (Gal. 6:2), to respect his calling and help him to realise it. In a word, it is to give myself to him (I John 3:16), as Jesus gave Himself to me. But it is not a matter of sentiment; it is a concrete attitude which expresses itself in acts (I John 3:18). That is why Jesus confirmed the Ten Commandments of Sinai (Matt. 5:17-19; Mark 10:19), which with their rigorous precision preserve us from vagueness, illuminism, and arbitrary judgments. He alone has truly observed them; it is only through Him, through faith in Him, that I can respect them myself. He has given them to us as precious life-lines, since we are not angels who would need only the formula: 'Love God and do what you like.' So Jesus confirms for me that to love my neighbour means to respect his authority, his goods, his home, his reputation—and his life (Gal. 5:14). It means far more, but in any case that.

So one cannot kill with love. Murder of any kind can never be anything but a refusal to love: it is the opposite of forgiveness. One cannot kill while remaining in Christ's communion (John 15:10; I John 2:4; 3:12, 15; 4:8, 20), any more than one can remain in it while stealing, slandering, or deceiving one's wife.

Henry Bois, however, has maintained that it is possible to love the person you are killing. 'Physical death,' he explains,[12] 'has not in the thought of Jesus Christ the importance which certain of his disciples have often attributed to it. . . .' In Bois' judgment, 'there is something more prejudicial to an individual than dying, and that is committing a sin or making others commit it.'[13] Surely such language has a smack of the Inquisition? He then quotes Mark 9:42, and concludes that 'it is perfectly possible to hang a great millstone round the neck of such a sinner and cast him into the sea, and to act in this way from love, if it is to prevent him from committing a heinous crime. Love for him, and not only for the victim I am saving. Yes, I can resist the evil-doer from love, and resist him by fire and the sword, with terrible severity. I can kill my enemy without hating him, not only without hating him, but actually loving him. . . .' 'Yes, according to Jesus' precept, we must love our enemies, and pray for them. Loving and praying are not absolutely incompatible with injuring or killing, because injuring and killing are external acts which can be dissociated from emotions of hatred and revenge. . . . It is the intention which gives the act its value. . . .' 'Even when a soldier is shooting at the enemy, he must do so in an attitude of benevolence and justice. . . .'

I find such a way of arguing outrageous. These distinctions between physical death and the death of the soul, between external acts and emotions, are contradicted by the whole of the Scriptures, which underline the bond uniting body and soul (e.g. Matt. 15:19). As to the text, 'It were better for him that . . . he were cast into the sea,' it leaps to the eye that Bois is completely misusing it. Jesus is merely describing the guilty person's objective situation in God's eyes, by no manner of means recommending his disciples to carry out such a judgment themselves! Many of His words could be quoted, in fact, as excluding the possibility of such a deduction (Luke 9:55-56; Matt. 13:29; John 8:7). Finally, Bois' mistake is to see in love essentially an emotion independent of the acts which condition it or express it.

To refuse the monstrous theory of 'killing with love', I cannot do better here than quote F. J. Leenhardt, who has devoted several pertinent and illuminating pages to the definition of Christian love. Discussing the two fundamental verses, 'Thou shalt love thy neighbour as thyself,' and 'Whatsoever ye would that men do unto you, do ye even so to them,' he writes:[14] 'Love of oneself is the most concrete and precise reality. . . . Whatever each one of us considers useful, desirable, necessary, urgent, pressing, where he is concerned himself, he is enjoined to realise that it is all those things equally for his neighbour as well. . . . I must measure my action to what I would expect from him if I were he and he were I. . . . To love your neighbour as yourself is to feel that his rights impose a duty on you. . . . Too often among Christians, brotherly love has lacked solidity and substance. Too often it has been ineffective because uninformed by a knowledge of these rights of our neighbour which must be satisfied. . . . You fall into romanticism, and the uncertainties of a generous improvisation, when you deprive Christian love of the substance given it by knowledge of the rights of your neighbour. . . . Love of your neighbour is also the movement of the heart which overcomes all the obstacles separating and estranging man from man.'

This is far indeed from Bois' line of argument. To claim that one can kill with love is to forget what these two words 'kill' and 'love' really mean. It is also to forget that the Ten Commandments were given us precisely so that we should know what it means to love our neighbour.

Perhaps I shall be reminded of that strange anecdote about a Christian in the Resistance who was charged with the duty of executing a man condemned to death, and who would not shoot till he had preached the Gospel to the man and prayed with him. It is scarcely a convincing story, and it also leaves a nasty taste in the mouth: it is reminiscent of the so-called Christian who periodically resorted to a prostitute after having carefully preached the Gospel to her and got her to say she was converted. In both cases there is a staggering incongruity between word and act. In both cases, too, the man is saying: 'the Gospel is good for you, but not for me.' Nor am I sure that the need impelling the former was so different from that impelling the latter: in both cases it was a need arising from the flesh and not the Spirit. In both cases that need was decided after an arbitrary human judgment, and in both cases it was a very relative need! One might also say that the anecdote really underlines how impossible it is for a Christian to make war—since in the vast majority of cases he has no chance to 'justify himself' by preaching the Gospel to those he kills.

Should anyone object that I am comparing murder and adultery too often, I would reply that I happen to take the Decalogue seriously, and that I find it salutary to look at the seventh commandment as a method of checking the validity of interpretations given to the sixth.

Moreover, H. Bois is setting his mind at rest too easily, I feel, when he writes that although it may be hard to kill with love, one can in any case kill without hate. For here is something I find most disturbing of all, in fact horrifying. Here is a result of technological advance which is scarcely a sign of moral progress. The slaughters of the Old Testament, the massacres of Vassy or St. Bartholomew, the bayonet charges of 1917, could be carried out only by men who had first been infused with a burning hatred against those who had to be exterminated. But the last traces of humanity in these men were to be found in this hatred. If the man in the artillery or air force today kills without hate, it is because he is completely dehumanised. In other days only the executioner used to kill without hate; but just for that reason he was a man apart, dreaded as a literally abnormal person from whom you kept away. In that he was like the prostitute; for it is basically quite as abnormal to kill without hate as to give yourself without love. Today almost all soldiers are executioners; human beings are killed in exactly the same way as rats are exterminated, coldly, without hate, without the executioner feeling any emotion. Not seeing the men he is killing, it is hard for him to see human beings in them; and therein lies his own dehumanisation.

In our day hundreds of men and women are first undressed—for even a dirty, torn, and lousy garment is worth more than a human being—and then crammed together in a building. Someone turns on a tap somewhere, releasing a gas which will liquidate them all in a few seconds: all that is done without hate or anger. It is a terrifying parody of the Sermon on the Mount: 'Ye have heard that it was said to them of old time, Thou shalt not kill . . . but I say unto you, that whosoever is angry with his brother shall be in danger of the judgment . . .'—so that Jesus would have sanctioned killing provided it was done without anger and without hatred! By this reckoning the torturers of Auschwitz and Ravensbrück, the men who dropped the bombs on Hiroshima and Nagasaki, were models of Christian morality.

But someone may remind me that 'death is not the worst thing that can happen to a person; far worse is the loss of his soul'—and object that I am according too much importance to the physical life of those we are likely to kill in war; as if I were obsessed exclusively with the need to save the body from death. To such an objection I would make several replies. First, my major concern is to be faithful to Jesus Christ. I have always considered that the whole testimony of the Bible constrained me to consider life, a human being's physical life, as a blessing in itself, because it is the unique occasion for this creature of God's to hear the call of his Creator and to respond to it, to receive by faith the Son of God's forgiveness and salvation, and to glorify the Father by the obedience which the Holy Spirit wishes to bring about in his day-to-day existence. 'What is the principal aim of human life?' asks Calvin at the beginning of his catechism; and replies: 'To know God.' The life of each human being has an inestimable price in God's eyes because Jesus Christ died for this man as well, so that he might know God. So it is impossible for a Christian to consider human life without remembering the price it has in God's eyes.[15]

Then again, God alone creates life. We can only transmit it. He alone is the master of life and death. Is it not man's characteristic sin to usurp the right to destroy the life given by God, and with it the potentialities God has put into it? Is it not here above all that man tries to take God's place. Is it not just in the field of the sixth commandment that man, in his relations with his neighbour, claims most brazenly to turn himself into God?

Thirdly, by participating in the war machine, I am not only afraid of causing my neighbour's death, but far more the death I shall bring on myself by my disobedience. To return to the actual words of the objection I have imagined, I would say most forcibly: in war, death is not the worst thing that can happen to *me*, but the loss of my soul. Shall I not be causing this by taking part in war—and perhaps the loss of my neighbour's soul into the bargain, because he will be led to blaspheme the name of Jesus Christ through my denial of Him? The real problem, in fact, remains very limited and precise: by killing my brother, am I not clearly showing that I do not believe Jesus is my Saviour or my brother's Saviour? Does not my presence in the armed forces signify that I have denied Jesus Christ, have cast myself off from Him?

Fourthly, if this objection means anything, it is this: better for my enemy (by definition, of course, the wicked aggressor) that I put him to death rather than let him go on perpetrating his crime. Both of us are therefore doing exactly the same thing; we are both obeying the government which has mobilised us to defend our country and our liberty; but he is a criminal, while I am both innocent and also conferring a benefit on him! Better for him that his body should be destroyed, so that presumably his soul be *ipso facto* saved! Why saved? Because I shall have stopped him carrying out the very crime I am committing against him. This is surely the most obvious sophistry, for my enemy could reason exactly the same way about me, But even allowing that I alone have the right to reason like this, what are we to think of this idea that it is better to kill someone than let him sin? Were the Inquisitors right by any chance? Did Calvin do well to have Servetus burned? And if, to save their souls, all who sin should be killed, who will be left alive anywhere? Where is the Good News in all this?

Frankly, I do not like such light-hearted disregard for human lives, other people's lives. For instance, certain Christian Churches carry their concern that human life be absolutely respected to the point of forbidding a Christian doctor to perform an abortion which will save the life of a future mother; yet they will authorise a Christian in the Air Force to drop a bomb exterminating thousands of human beings who ask only to live. The flagrant contradiction between these two attitudes is an outrage not only to the intelligence, but above all to their faith.

Why does Christ call us to love our neighbour unconditionally? Because in this way we can thank God for the salvation He has given us. In this way we can show that we have grasped it by faith. For faith without works is dead (James 2:14-26). Love of our neighbour is the recognition of our faith (I Tim. 1:5.) Anyone who has discovered that God so loved him that He gave His only Son for him cannot do otherwise than love God in return, and in consequence love his neighbour (John 15:12; Romans 15:7; I John 4:11). Anyone who has been forgiven cannot himself refuse forgiveness to others (II Cor. 2:10-11; Col. 3:13). Anyone who has been saved cannot but bear witness of this salvation to others (Matt. 5:16; Mark 5:19; 1 Peter 2:12). The whole Gospel strongly insists on the indissoluble link between the two commandments in the Summary of the law: you cannot love God without loving your neighbour (I John 2:9-11; 3:10; 4:21). 'By this we know that we love the children of God, when we love God and keep his commandments' (I John 5:2). There seems little need to press the point further.

To stress that love of God and of our neighbour are a unity, Jesus has reminded us that we love Him in the person of our neighbour: 'Inasmuch as ye did it unto one of the least of my brethren, ye did it unto me' (Matt. 25:40); see also Matt. 10:40; Luke 10:16; Acts 9:5; I Cor. 8:12. To kill my neighbour is thus to cast myself off twice from Christ Himself, both subjectively and objectively, as it were: for when I kill, my personal attitude takes me away from His communion; and the person I kill is Jesus again. For all our hair-splitting and fine distinctions, we shall never drown the cry of Christ: 'When you kill your brethren, you kill me. When you take part in war, you crucify me.'

The obedience of our faith is the fruit of the Holy Spirit in us. But the Holy Spirit cannot contradict the Scriptures (II Tim. 3:16; Acts 17:11), or we are in the realm of illuminism and have left the Christian faith behind. The Scriptures are quite categorical: besides all the texts I have quoted, they specify that the fruit of the Spirit is kindness, gentleness, compassion, peace, love. (Gal. 5:22; Col. 3:12 & Titus 3:2); whereas bitterness, anger, strife, seditions, murders, anger are castigated as the work of the flesh (Gal. 5:20; Eph.

4:31; Rom. 1:29; 13:13; I Cor. 3:3; Col. 3:8; I Tim. 1:9). Everything that is not the product of the faith is sin, the apostle insists (Rom. 14:23); and who will dare say that his faith impels him to kill, under the inspiration of the Spirit? The whole New Testament proclaims that such language is impossible, nay blasphemous.

2. Loving Your Enemies

I dare say I shall be told that all this is theoretically true, but that we live in a cruel world where our very existence is threatened by implacable enemies, and that the Gospel does not expect us to be so far in the clouds that we refuse to defend ourselves. We must take care here not to substitute a human wisdom for the wisdom of Christ. For after all were Jesus and the apostles living in a world less cruel than ours? The New Testament is surely full of this admittedly tragic problem: what should be the Christian's attitude towards his enemies?

According to the Gospel, to love your neighbour is also and more particularly to love your enemies: we should know this already from the parable of the Good Samaritan. But Jesus expressly commands us: 'Love your enemies,[16] bless them that curse you, pray for them that persecute you' (Matt. 5:44; Luke 6:27-28; Rom. 12:14). 'For if ye love them that love you, what do ye more than others?' (Matt. 5:45-48; Luke 6:31-36). When evil men do grave harm to us by word or deed, Jesus asks us to forgive them (Matt. 6:14-15; 18:35; Mark 11:25), over and over again (Matt. 18:21-22). 'Ye have heard that it was said: an eye for an eye and a tooth for a tooth; but I say unto you, resist not him that is evil' (Matt. 5:38-42). In fact the whole of the New Testament calls on Christians not to return evil for evil, but to overcome evil with good (Matt. 5:44; Rom. 12:17-21; I Thess. 5:15; I Peter 3:9). 'Behold,' says Jesus, 'I send you forth as sheep in the midst of wolves' (Matt. 10:16). For there are certainly wolves, but the sheep of the Good Shepherd must count only on God to give the wolves their deserts (Rom. 12:19-20; 16:20), for retribution depends on Him alone (Col. 3:23-25; James 5:9). While awaiting the last judgment, Christians must persevere in the path of peace and goodness (I Peter 4:12-19; II Peter 2:18-25). The disciples, who are not more than their Master, must bear in silence all persecutions and injustices, following the example of their Master (Matt 10:24-25; John 15:18-21; I Peter 2:18-25), who urges them to have no fear of death itself (Matt. 10:28; Phil. 1:28). For patience in their afflictions is their best witness amidst the pagans all round them (Matt. 10:17-20; Luke 21:12-19; I Peter 2:12; 3:8-17). It is a grace and a joy for them to be unjustly maltreated, while continuing to do good from love of their Master (Matt. 5:10-12; II Cor. 12:10; James 5:9-11; I Peter 4:12-19).

Remarkably enough, it is never in the New Testament a question of 'defending yourself' from your enemies by your own strength or with arms. This term is never used except to designate Christians' verbal defence before a tribunal (Luke 12:11; 21:15; Acts 22:1; 24:10; 25:16; 26:1; I Cor. 9:3; II Tim. 4:16). It is surely disturbing to find that this idea of defence, self-defence, which is the basis of the traditional militarist[17] doctrine has no Biblical support, and that the expression itself does not appear a single time in the New Testament. No single text can be invoked that would explicitly justify 'self-defence'; on the contrary, Jesus seems to have excluded it (Luke 9:24; 17:33). In fact there is not even a passage positively justifying or recommending the legitimacy of active and violent 'resistance' to injustice. In the New Testament, if there is a question of resisting, it is only resisting the devil, or God, never of resisting men.[18]

3. The Distinction of the Two Orders

Another objection might run like this: in all these New Testament passages it is always a question of the struggle of pagans against the rise of Christianity, against the Church as such. When the Gospel is threatened, Christians must endure everything in silence, even martyrdom. But you cannot conclude from that that Christians should keep this same attitude of non-resistance in the material affairs of this world. You are confusing the order of redemption, in which the Church is called to preach without any violence the Gospel of reconciliation, and the order of conservation, in which justice should be defended forcibly, if need be, by the city's magistrates, or if that fails by the citizens themselves. Armed defence is obviously legitimate only in this second context, but it becomes legitimate immediately it ceases to be a question of propagating the faith.

Luther in his 'Table Talk' admirably expresses this distinction: 'If anyone breaks into my home, tries to do violence to my family or myself, or to cause us harm, I am bound to defend myself and them in my capacity as master of the house and head of the family. If brigands or murderers had tried to harm me or do me wrongful violence, I should have defended myself and resisted them in the name of the prince whose subject and servant I am. These people would not have been attacking me because of the Gospel, as a minister and member of the Church of Christ, but as a subject of the prince and obedient to his authority. So then I must help the prince to purge his country of bad subjects; and if I have the strength to cut this bandit's throat, it is my duty to take the knife to him, and I shall feel no remorse on receiving the sacrament. For it is part of my duty to save a good citizen from peril, and still more to save my prince's country. But if I am attacked on account of the divine word, in my capacity as preacher, then I must endure it and leave God to punish him and avenge me. A preacher must not defend himself. So you do not see me taking a poniard when I go up into the pulpit, but only when I go on a journey or a walk in the country. As to the Anabaptists, I despair of these bad subjects: they refuse to bear arms and boast of their unlimited patience.'

Now, first of all, however well Luther's distinction between the preacher and the citizen may be founded, it is impossible to find a single text in the New Testament justifying this right and 'duty' he claims, 'if I have the strength to cut the bandit's throat, to take the knife to him.'

But does the New Testament really call believers to non-resistance only in cases where sufferings are imposed on them because of Jesus and on the occasion of their preaching the Gospel? Among the many exhortations to non-resistance quoted above, there are some, it is true, which apply beyond dispute to those who are persecuted because of the Gospel; it does not follow, however, that these exhortations have no validity at all for believers who may be persecuted for reasons independent of their being Christians. And there are also exhortations to non-resistance which do not specify the cause of the ill-treatment to be endured (I Peter 2:18-20; 3:9; Rom. 12:17-21; I Thess. 5:15; Matt. 6:14-15; 18:21-22): by what authority can it be asserted that these texts are strictly concerned with persecutions undergone by Christians because of their faith, and that consequently they do not apply to so-called cases of 'self-defence'? Finally there are exhortations concerned with attacks clearly not provoked by preaching the Gospel, which are therefore clearly part of the order of conservation (Matt. 5:38-41; Luke 6:27-30; I Cor. 6:7-8).

The whole Gospel condemns the use of murderous violence to defend ourselves against injustice, without specifying what injustice. So what can one think of the distinction illustrated by Luther? It is not so easy to distinguish between the order of redemption and that of conservation, between the preacher and the citizen. There may be a shade of difference useful for clear thinking, but no sharp, unambiguous dividing line can be drawn between them. If Luther is attacked by a brigand, will he have the time to call to the brigand, before deciding what attitude he should take: 'Whom are you attacking, the preacher or the citizen?' For after all, he is still a citizen when in the pulpit, nor in the street does he cease to be a preacher. If a demented lunatic hurls himself on Luther during his sermon, has he not the 'duty of saving a good citizen from peril'? And if he is attacked in a forest, must he not proclaim Christ to the brigand by his attitude of firm kindness and non-violence, since preaching is also carried out in every act of our daily lives? And if instead of taking a preacher as example, Luther had spoken of an ordinary believer, the distinction would have been still more obscure.

No, religion and politics are not so easily distinguishable. When the Churches are persecuted, whether by Nero, Louis XV, Hitler, or Stalin, which part of the ills they suffer, and the causes of those ills, come under the order of conservation and which under the order of redemption? For the Church is also a natural community—and the book you are now reading is at once political and theological!

The distinction cannot be rigorously applied to life. 'It is radically false,' writes Ch. Westphal,[19] 'to say that religion is a private matter, as if there were a religious domain independent of life's other domains. Man is not divided, and here one can say that Christ is not divided . . . the religious part is everywhere, or it is nowhere.' There is no subtlety which will refute the Gospel's express testimony 'Render to no man evil for evil' (Rom. 12:17).

4. The Unity of the Church

All the above is further confirmed when we consider the universality of the Church. In accepting the salvation of Christ, I find myself thereby reconciled not only with my heavenly Father but also with my brethren in the faith (Gal. 3:27; Eph. 2:13-18); united with them by His forgiveness, I discover that I am united with each one of them whatever his race (Rom. 10:12; Rev. 7:9), his nationality, (Col. 3:11), his social situation (Gal. 3:28), by the love we owe each other because of Him. There is a single body (John 10:16;11: 52; I Cor. 12:12; Eph. 4:4-6; 2:19-22; Col. 3:15), Christ's body, and I know that we are all members of that body[20] (Rom. 12:4-5; I Cor. 12:20-27). Nothing in my attitude should risk breaking, or even

c

weakening this unity of the children of God (Eph. 4:25; I Cor. 1:10; Phil. 2:1-5). All the barriers which may otherwise estrange me from my brother believers must therefore be overcome by the charity which is our fundamental bond (I Cor. 13; Eph. 4:1-3). To be estranged from a brother believer is to be estranged from the Church (I Cor. 12:21). Brutally to oppose a brother believer is to break Christ's body (I Cor. 1:13; 3:16-17; Rom. 14:19-20).

This is why the New Testament insists so strongly on the need to drive quarrels and divisions out of the Church (I Cor. 12:23; Rom. 16:17-18; Gal. 5-15). For the Church, by its oecumenical unity, must be in the world a striking witness to the truth of the Gospel (John 17:21-23; I Peter 2:9-10), and even more a sign of the Kingdom of God. That is why the Christian's membership of the community of the Church should take precedence over every other human bond, every other natural community he may belong to (Acts 2:40; II Cor. 6:14-18; Phil. 3:20; Heb. 11:13-16; 13:13-14; I Peter 2:11; II Peter 3:13).

It would therefore seem impossible for believers to take up men's necessarily carnal quarrels to the point of tearing asunder the body of Christ. It would seem impossible for a French believer, on the grounds that his government was in conflict with the German government, to resign himself to taking part in the slaughter of Germans, when there are believers among them who like him form part of Christ's body. For, after all, in the last resort war between Christian nations is nothing else but the introduction of carnal quarrels and divisions into the bosom of the Church. If we are shocked by such language, it is because theology is suspect today and we have grown used to thinking that the national community takes precedence over the community of Christ's body, the State over the Church.

We shall see later on that the State does have an importance in the context of the Kingdom of God; but to give it priority over the Church is to take a position beyond the limits set by the Scriptures. When there is a conflict between the demands of the Church and those of the State, it is the former which must prevail (Acts 5:29). Nothing in the Scriptures gives the Christian authority to tear apart the body of Christ for the State or anything else. Do we believe in the Universal Church, in the communion of Saints, or do we believe in the eternal mission of our country? One cannot believe in both at once; one cannot be Christian *and* nationalist.

'Christians of all denominations, languages, and races,' Daniel

Parker proclaims[21], 'must stir up their respective clergies, and work, with the violence of the faith, to re-establish in the international community of Christians the sense of deep solidarity which unites all His disciples in Christ.'

5. Conclusion

Of course this non-resistance to evil is disconcerting to the admirers of force, the worshippers of Mars, the fanatical pragmatics that most of us are. In any case, perhaps we should rather talk of non-violent *action* or even non-violent resistance; for the non-violence of the Gospels never implies acquiescence in evil. All the texts I have just quoted present mostly the negative side of an attitude which is in fact very positive and active—the attitude described in amazingly concrete terms in the Beatitudes (Matt. 5) and the hymn to Charity (I Cor. 13): the attitude of Christ and the apostles. These two texts have always been known to give a vivid portrayal of the charity of Jesus Himself. It is therefore something quite different from passive resignation and weak surrender to someone stronger. The Christian is certainly not disarmed in the struggle he must carry on; but his arms are those of the Spirit—unless we say that the Crucified and the martyrs were passive cowards. But this brings me to my second point.

Chapter 2

THE EXAMPLE OF CHRIST AND THE APOSTLES

1. *They Always Refused to Fight*

HAVING considered the teaching of Christ and the apostles, let us now look at how they put into practice this Truth they preached: one is immediately struck by the way in which they sometimes fled from the enemies who wished to kill them. And when eventually caught by such enemies, instead of defending themselves, as would seem natural for men with any 'guts,' they let themselves be manhandled, tortured, executed, without trying to hit back. Indisputably, they practised as well as preached the refusal to take part in murderous strife.

On several occasions the Gospels relate how Jesus, directly threatened with death, rather mysteriously 'passed through the midst' of His enemies and 'escaped from them' (Luke 4:30; Matt. 12:15; John 8:59; 10:39; perhaps also Matt. 14:13). It is incontestable that He several times sought refuge in hiding (Mark 7:24; 11:19; 14:12-16; Matt. 21:1-3; 26:30; John 7:1-10; 11:54). So long as His hour was not come, He always avoided the danger without committing any violence (John 7:6 and 30:8-20). Then, on the eve of the Passover, He let Himself be caught, when He could have escaped a thousand times over, and literally offered Himself to the tortures and execution which He knew awaited Him (Matt. 26:47-50, *et al.*). His cross was the consecration of this non-resistance, this non-violence which He had preached (Luke 23:33-34); it was just because of it that He was mocked at Golgotha (Matt. 27:29-44).

Jesus stopped His disciples using violence against their adversaries and rebuked them for having wished to use it (Luke 9:51-56; John 18:11). He expressly instructed them not to persist in face of their hearers' hostility (Matt. 10:14) and even to flee from the persecutions that would threaten them (Matt. 10:23). And it must be said that before that first Pentecost they obeyed the instructions all too well, for their successive flights seem to have been more an expression of cowardice than of concern to obey their Master's command (Matt. 26:56 and 75; 27:55).

But after Pentecost, although the Holy Spirit had filled them with boldness and courage, we see the Apostles still following their Master's tracks on the path of non-violence: they too fled before threats of death (Acts 8:1, 4; 9:25, 30; 14:6; 17:10-14); and when they were brought to bay by their adversaries, they let themselves be taken without resistance (Acts 4:3; 5:26, 41; 21:30-33) and put to death without opposition (Acts 7:54-60; 12:2). Sometimes beneath the blows they feigned death (Acts 14:19-20); Paul even escaped by appealing to human justice (Acts 22:25; 25:10-12); but these were certainly not instances of recourse to violence or going back on their moral rule. For the non-violence of the Gospels certainly does not imply abdication before injustice. Many were killed; like their Master, they were martyrs (literally, in the Greek, 'witnesses'), in that their death was in itself the best way of preaching the Gospel— as, afterwards, with the martyrs of the first century and those of the Reformation.

2. *Except at Gethsemane, They Never Bore Arms*

Their only arms were in effect the arms of the light (Rom. 13:12) and of justice (II Cor. 6:7), all the panoply of God so proudly enumerated by the apostle Paul (Eph. 6:10-17; I Thes. 5:8). They were certainly not of the flesh (II Cor. 10:4), let alone material arms! In fact, there is not a single text in the New Testament to show that Christ or the apostles ever 'bore arms,' in the usual sense, apart from the exceptional and obscure episode of the two swords of Gethsemane (Matt. 26:51-54; Luke 22:35-38, 49-51; John 18:10-11). This is exceptional, because it is absolutely the only mention of arms being borne and used by the disciples; and obscure, because it contains elements which are hard to explain and reconcile with each other. Three different interpretations have been suggested:

(*a*) Luke's account contains an explanation given by Jesus Himself for His surprising order: 'He that hath no sword, let him sell his garment and buy one. For I say unto you, that this which is written must yet be accomplished in me: And he was reckoned among the transgressors; for the things concerning me have an end.' By this interpretation Jesus was impelled by His desire to accomplish the Scriptures, a desire which is particularly evident during the last period of His ministry; He therefore asked His disciples at this tragic hour to obtain purses and swords, so that when He was arrested and executed it could be said of Him that He was considered as a criminal, having been taken among people who were suspect and armed. In fact He asked them to *play the part* of criminals, so that it would afterwards be recognised that the prophecy of Isaiah 53:12 did apply to Him, and that He was therefore the Messiah.

This interpretation has a double advantage: it is drawn from the Scriptures, in fact from the text itself; and it also accords well with the sequel. It is then perfectly understandable that Jesus is content with two symbolic swords (only two swords to defend twelve men); also that when one of the disciples, not having understood His intention, effectively uses his sword, Jesus stops him at once: 'Put up the sword,' He cries. And to demonstrate that He had only meant the disciples to *make a show* of these swords, He there and then heals the ear of the injured servant. This bloodshed has resulted from an action contrary to His real intention.

If we adopt this explanation, what conclusions can be drawn? That Jesus considers as transgressors the citizens who carry a sword! That He rebukes murderous violence! That in any case, even if He asked His disciples to buy swords, He certainly did not want them to use the swords in earnest. The episode would then cease to be unique of its kind. Far from invalidating my thesis that the disciples never bore arms and never used them, the text confirms it: that evening Jesus was presenting a symbolic scene of Messianic significance, but He neither recommended nor authorised the *use* of arms.

The interpretation is open, however, to two serious criticisms. For one thing it seems hard to reconcile the express command Jesus gives *all* His disciples, that they each buy a sword, with the symbolic and harmless demonstration, the little 'play' He intends to produce, for which He needs only two swords. For another thing, it is rash to base the interpretation of so obscure and difficult an episode on a prophetic text which might very well be a gloss by the Evangelist himself.

(*b*) According to the second interpretation, when Jesus gave all His disciples the command to buy a sword, He was speaking seriously and unambiguously. He gave His express approval to their bearing arms, and implicitly to their using arms. Obviously this literal interpretation is the one the defenders of traditional militarism fall back on; and, if it can be shown to be tenable, the testimony of all the rest of the New Testament concerning the apostles' arms certainly loses a great deal of its weight.

But this explanation of the episode faces difficulties which in my opinion are insurmountable. First of all, one may wonder whether Jesus really thought His disciples would find a chance to obtain twelve swords, except by barter, at the late hour when He asked them to buy the swords. The fact that among the crowd which came to arrest Him there were men armed only with staves (Matt. 26:47) suggests that it was relatively difficult to obtain arms at that time, no doubt because of the Romans' surveillance.

Secondly, if Jesus has expressed the wish that all His disciples should get themselves a sword, it is strange, to say the least, that He should show Himself so quickly satisfied—'he said unto them, it is enough'—when they tell Him they already have two swords, or more likely have just found them while rummaging in the house (as suggested by the text: 'behold, here are two swords'). Whatever may be the exact sense of 'it is enough' (I shall return to this later), Jesus is obviously disinterested in the ten other swords which He has declared necessary just before. In the space of a few seconds (by this interpretation) He contradicts Himself blatantly enough to make one wonder whether He really knows what He wants; moreover, how could two swords be enough for twelve men? Jesus was not a fool, and we can hardly suppose He was playing a trick on the disciples; so the words 'it is enough' remain inexplicable.

H. Bois[23] suggests that Jesus was momentarily overcome by the frenzy of His disciples, 'terrified as they were by the turn events had taken. But the idea of resisting by arms was only a passing idea, a temptation soon rejected by Him. . . . As soon as He sees the two swords His disciples hasten to bring Him, He pulls himself together . . . changes his mind. And when He says, It is enough, He is really contradicting his previous order.' This explanation, though psychologically ingenious, nevertheless assumes that at least for a few moments Jesus succumbed to temptation, which seems inadmissible, as is the insinuation that Jesus was no longer in control of Himself and His words, since He contradicts Himself pathetically within a few minutes. Finally, it implies that the thought of having recourse to arms was in itself a temptation for Jesus—which at once eliminates all possibility of invoking this text to justify the use of arms!

But here is a new contradiction: when Peter at the critical moment effectively uses his sword, Jesus stops him at once, rebukes him severely, and miraculously cures the servant's ear. Why should Jesus have asked the disciples to take swords if He was then going to stop them using the swords at the opportune moment? Could it be that He preferred to give Himself up, having established at a glance that His enemies were too numerous, so that the battle was lost in advance? But in that case why was He satisfied with the two wretched swords? Obviously, however, these suppositions would make Jesus a faint-hearted coward, and they are all quite untenable.

So it cannot really be thought that He asked His disciples to get swords for the purpose of opposing His arrest. Some will try to bolster up the literal interpretation of the 'two swords' episode by suggesting that Jesus was thinking of the period *after* His arrest, which would be a tragic one for His disciples. This would certainly make better sense of the spirit and words of Jesus' recommendations in Luke 22:36. The same question still comes up at once, however: what was His precise intention, what purpose were these swords to serve after His own disappearance?

One is lost at once in improbable guesses: were the disciples to avenge the Master's death by summary executions? Or were they to join up with the Zealots as a 'Maquis' and form an armed band of patriots who would assassinate Roman soldiers? Were they to seize Jerusalem by violence after Christ's death, so as to set up the Messianic rule there? But then why only two swords? Why did Jesus let Himself be arrested so meekly? Moreover, He had expressly declared that His Kingdom was not of this world, and so His disciples should not fight for Him (John, 18:36). Was He contradicting Himself, and lying to Pilate? On the contrary, His proud reply to Pilate disposes once and for all of the suppositions I have just enumerated, already absurd in themselves.

One possibility remains: Jesus authorised His disciples to resort to self-defence *after* His arrest. But against whom would the disciples have needed to defend themselves? Against the police who would come to arrest them as well? But all Jesus' teaching, and the whole of the New Testament, calls on the contrary for submission to the proper civil authorities; He was to give them an example of complete submission before the police; so He cannot have recommended them to armed insurrection. (Calvin rightly says of Peter's ill-considered act: 'By doing violence to the police, he acts like a brigand, because he is resisting the power God has ordered.' And further: 'It was by no means lawful for a private man to rise against those who were furnished with public authority.')[24]

Perhaps it will be suggested that Jesus allowed them to defend themselves against personal enemies who might attack them individually. But who would have an interest in attacking them? They were neither rich nor powerful, and it was clear that after their Master had gone they would represent absolutely no danger to anyone. (In the passage quoted above Calvin, who cannot be suspected of weakness, continues: 'So let us refrain from repulsing our enemies by force or violence, even when they give us wrongful provocation, unless the law permits it.' And if it is the Gospel someone might want to destroy by attacking the disciples, that raises a very delicate problem: would Jesus have allowed them to defend His teaching by arms? It would be most surprising, but I shall return to the point later. Anyhow, one can scarcely admit that Jesus was ready, by arming His disciples, to issue a blatant challenge to the Romans: obviously like all armies of occupation, they could not tolerate the bearing of arms by private individuals. The literal interpretation imputes to Jesus an offence against the *de facto* authority, an offence of insubordination which would come very near to being a sin.

So one cannot see at all what Jesus might have meant by re-commending His disciples to get swords for possible use after His arrest; and there are three more decisive objections to such an inter-pretation. First, He tells them to buy swords *now*, not for some time in the future: 'But now . . . he that hath no sword . . .' also, in verse 37 (of Luke 22) Jesus refers explicitly to His death. Secondly, it is undeniable that in saying: 'Put up thy sword again into its place; for all they that take the sword shall perish by the sword,' He con-demned the use of arms generally, and in particular the use of these famous swords which He had ordered them to obtain a few hours before. This statement of His is absolutely irreconcilable with the hypothesis that He would have allowed His disciples to *use* their swords after His arrest. Indeed, one may even think that He spoke in this manner precisely to remove from their minds any sort of misunderstanding concerning their two swords, and to forbid them expressly from using the swords in the future.[25]

Thirdly, the testimony of the New Testament confirms that in fact after Jesus' arrest the disciples did not use their swords; there is no text suggesting that they even kept the swords in their possession.

It remains to develop two important arguments against the literal interpretation of the episode, taken as a whole. First, when before leaving the high chamber Jesus recommended His disciples to take a purse and a scrip, such a recommendation modifies the instructions He had given them on first sending them out (Luke 9:3), but it by no means contradicts the rest of His and the New Testament's teaching. Whereas when He tells them to buy a sword, if this is to be taken in its usual sense, such an order contradicts not only his previous instructions but also the New Testament in its entirety. Of

course a text does not lose its authority simply because it is unique
of its kind, but I find it hazardous and false to interpret a text unique
of its kind in such a way that it is also unique in contradicting the
whole of its context. When possible, one should interpret it in the light
of its context: this is one of the principles of sound Biblical exegesis.

Secondly, those who would stick to the literal interpretation of
Jesus' order are caught on the horns of a dilemma. They are telling
us that Jesus is commanding His disciples, as disciples, to buy
swords for possible use in self-defence. Jesus is thus speaking here
to the Church as such, for it would be absurd to imagine that by
these words He is discharging His disciples from their mission as
apostles. He is clearly giving them new instructions for a new mission
which will begin with His own departure from their midst. Now,
much of the traditional doctrine justifying military service is founded
on the distinction of the two orders which I have already mentioned.
According to this doctrine the use of murderous violence would be
lawful in the framework of the civil society, but not in the framework of the Church and its mission. To revert to Luther's concepts,
quoted above, the use of the sword is lawful for the defence of the
citizen, but not for the defence of the preacher. Here, however,
according to the literal interpretation, Jesus is authorising His
disciples as preachers, not as citizens, to make use of the sword.

In this embarrassing dilemma, the militarists have to choose between the literal interpretation and the distinction of the two orders.
It is probable that they will eventually sacrifice the former.

(c) If the literal interpretation is so extremely illogical and contradictory, we must look for a quite different one. According to a
third hypothesis Jesus was using the word 'sword' not literally but
figuratively. Perceiving a terrible storm coming upon his disciples
(Luke 22:31), and foreseeing that once the shepherd was struck the
sheep would be scattered (Matt. 26:31), He was trying to give them
moral stiffening, preparing them to face the tempest hovering over
them (Matt. 26:41). By solemnly commanding them to take a purse,
a scrip, and a sword, He wanted to make them understand through
striking imagery that the hour had come for them to prepare themselves for a tragic spiritual battle. They would need a supply of
moral forces[26] and a spiritual pugnacity to help them overcome the
ordeal of their dispersion and the despair in which He would leave
them by His death. For then each of them could count on his own
resources alone.[27]

Such an interpretation would fit in well enough with Jesus' habit of using language full of imagery, sometimes even in a frankly extravagant manner (Matt. 5:29-30; 7:5; Mark 10:25; Matt. 23:24); nor would it be the first time His hearers made the mistake of taking literally an expression He had used figuratively (Mark 8:15-16; John 3:4; 6:42, 52). This time His simple-minded disciples took literally the use of the words 'swords,' which was obviously intended to give them a shock. To quote Calvin's commentaries again:[28] 'Here is another example of dull and most shameful ignorance on the part of the disciples, that after being warned and admonished so often to bear the cross, they nevertheless think they will have to fight with swords of steel . . . they were so stupid they never thought of the spiritual enemy.'

Then again, one can hardly take these last recommendations of Jesus solely in their literal sense: would He have nothing more important to say to His disciples in this tragic hour than to take on their persons these three material objects? And if we try to imagine the scene, when He went to the high chamber on that dark and anxious night—what on earth were these poor disciples to put in their purses and their scrips? What would they look like carrying their swords as well? When the text is compared with Jesus' instructions concerning their first mission (Luke 9:3-5; Mark 6:7-9; Matt. 10:9-10), it can be seen that those instructions, to which He refers expressly here (22:35), must also be understood in their figurative sense; only St. Francis of Assisi and Pierre Valdo have taken these too in their literal sense. But it is clear that the Church, from its first days, has always interpreted Luke 9:3 figuratively; so why should it do any different with Luke 22:36? Why take the word 'sword' literally, when you do not take literally the words 'purses,' 'scrips,' 'money,' 'staves,' and 'shoes'?

In favour of the symbolic interpretation of the word 'sword' one can also invoke its general use in the New Testament: outside this episode, it is used seven times in the sense of a material weapon and nine times in a figurative sense. Among these latter texts, let me quote Jesus' characteristic phrase: 'I am come not to bring peace but a sword' (Matt. 9:34), where Luke (12:51) gives 'Not peace but rather *division*.' Again in Luke 2:35 Simeon tells Mary that a sword shall pierce through her soul. Paul quotes in his divine panoply 'the sword of the Spirit, which is the word of God' (Eph. 6:17, see also Heb. 4:12). The mere enumeration of these texts is enough to give plausibility to a figurative interpretation of Jesus' phrase.

An objection will be made which at first sounds more serious than it is: when the disciples say, 'Lord, behold, here are two swords,' Jesus answers, 'It is enough'—as though He found it natural they should take His order literally. And if they were in fact misunderstanding Him, He does not rebuke nor correct them. But to begin with let us imagine Jesus tired, anxious, discouraged by His disciples' incomprehension, simply wishing to cut short, perhaps with some irony in His voice, their stupid and untimely search for material arms, perhaps feeling there was no time to explain how they had misunderstood Him. In fact, however, it is clear from the Greek text that He is *not* saying 'they, these two swords, are enough,' for He uses the singular ἱκανόν ἐστιν, 'it is enough': in other words, 'that's enough, don't say any more.'

Another objection might be that anyhow Jesus let His disciples take these two swords with them, so that they had them at Gethsemane. But we cannot be sure He knew they were slipping these weapons under their clothes, or if He did know that He agreed to their doing so. Even if it could be established that He deliberately let them do so, it would still not be proof that He explicitly gave them permission, far less approved of their taking these swords with them. After all, He let Judas betray Him.

If, despite all these doubts our objector still thinks Jesus agreed to two of His disciples being armed that night, I would suggest a combination of the first and third interpretations of the episode: He talked of their buying swords in a figurative sense; but when He realised two of His disciples were taking His words literally, were childishly presenting Him with two real swords, He resigned himself to not opposing their action; for He thought of the prophetic and messianic significance that would be given by the presence of real arms among the little group of His disciples when He was arrested. He could thus validly be charged with being taken 'in the midst of transgressors' and Isaiah's prophecy would be fulfilled in His person. This is why, before they even announce with their naïve pride, 'Here are two swords,' He explains to them the use He will make of their arms. It is also why He then simply tells them 'it is enough,' as if to say, 'no more about that, let's go on to something else.' For these two swords would be quite enough to have Him considered the head of a gang of criminals; if there had been any more, He could have even feared a real battle with bloodshed. Two swords were just right for His little Messianic 'production,' and this loses its somewhat childish character if the idea only came to Him by chance when He realised how His disciples had misunderstood Him.

So He would not have been thinking of it in verse 36, where He was certainly speaking figuratively.

In conclusion, I think we may say that this episode, whatever the obscurities still hanging over it, is far from contradicting my assertion that Jesus never permitted His disciples to use murderous arms. If in the exceptional and particularly tragic circumstances He did let two of them carry a sword for a few hours, it was certainly not so that they should use the swords effectively; for He severely rebuked the disciple who used his to wound a servant of the high priest. So no basis can be found here for a Christian justification of murderous violence.

3. They Never Carried Out Acts of Violence

Never—except, of course, for Peter's action at Gethsemane, of which we have just spoken, and which was strongly enough condemned by Jesus. The partisans of militarism, however, may invoke three other texts in their attempts to prove that the founders of Christianity made use of violence in other circumstances too.

(a) First of all, they may cite the whip which Jesus used to chase the merchants and money-changers out of the Temple in Jerusalem. Their formidable syllogism will run: in striking with a whip Jesus gave His sanction to violence; war is a form of violence; so Jesus gave His sanction to war.

The first thing that might be said about this is that war is not fought with whips. The fallacy of the syllogism lies in the ambiguity caused by taking the word 'violence' in an abstract sense; abstractions are always dangerous in considering Biblical texts. There is violence and violence: there is a difference of kind as well as of degree between a whip and a sub-machine-gun. That is why in this study I generally use the expression 'murderous violence' to distinguish it from the use of force which is not lethal and against which the Christian need not always object. Bois, for instance, takes a lot of trouble to show from this text that 'force can and should be employed against evil.'[29] But who would deny this? The only problem is about lethal violence, homicide. The syllogism's major premise would be sound only if it were restated thus: by striking with a whip, Jesus sanctioned a certain form of violence. And this destroys the syllogism at once.

Besides, what exactly happened that day? It is undeniable that Jesus was animated by a fine fury, expressed in impulsive authoritarian actions. On an irresistible impulse He overturned the tables of the money-changers and the stands of the merchants, and caused all these traders a considerable loss of money. The Gospel of John, however, is the only one to mention a whip of cords. The three Synoptic Gospels say that Jesus 'began to cast out them that bought and sold in the temple' (Mark 11:15) without specifying if it was done with a whip or any other instrument. We must therefore consider the 'whips' question with care. Even John does not state explicitly that Jesus struck *the money-changers* with His whip, or even touched them. He simply says: 'And when he had made a whip of small cords, he drove them all out of the temple.' It is not even probable that He touched them; on the contrary, it seems quite likely that the sight of Jesus, filled with rage, the whip in His hand, was so terrible that the people ran away without waiting for their money.[30]

On the other hypothesis, if one tries to picture the scene concretely, there is something unprecedented and even repugnant in imagining Jesus lashing out at people who have been taken unawares and believe themselves quite in order with their secular trading. To assert that this was a good way for things to happen, one would need a solid Scriptural base. Now, the only indication the context can bring here to illuminate the incident, is that the chiefs of the people afterwards reproach Jesus, not for having used violence and injured people, not for His blows, in fact, but for arrogating an authority He did not have (Mark 11:28).

One thing we should notice about this passage is that the word translated here by 'drive out' ($\epsilon\kappa\beta\acute{a}\lambda\lambda\epsilon\iota\nu$) is often used in the New Testament without this idea of violence.[31] For another thing, it is known that there were Temple ushers who were armed guards charged with maintaining order there; it was they, in fact, who would come to arrest Jesus at Gethsemane (Luke 22:52; John 18:3; and cf. Acts 5:26). Considering the mass of people there would be in Jerusalem with the Feast of Passover approaching, there must have been a good number of these ushers on duty when the incident took place.[32] It is psychologically inexplicable that they did not intervene if Jesus drove out the money-changers with blows of a whip, especially as intervention would certainly have had the approval of the chiefs of the priests; they would not have allowed an agitator to cause such a disorder and injure so many interests. Their abstention is very understandable, on the other hand, if it was by His moral ascendancy and authority alone that Jesus drove out the money-changers.[33]

Moreover, the text states: 'He drove them all out of the temple, the sheep as well as the oxen.' The word 'all' (πάντας) is in the masculine; it could agree with the merchants, but even better with the oxen. The construction of the Greek sentence suggests that these 'all,' driven out by Jesus with His whip, are the animals, 'namely' the sheep and the oxen. Surely it is quite natural to think that Jesus took a whip not for the merchants but for these animals who are expressly referred to twice in this short passage? For after all, while one can perfectly well imagine Jesus driving out the money-changers without using his whip on their persons, He could scarcely have driven out the sheep and oxen without using a whip or a stick.

The upholders of militarism have exploited this text so much that it is hard to approach it objectively without preconceived ideas. By a sort of atavism, the picture of Jesus whipping out the money-changers haunts our minds. Yet it is more than probable that they fled of their own accord, cowed and stunned by the Master's indignation and angry words; but that the animals stayed where they were, being doubtless tied up as in any other stock market. Jesus would then have untied them, and as they were probably running in all directions, He got hold of one of the ropes they were tied up by and used it to drive them all out of the Temple. To make the text say more than this is to venture into the field of unnecessary hypotheses.[34]

So our major premise must be amended again: in *using* a whip, Jesus sanctioned a certain form of violence.

But what exactly did He sanction by His action? The theorists of militarism obviously wish to use this text to justify 'self-defence.' Now Jesus, quite rightly, is not defending Himself here; He was not threatened in any way, nor even disturbed by these peaceable traders. On the contrary, He is indisputably the aggressor! So if His action provides a sanction for anything, it is for the right to attack violently men who have not done you any harm—which is rather more than our theorists need.

Furthermore the theory of the distinction between the two orders is once more invalidated by a Scriptural text. For the quarrel between Jesus and the traders in the temple lies in the order of redemption, not the order of conservation. There is no sort of conflict of material interests here, but a discussion concerning ritual and liturgical fidelity. It was not social justice, people's right to live honourably and in freedom, that was at stake, but solely the integrity and purity of the worship offered to God in His temple. Was Jesus sanctioning violence in this latter context? Here again, it is far more than our theorists need, and their argument boomerangs most un-happily for them. It is the same dilemma again: if Jesus sanctioned anything with His whip, it was the intrusion of aggressive violence and brutal coercion into the realm of the practice of the cult; but then the distinction of the two orders is irremediably contradicted once more. If this distinction is to be kept, all hope must be aban-doned of using this text to sanction anything. All the major premise can properly state is: in using a whip, Jesus used a certain form of violence!

It is time to ask what Jesus' real intention was. It was certainly not to make a public demonstration of the legitimacy of violence. All the Biblical scholars seem agreed in giving this text a Messianic inter-pretation. His adversaries were always trying by insidious traps to catch Him contradicting the law; and He wanted to prove to them that He really respected the Mosaic observances more than they did. John actually notes this concern on Jesus' part to show Himself very respectful of the Law in all its details, quoting Psalm 69: 'The zeal of thine house hath eaten me up.' By His act of authority the Master wishes to manifest Himself as King of Israel; as Calvin writes[35]: 'He wanted to take possession of the Temple, and to perform an act to make known His divine authority.' And as by His entry into Jerusalem He had that very morning deliberately fulfilled the pro-phecy of Zechariah (11:9): 'Behold, thy King cometh unto thee . . . riding upon an ass,' so by driving the merchants out of the Temple in a dramatic manner, He may well have been wanting to fulfil to the letter two other Messianic prophecies: that of Malachi (3:1-3) '. . . and the Lord, whom ye seek, shall suddenly come to His temple . . . He shall purify the sons of Levi . . . that they may offer unto the Lord an offering with righteousness'; and that of Zechariah (14:21)— 'There shall be no more merchants in the house of the Lord of Hosts in that day.' Finally, if Jesus' act is the fulfilment of prophecies, it is perhaps also a sign prophetic of the Last Judgment, as if to say: 'God will not always be mocked.' For the bridegroom shall rise one day, like a thief in the night, to sit upon his Judge's throne (Matt. 25:6, 31): 'happy the servants whom their Master on His coming shall find vigilant and faithful' (Matt. 24:42-51).

Jesus' act, then, was essentially a Messianic act; it could not be normative for us, and it does not sanction anything at all. Let us conclude with Calvin[36]: 'But nevertheless, we must take good care that no one goes beyond the limits of his vocation. The zeal must be common to all with the Son of God; but it is not permissible to seize a whip in order to correct vices by acts of violence. For we have not received even the power nor the warrant.'

(b) I now come to two texts which might be advanced to prove that the apostles made use of violence. One relates the supernatural death of Ananias and Sapphira, who deceived the apostles on the sale price of the property they had decided to offer to the Church (Acts 5:1-11), the other the blindness with which Paul miraculously struck the sorcerer Elymas, who was hindering him in his preaching.

Some readers may feel I am wasting my time in refuting such arguments. But the sad thing is that Christian theologians have used them (including Karl Barth, for instance).[37] Calvin himself gave them an example of this, his commentaries on these two episodes being highly ambiguous.[38] Speaking of the sudden deaths of the liar husband and wife, he writes: 'St. Peter, then, did nothing contrary to his office when he unsheathed in due time the sword which the Holy Spirit had given him.' He adds at once, it is true, 'that this was an extraordinary thing,' by which we are doubtless to understand that the case was unique of its kind, and therefore perhaps not normative in his eyes. His thought is not firm on the subject.

On Elymas, his language is still more misleading: 'But when Paul sees that maliciously, and by deliberate intention, Elymas is making war against the pure doctrine of the true religion, he treats him as no more nor less than a slave of Satan. It is thus that we must treat the desperate enemies of the Gospel, who clearly show a stubborn contumacy, and a profane condemnation of God, and principally when they close the passage to others.' One must not forget that this was written in the middle of the sixteenth century. Moreover, Calvin was obviously alarmed himself by the inferences which could be drawn from his own words, so that before concluding on this passage he tries to close again the sinister door he has half opened: 'However, I know how easy it is to stumble in this place; and faithful doctors must be all the more sure to be on their guard. First, that under cover of zeal they do not take the rein off their carnal affections; and afterwards that they are not boiling with too hasty a vehemence, too quick an ardour, when moderation can still be used; thirdly . . .', etc. Here is Calvin getting entangled in casuistry without even taking the trouble to justify his assertion in principle.

First I would point out that in both cases, once more, the episodes related come within the framework of the order of redemption, not that of conservation. With Ananias and Sapphira we are confronted by an incident arising strictly out of ecclesiastical discipline: an internal affair which shatters the Church but in no way touches the social order and people's right to live in peace. With Elymas it is a matter of the Church's missionary preaching, and of that alone: we watch an episode in Paul's spiritual battle which has no concern at all with social justice. So if you admit with Calvin that the apostles were right to punish these three people, you are justifying the use of murderous violence within the Church and in the service of its preaching. You could then infer the lawfulness of any holy war the objective of which was strictly religious; to follow Calvin here, in fact, may lead absolutely anywhere.

Calvin's interpretation, however, must be rejected for three reasons. First, it is regrettable that he did not pay sufficient account to the miraculous, spiritual character of the punishments in question, did not see that they come within a whole succession of marvels which fill the Acts, from Pentecost's 'Speaking with Tongues' to the Viper of Malta (Acts 2 and 28). Clearly, all these form a set, intended to affirm the growing faith of the apostolic Church and to confirm the apostles' preaching by 'acts of power' capable of impressing the multitudes. This is what Jesus had expressly promised to His disciples (Mark 16:17-18), and what the apostles deliberately ask for in their prayers (Acts 4:40). So these are essentially miraculous events meant to accompany the apostles during the apostolic period (Acts 2:43; 5:12). Were such events to continue after that period? Calvin faces such questions for the other miracles, for instance the speaking with tongues, and readily concludes that they were destined for the apostolic period only. But astonishingly enough, he never asks himself whether the miraculous punishments too may not be strictly confined to that period. Their extraordinary character, the fact that these punishments seem to us so very much in excess of the crime, compels the realisation that they are marvels *sui generis* whereby God is glorified while confirming the apostles' work; but it cannot be admitted that they are part of an ecclesiastical discipline for which they would be normative models.

Secondly, Calvin did not distinguish in these supernatural punishments which part came from God and which from the apostles. For after all, when he writes concerning Elymas' blindness, 'it is thus that we must treat the enemies of the Gospel,' he is speaking of something easier said than done; did he himself ever administer physical punishment to an adversary by the power of his words alone? Moreover, it is strange that so skilled a jurist should not have seen that if it was the apostles who meted out these punishments, they would have rendered themselves guilty before God, and would have had to give an account of their actions before the political authorities of their time; for neither Peter nor Paul were qualified to execute such summary judgments or even to deliver them!

It is equally surprising that a theologian as assured as Calvin did not see that he was here attributing to the creature what belongs to the Creator. He is so luminously clear, for instance, on the effectiveness of the sacraments, showing that this resides not in the officiant nor in his act but solely in the Word of God of which the sacrament is the sign. Yet he did not see that here too it is the Word of truth which alone was effective to punish the three guilty people. To revert to Calvin's own words, that which was 'naturally beneficent' but 'was mortal' for Ananias and his wife, was not any power residing in Peter's person, which was available for his use and was also available for the Church's use, but the power contained in God's Word pronounced by the apostle and made effective by the Holy Spirit. So it would be dishonest to compare the 'physical' punishment of Ananias and his wife to the capital executions of which the Church, alas, has carried out all too many, with or without the hypocritical aid of the secular arm. There is no common measure between the punishments of God and those of men; and in these two cases Calvin has dangerously confused them.

Thirdly, he gives these texts too hasty and direct, too legalistic an interpretation. Should we not always go through the Gospel to explain a Biblical text, and make sure that the explanation will fit naturally into Christian 'doctrine'? Now, there seems little enough connection between Calvin's interpretation and the Good News: but also, we should note, he has not sought to illuminate our two episodes by other texts in the Gospels. Let us remember, for instance, that Jesus, after confirming that the adulterous woman deserved condemnation, nevertheless withdrew from sinful men the right to execute her, and refused Himself to take the responsibility for her execution. Again, we read in Luke how one day the Sons of Thunder wanted to bring down fire from Heaven on a village that would not receive Jesus. Jesus severely rebuked them. 'Ye know not what manner of spirit ye are of,' He tells them; 'for the Son of Man is not come to destroy men's lives, but to save them' (Luke 9:54-56). Had Calvin thought of these two texts, he might have been more careful about saying that we ought to 'treat' the enemies of God as the apostles 'treated' Ananias, Sapphira, and Elymas.

I do not like arguments *ad hominem*. But it may have already occurred to the reader that Calvin's erroneous interpretation has a sinister light thrown on it by the burning of Servetus and others. I myself would only conclude by asserting that in these two episodes the apostles did not make use of violence.

There is one other text which might be invoked to show they did use violence; but I shall not spend much time on it, partly because its exact interpretation is obscure, and partly because even if the 'violent' interpretation is adhered to, all I have said in the preceding paragraph is still true here and needs no repetition.

Was the curse uttered by Paul against the incestuous man of Corinth an execution to death? Some have maintained that it was, but I share the opinion of most scholars, who see it as an excommunication like the one referred to in I Timothy 1:20: to deliver someone over to Satan remains an educative disciplinary measure and therefore not mortal. It is also quite impossible to see how putting a guilty person to death would deliver him automatically to Satan. It is not the death which delivers him to Satan but the rejection of Christ, the separation from His presence. By the excommunication the incestuous man is to be delivered to himself, that is, to the mortal power which rules over his flesh. 'Paul,' explains Goguel[39], 'asks the Corinthians to judge the guilty man, and to deliver him to Satan, that is to pronounce the curse on him, so that he dies as a consequence of that curse, and that his spirit should be saved in the day of the Lord.' For 'This curse, following Jewish ideas, was to bring on the death of the person who was its object.'[40] Paul is not asking for the execution of the incestuous man but for his solemn expulsion from the community, after which (in Paul's thinking) the guilty man's death could not help following in some way or another.

One could go on discussing indefinitely whether Paul was justified in introducing into the Church this Jewish practice of pronouncing curses. In any case it was not a question of violence in the ordinary sense of the word, and I cannot see how this text could possibly be quoted in favour of war.

Chapter 3

THE NEW TESTAMENT NEVER SANCTIONS VIOLENCE

NEITHER Christ nor the apostles ever recommended lethal violence. They did not justify it nor sanction it. The only text which might be invoked as exception to this rule is Romans 13, where Paul seems to be sanctioning the use of violence, even of a lethal kind, on the part of the magistrate, that is to say the pagan judge, charged with the punishments of common law criminals. This is a text which I shall later be discussing in detail; but for the moment I would exclude it from consideration as not dealing with *Christian* judges. Let us now go quickly through all the other texts in the New Testament which are usually advanced to prove that Christ and the apostles would have sanctioned violence, and particularly the violence of soldiers.

(*a*) First, the examples may be quoted of John the Baptist giving instructions to the soldiers who came to ask him what they should do (Luke 3:14); of Jesus talking to the centurion of Capernaum (Luke 7:1-10), and to the royal officer whose son and servant He cured (John 4:46-53); of Peter when he converted the centurion Cornelius. None of the three reproached any of these men for being soldiers, nor asked them to leave the army. Therefore, it is suggested, Christ and the apostles saw no incompatibility between the profession of soldiering and Christianity. 'John the Baptist recognises the activities of the military as legitimate,' proclaims Luther, for example.[41] This conclusion seems very hasty, for the argument from silence is often fallacious.

You could justify anything by such reasoning in these cases. Jesus did not reproach Pilate for his presence in Palestine as *Gauleiter* of an occupying power; so He sanctioned the Roman occupation, and all military occupations generally; implicitly He must then condemn all defensive wars against a foreign invasion. He did not reproach the Herodians for their servile collaboration with the Romans; so He sanctioned all collaborations, including Vichy's. He did not reproach the Pharisees for their patriotism and their hostility to the Romans; so He also sanctioned patriotic resistance to the invader. He did not reproach His disciple Simon the Zealot for having been 'in the Maquis' and offered violent resistance to the Romans; so He sanctioned all resistance movements. He did not ask Zacchaeus to give up his job as head of the publicans; so He approved of the Roman occupation, its system of collecting taxes, and implicitly a powerful nation's right to colonise and exploit a weaker. He did not rebuke Pilate for having massacred the Galileans in the middle of their sacrifices (Luke 13:3), so He sanctioned the most brutal police measures. He did not reproach His own judges for the injustice and irregularity of their procedure in His case; so He sanctioned the trials used by dictatorships (and others) today. One could go on indefinitely in this vein, but to take one more argument *ad absurdum*, it would make the Bible approve of prostitution because Rahab the prostitute is often mentioned without her profession being condemned.

The whole argument would only begin to have some importance if it could be proved that in the instances quoted John the Baptist, Jesus, and Peter said nothing more than what is given to us in our extant New Testament accounts. But of course we have nothing like 'short-hand reports' of their conversations with these soldiers. Also, we can have no idea what these officers did or would have done once they had entered the Church; in the first two cases we are not even sure that they did effectively enter it. It would, too, have been a spiritual error to ask them to begin by changing their moral and professional life before being genuinely converted to the Gospel. The case of Zacchaeus (Luke 19) shows that Jesus knew how to wait for His hearers to deduce for themselves the consequences of His teaching and His love for them.

Those who make so much play with these four 'silences,' and deduce therefrom that the profession of arms is legitimate, do not seem so keen to deduce that the military occupation of a foreign country is legitimate (seeing that these soldiers had come to Palestine as troops of the occupation). If it *is* legitimate, why do we need a (defensive) army? The justification of military service is destroyed at its roots. And if not, why do they refuse this second deduction, having accepted the first?

Furthermore, if it is claimed that since Jesus admires that officer's faith, He admires his moral conduct also, this leaves out of account that the episode occurs before the Cross, before Ascension, and thus before a life of true Christian obedience was even possible. A reading

of the Gospels shows us that the sanctification of the disciples themselves was scarcely very advanced at that time—'For the Holy Spirit
was not yet given, because that Jesus was not yet glorified' (John
7:39). Jesus could not demand the fruits of the Spirit before the hour.
Any deduction from the centurion's faith as regards his personal
sanctification is therefore mistaken *a priori*.

The New Testament never speaks of the *principle* of military service, nor of the problem raised by the Christian's submission to this
service, for the good reason that the problem did not then arise.
The Roman army was made up of volunteers, who were called on
not only to carry out the brutalities of their calling but also to take
religious oaths incompatible with the Christian faith. They had to
arrest, torture, and execute believers—who had soon become suspicious characters. For another thing, it was doubtless hard for the
first Christians to forget that their Master had been crucified by
Roman soldiers; so they would never even have considered choosing
such a profession. As to the soldiers who became Christians, the
New Testament gives us absolutely no suggestion of how they
resolved their personal problem; it would be rash to try to fill in this
silence. According to certain texts of the early Fathers, it seems
that most of them put off their baptism till the day when they would
be released from their service.[42]

I readily accept that the Baptist's recommendation, 'Do violence
to no man' (Luke 3:14), cannot be considered as a criticism of the
soldier's calling, for it is obvious from the context that he was
referring not to the violence inherent in the principle of armies, but
to the unauthorised violence soldiers might commit for selfish reasons
and outside their orders. The silence of Jesus and the apostles, or
rather the fact that the New Testament does not report any speech
in which they pronounced a moral judgment on the soldier's calling,
cannot be exploited either for or against that calling. This is an
important element lacking, alas, for our study. But perhaps after all
it is a good thing, because it means that our judgment on the army
must be taken from the Gospel itself, and not from some phrase
of approval or condemnation which would make it dangerously easy
to do without a sound theological basis for our position.

(*b*) Then there is the parable in which Jesus describes 'a strong man
armed who keeps his palace, his goods are in peace' (Luke 11:21-22).
But Jesus is speaking here of the devil and not of us; and He presents
Himself as the one 'stronger than he' who 'shall come upon him and
overcome him.' So it would be absurd to claim that this text justifies

Christians in bearing arms. Here is how R. de Pury interprets this short parable:[43] 'No one can take the world out of the domination of the Power of darkness, unless he has first eliminated the use of all the means of that Power.' There is absolutely no question here of the army or of self-defence; on the contrary, Jesus compares himself to the aggressor.

(c) Paul several times makes allusions to military service, but only in metaphor or analogy to use in discussions concerning the Christian life. There is never the slightest moral sanction from him; he never expresses any moral judgment on the soldier's profession. 'What soldier ever serveth at his own charges?' (I Cor. 9:7). Here is Calvin's commentary:[44] 'Now, by this analogy taken from men's ordinary life, he confirms that he could have lived, had he wanted, at the expense of the Church . . . for it was the custom to supply food to the police from public money.' Paul was by no means justifying the army, but only the apostles' salary. He also wrote to Timothy (II Tim. 3:4): 'Thou therefore endure hardness, as a good soldier of Jesus Christ. No man that warreth entangleth himself in the affairs of life, that he may please him who hath chosen him to be a soldier.' And here again is Calvin's commentary:[45] 'All those who serve Christ wage war, and their way of waging war consists not in doing ill to others but rather in patience'—which might well bring a frown to the faces of our militarists. Then Calvin mocks those who 'know no other way of fighting their adversaries except by haughtiness and violence, and cannot accept the lesson that it is to possess their souls in patience. . . . Paul persists in the analogy of war he has adopted . . . he compares the profane way of waging war, that is the way in use in the world, with the spiritual and Christian way. . . . All those who wish to wage war under the standard of Jesus Christ must leave all delays and hindrances of this world, and give themselves totally to his service.'

(d) The same arguments apply to the parable where Jesus presents a king, who before making war on another king, sits down to see if he has enough soldiers to attack his enemy; otherwise he will ask him for peace (Luke 14:31-32). The context leaves no doubt whatever: Jesus is simply arguing from the prudence of this king that His disciples should 'count the cost' just as carefully before enrolling in His service. The parable carries no value judgment, favourable or unfavourable, on the principle of war as a method of resolving conflicts between kings. He is arguing from what actually happens, without presuming any sort of judgment as to what ought to happen.

(e) The same applies again to several parables where Jesus presents a king who wipes out his enemies (Matt. 22:7; Luke 19:27; 20:16). It scarcely needs repeating that the behaviour of the characters in Gospel parables are not normative from the ethical point of view, since the point and purpose of the parable are always elsewhere; and that Jesus presented in His parables a good many characters whose behaviour is morally more than suspect: e.g. the unjust judge, the man who finds a treasure in a field, and the man who made friends for himself with ill-earned wealth. No one has ever had the absurd idea of taking them as moral examples to be followed. Then again, Jesus compares Himself to a thief, but no one considers this a justification of theft. (In any case, if the massacres ordered by the kings in these parables are the sign of anything, it is of the Last Judgment and not of the wars whereby men seek to obtain justice for themselves in their mutual conflicts.) The parables speak to us of the Kingdom of God and not of Christian morality. In them Jesus exhibits men as they are, not as they ought to be.

(f) At the risk of wearying the reader, I would point out once more that when Jesus announced to His disciples that they would hear tell of wars and rumours of wars, that the nations would rise against each other (Matt. 24:6-7), and that the children of Israel would fall by the edge of the sword (Luke 21:24), He was certainly not suggesting that His disciples should take part in these wars.

(g) Hebrews 11 might be invoked with more reason. Among all the witnesses of the Old Covenant whose faith the writer gives us as examples, he quotes warriors like Moses, Gideon, Barak, Samson, Jephtha, and David. He recalls too the faith of those who 'subdued kingdoms . . . were valiant in war and turned to flight the armies of the aliens.' Therefore, the argument runs, participation in war is not incompatible with the faith.

I shall be considering in the next chapter the relationship between the Old Testament and the New. Here I would say two things only to refute this argument. First, the faith in Jesus Christ of the New Testament is different in ethical content from the faith of the men of the Old Testament—this is surely undeniable—and the two types of faith cannot be assimilated. If they could, it would presuppose that in relation to the Old Covenant the Gospel brought no new implications or demands. Plainly, Christians cannot model their ethical conduct on the men of the Old Testament.

Secondly, the author of Hebrews gives us as an example these warriors' *faith*, not their moral behaviour: their fundamental

religious attitude of creatures relying on their God's promises to
them. Abraham also showed his faith when he prepared to cut his
son's throat, and Jacob showed his when he deceived his kinsmen
and lied to them. Most decisively of all, Rahab the harlot is enumerated in the same passage as an example of faith; so we are surely not
expected to imitate the warriors' moral conduct, their adulteries and
polygamies and ritual murders (Jephtha's daughter) and trickery in
war. Their faith was manifested not so much by the act of making
war as by the miraculous way in which they made it. As Javet says[46]:
'In this enumeration faith is manifested by extraordinary events.
Whether they are triumphs or sufferings, they are always manifestations which are striking by their unprecedented character.' The accent
is on the miraculous character of the deliverances obtained, not on
the legitimacy of war itself—a question which does not seem to have
been raised before the coming of Christ, and which the author of
Hebrews certainly does not mean to raise here. So this passage
cannot offer a justification of war itself.

Chapter 4

THE TESTIMONY OF THE OLD TESTAMENT

DISCUSSION of Hebrews 11 has brought us to the testimony of the Old Testament. What guidance can we draw from it on the problem of war? From the point of view of the Christian ethic a study of the Old Testament is bound to be disappointing, because—as already pointed out—Old Testament texts cannot be normative for Christians, except when they can be interpreted Christologically; and this is particularly true for ethical questions. That is why I had to begin with the New Testament.

Calvin's fundamental error over the problem of war seems to lie precisely in the fact that he founds his ethic indifferently on the two Testaments, giving the same authority to both. And as the New Testament is very reserved on political questions, he has succumbed to the temptation of leaning heavily on the Old Testament, which of course is infinitely more explicit on everything concerned with war. This has led him to surprising contradictions, as witness the arguments by which he tries to justify war.[47] He first deduces the justification of war from the legitimacy of the death penalty, which he then bases on texts taken almost exclusively from the Old Testament, the only one from the New Testament being naturally Romans 13; yet he recognises the juridical ordinances given by Moses to the people of Israel alone as being out of date and not necessarily valid for other peoples (except, of course, for the 'moral law' of the Decalogue which remains valid for Christians), since 'the said judiciary laws can be broken and abolished without in any way violating the duty of charity.'

But here is the brutal fact: one can say by and large that the Old Testament ignores that respect for human life, that unconditional love, that non-violence, which as we have seen forms the general climate of the New Testament. There is a striking contrast here between the two parts of our Bible. It is remarkable to find, for instance, that the three great personalities of the Old Testament most often mentioned in the Gospels and to some extent associated with Jesus' ministry, of whom He often spoke and who have been seen as His remote forerunners, are all three of them men who never hesitated to shed blood, often in a most brutal manner. Moses had three thousand men slaughtered for having worshipped the golden calf (Exod. 32:28). David spent a large part of his existence making war, and killed almost the whole household of Nabal because the latter had doubted his Messianic royalty (I Sam. 25). As to Elijah, we know that he had four hundred prophets of Baal all massacred together after their spectacular defeat (I Kings 18).[48] Such is the contrast between these three men, the spiritual elite of the Old Covenant, and Jesus, gentle and meek of heart, who was concerned to spare the life even of the adulterous woman. Everywhere in the Old Testament human life is cheap, and the best believers have scarcely felt any scruples about shedding blood. This is one of the reasons why some Christians find it so disheartening to read the Old Testament: its believers are almost all warriors; only Jeremiah is non-violent in the manner of Jesus and the apostles.

Scattered through its pages, of course, there is another strain, universalist and pacific, which can be found especially in the prophets. There are even passages implying disapproval of massacre and bloodshed (I Sam. 25:31-33; I Chron. 28:3). But they may well be deplored more for ritual than moral reasons. There are some fine prophetic texts announcing the end of wars, such as the famous one identical in Isaiah (2:4) and Micah (4:3): 'and they shall beat their swords into plough-shares, and their spears into pruning-hooks: nation shall not lift up sword against nation, neither shall they learn war any more.' (Cf. also Isa. 11:6-10; 23:17-18; Hosea 2:18; Zech. 9:10; Psa. 72:3 and 14.) But what exactly do these Messianic prophecies signify? Will this pacifism be realised only at the end of time, at the return of Christ; or does it imply that from now on Christians must cease to go to war? One can hardly decide between these two opposing opinions without reference to the New Testament; or rather, the question only comes up because of the New Testament.[49]

At any rate, while the prophets did sometimes recommend their people to surrender to their enemies (Isa. 20; Jer. 21:8-10; 27:8-13), it was clearly not because they disapproved of war, but because God had revealed to them His certain intention of punishing His people by means of foreign armies, so that any attempt by Israel to resist the invasion of the Assyrians or Babylonians could only be foolish and also sinful, a mad attempt to escape divine punishment, which in the long run was bound to make the punishment more severe. The prophets did denounce the false security given by the weapons of war and warlike alliances (Isa. 30:1-7; 31:1-3; 36:6; Jer. 17:5). But it must be recognised that these fine pages, so scathing for the army, are denouncing war's futility rather than its immorality, the folly of concluding alliances without God's will rather than the principle of war itself.

Ritual ecstasies and frenzy, alcoholic and sexual orgies, human sacrifices and holy wars, were normal for the pagan tribes surrounding Israel; and the prophets fought fiercely against such excesses being introduced into the Jewish religion. But their protests against ritual drunkenness,[50] prostitution,[51] and the sacrifices of new-born babies[52] are much firmer and more intransigent than those against war. If by no means a bacchic or erotic God, Israel's 'Lord of Hosts' was certainly a warrior God.

There is no getting away from it: as far as the problem of war is concerned, the climate of the Old Testament is very different from that of the New. It contains declarations which are disconcerting and even scandalous (in the literal sense of the word) regarding the wars of extermination which God had explicitly ordered (Num. 31:17; Deut. 20:13-18; Joshua 8:22-24; 10:28, 35; Judges 21:10; I Sam. 15:3). Can the God of Jesus Christ really have ordered these massacres worthy of Hitler's gas chambers, or were the writers of the Old Testament attributing to God orders which came from an incomplete, primitive revelation? I will leave the reader to decide. This, in fact, is not a problem of Christian ethics but of Biblical theology which has no direct relevance to our subject; for even if God really gave such orders to Israel in pre-Gospel days, it would still not be proved that they were normative for the people of the New Covenant. The Old Testament does not know of gentleness, the benevolence towards all creatures of God, the charity towards enemies, which appears everywhere in the New Testament. The wonderful Psalms themselves are studded with ugly curses (e.g. Ps. 137:7-9), which Christians delicately take as symbolic whenever possible.[53]

It is understandable enough that the Marcionite heresy, whereby the Old Testament is rejected as contrary to the Gospel, should have been one of the first big temptations of Christian theology. But sometimes the whole of the Christian Church seems to have sunk into the opposite heresy, which would reintroduce into the New Covenant the bloodthirsty brutality of the Old Testament. In the last resort it is perhaps the same heresy, the same refusal or incapacity to overcome the antinomy between the two Testaments as regards loving one's neighbour. Marcion, to keep the charity of the Gospel, eliminated the Old Testament; the Church of Constantine, to keep the Old Testament, sacrificed the charity of the Gospels; but the two heresies are complementary, for both the Old Testament and non-violent charity must be kept.

But here is a decisive question: where does the non-violent gentleness of the Gospel come from? Where are its deep roots if not in the Old Testament? What can be the source of this Gospel doctrine of non-resistance to the evil-doer, of forgiveness for enemies, of unconditional charity? Could it come from the Glory that was Greece, the Grandeur that was Rome, the Syrio-Phoenician peoples, the mystery cults of the Middle East or the religions of the Far East? We must surely reject all these suppositions as unfounded. What seems certain is that Jesus was nurtured on Hebraic literature, and to all practical purposes on that alone; the same applies to the apostles. Yet the Gospel, with roots that go deep into the Old Testament, suddenly gives off an atmosphere which is radically different. How does this come about?

I can see only one satisfying answer: the systematic refusal of violence was a personal contribution by Jesus of Nazareth, His original discovery. It would be fascinating to know the way in which, through His patient study of the Law and the Prophets, Jesus gradually reached this completely new conviction. He was doubtless influenced by the sect of the Poor of Israel, and of course there are many texts in the Old Testament which speak of the kindness, the infinite mercy, the 'humanity' of the Almighty. Of course, too, the Old Testament already contains the Gospel in embryo. It is probable that Jesus was deeply impressed by the account of the 'still small voice' that spoke to Elijah (I Kings 19); by the fifty-third chapter of Isaiah; by the tragic destiny of Jeremiah, man of sorrows, and by the way in which David made absolutely no attempt to grasp by force or trickery the kingdom God had promised him through Samuel: he waited patiently for his royal crown on the sole good pleasure of the Almighty.[54] It remains true that up to this day the Jews have been waiting for a Messiah who will *not* be a suffering king, weak, non-violent, and vanquished! The synthesis of these scattered elements is therefore the new and original element which we owe to Jesus Himself.

Let us remember also that before and after Jesus several false Messiahs appeared, who all had this in common: they used violence —those of whom Gamaliel speaks in Acts 5:36-37, and also the one referred to in the recently discovered Dead Sea Scrolls. Compared to these apprentice Messiahs, Jesus was a completely original King of the Jews, which explains the mocking tone of Pilate's question: 'Art thou the King of the Jews?' (John 18:33) and hesitations about condemning him; for the Governor saw clearly that this was not a Messiah like the rest, precisely because He represented no *military* danger for Rome.

This is part of the crucial misunderstanding between Jesus and His people. His method of non-violence was strange by comparison with the Old Testament: neither military nor political, it bewildered His contemporaries and disappointed even His friends and disciples. His own mother and brothers failed to understand Him because they had hoped He would manifest Himself to Israel after the manner of the world, with the methods of violence. In the crisis the crowd deserted Him at once because *they* were ready to use violence and could not see why He still would not use it.

Yet from one end of His ministry to the other it remained the great temptation for Him, all the more terrible because by resisting it He was carving out an entirely new road. This is how all the Biblical scholars interpret the third temptation (Matt. 4:8-10), when the Devil offers Him the conquest of the world 'if thou will fall down and worship me,' that is to say, if Jesus will agree to use Satan's means, including violence, to conquer the world. Then there is the plot whereby the crowd try to take Him away by force to make Him King (John 6:15), that is, compel Him to be a military king. There is the entry into Jerusalem on Palm Sunday when Jesus deliberately chooses to ride an ass instead of the horse of a political chieftain. There is the agony at Gethsemane where He must accept the need to be conquered without resistance. Several sentences He lets slip during his Passion help one to guess the inward drama developing in His heart, because right to the end He is still tempted by the use of violence: 'Thinkest thou,' He says to Peter, who has just brandished a sword, 'that I cannot pray to my Father, and he shall presently give me more than twelve legions of angels?' (Matt. 26:53). And Pilate is treated to the same echo of His inner conflict: 'If my kingdom were of this world, then would my servants fight that I should not be delivered to the Jews . . .' (John 18:36). Finally, of course, the temptation reaches its paroxysm at the Crucifixion when the crowd mock Him: 'He saved others, let him save Himself, if he be Christ . . .' (Luke 23:35). But He stands firm, faithful to the line of conduct He has set Himself, however disastrous it may appear: 'Father, forgive them, for they know not what they do.'

The whole Gospel drama cannot be reduced, of course, to this question of violence. But I think it will be agreed that the stubborn rejection of violence is a positive and illuminating factor in the development of Jesus' ministry. His independent attitude in this, compared with the tradition of violence emanating from the Jewish Scriptures, is found again among the writers of the New Testament and the Fathers of the Church. They too were brought up on the Old Testament, with all its glorifications of nationalism and militarism; they saw in it the Word of God in its full sense; yet they were unanimous in following Jesus on the road of non-violence.[55]

And the Christians who so readily invoke the Old Testament to justify war are a little presumptuous, since they are thereby claiming to know and interpret the Old Testament better than the Christians of the first three centuries did, including the apostles and Christ himself.

Let us fall neither into the Marcionite heresy nor the Constantinian. Let us keep the Old Testament because Jesus and the Gospel were nurtured on it and because it is orientated towards the Messiah's coming. It remains for us the Word of God, even though some of its ordinances are superseded because of the Gospel. But let us keep also the non-violence of the Gospels, because its new note compared with the Old Testament is evidently a personal and original affirmation by Jesus Himself. To muffle this note by linking the Church once again with the use of violence seems to me a betrayal of the Master's thought and intention, which He expressed clearly and forcibly enough, and for which He certainly paid a heavy enough price. It has always been the Church's temptation to construct a theology of glory which dispenses with the Cross (I Cor. 2:2).

Chapter 5

WEAKNESS ACCORDING TO THE GOSPEL

FOR the sake of convenience I have so far been using the term 'non-violence'; but this too is unbiblical, and another disadvantage is that the term is liable to be misunderstood, suggesting an interpretation of Christian charity as something soft and spineless. The Gospel, however, implies a certain violence, spiritual, certainly, never leading to brutal coercion and bloodshed, but nevertheless a kind of violence, a concentrated and active moral energy. It is illustrated by Jesus' attitude in driving the money-changers out of the Temple, and we find it again in his invectives against the Pharisees (Matt. 23). He was aware of having come to bring a fire upon the earth, not peace but a sword: the spiritual division, that is, between those who believe in Him and those who refuse to believe. He recommends his disciples to 'hate' their kin, and even their own life (Luke 14:26). It is clear that life according to the Gospel is a perpetual tension, a continual strife which is no less bitter for being fought out on the spiritual and not the material plane.[56]

The apostle Paul, who often uses analogies with physical force (Gal. 1:8-9; 2:11), explains (Eph. 6:12): 'For we wrestle not against flesh and blood, but against principalities, against powers, against the rulers of this world of darkness, against spiritual wickedness in high places. Wherefore take unto you the whole armour of God. . . .' Yes, the Christian is a soldier who must fight the good fight of the faith (Timothy passim.). And it is doubtless in this sense too that we must understand Jesus' words, obscure though they are, when He says that 'the violent' take the Kingdom of Heaven by force (Matt. 11:12). He is demanding of His hearers a true faith which He compares to spiritual 'violence': in Calvin's words (*Comm.*, 1, 277), 'ardent affection' and 'vehement impetuosity' with which believers take possession of the Kingdom and enter into it.

No, the non-violence of the Gospel certainly does not imply cowardice and abdication before evil; on the contrary, it demands great moral strength and full self-mastery, stubborn refusal to let sin

E

triumph in one's own heart: which is no small thing! For the non-violent man in this sense is one who, when his enemy's attitude fills him with indignation, suffers also from the access of sinful anger in his own heart; so he refuses to indulge his own longing to hit back and get his revenge, to justify himself by hurting his adversary (Matt. 15:18-19; 5:21-22; I John 3:15). For violence is a reaction from pride, whereas Jesus asked us to look first at our own faults before considering those of others (Matt. 7:3-5; John 8:7; Rom. 2:1; 12:3; Gal. 6:1-5; Phil. 2:3). The Christian who indulges in material violence forgets that he is a sinner who lives by grace. He seeks his justification in his own vengeance and not in God's pardon (Rom. 12:17-21). This is true for communities as for individuals.

We can see here, in fact, that the 'violence' and 'non-violence' of the Gospel have come together and bear a strange resemblance: far from excluding each other, they both signify the same refusal to make any compromise with sin. They often co-exist, and are indeed two complementary aspects of the Christian attitude.

Perhaps it would be better to speak of 'weakness' according to the Gospel, for this term is often used in the New Testament to designate Christ's deep-rooted attitude. 'For though he was crucified through weakness, yet he liveth by the power of God' (II Cor. 13:4). 'For . . . the weakness of God is stronger than men' (I Cor. 1:25). The cross is in the whole line of Jesus' teaching. There were not two different and alternating moral attitudes in His life, so that He was 'violent' in some cases and 'non-violent' in others; He always acted and lived looking towards the Cross, which He knew was the natural and logical end to his ministry (Mark 10:38, 45; Luke 12:50; Matt. 16:21) —and for which He had prepared from the first day in full awareness of what it meant (John 9:4; Luke 13:32).

What does it signify—this 'weakness' of Christ? First it reveals the infinite respect in which God holds His human creatures, whose conscience and heart He will not force or violate, and the humble hope He has of winning them to Himself nevertheless. In this sense violence and physical coercion, because they exclude respect and hope for the person on whom they are practised, are very much the opposite of the love incarnated in Christ and lived by Him. This courageous weakness is also the sign of God's forgiveness; for God is wounded by my sinning, and if He nevertheless loves me, the sinner, it implies that He is bearing the weight of the sin and Himself enduring its consequences. This is the only road which leads to reconciliation, and here again there is an absolute opposition between the forgiveness expressed by this 'weakness' and murderous violence, because the latter shows you refuse to endure the injury, to bear the cost of your neighbour's ill-doing. Like God, man has no other choice between destroying the sinner and forgiving him freely. The weakness of Jesus is our wonderful proof that God has resolutely chosen the second method with us; but He also points us to the same path.

Finally, this weakness is Christ's best arm; for it is the spectacle of His love and His complete self-sacrifice which alone can break down in us the very roots of sin, and disgust us with evil. Gratitude towards Him who gave His life for us is the only force strong enough to overcome in our hearts the attractions of sin. This is where Christ's power and victory are seen, but it is again the opposite of violence, which always hardens the evil-doer's heart, which can only aggravate evil, not resolve or extinguish it. Violence breeds hatred, resentment, and more violence; never peace or love. Tragically, we reap what we have sown (Gal. 6:7), and grapes are not gathered from thorns (Matt. 7:16). In this sense the Cross is the only true victory over the power of evil.

Jesus expressly called His disciples to follow Him on this path of weakness or non-violence, of complete service to humanity. For to quote Macgregor again:[57] 'We err if we isolate the Cross, as if it were a unique divine transaction without any relevance to the morality Jesus taught or the sort of life to which He called His disciples after having first lived it Himself.' 'He that taketh not his cross, and followeth after me, is not worthy of me' (Matt. 10:38). 'If any man will come after me, let him deny himself, and take up his cross and follow me. For whosoever will save his life shall lose it: and whosoever will lose his life for my sake shall find it' (Matt. 16:24-25; Luke 9:23). 'Ye shall drink of the cup that I drink of; and with the baptism that I am baptised withal shall ye be baptised . . .' (Mark 10:39-45). 'Behold, I send you forth as sheep in the midst of wolves' (Matt. 10:16). One could go on indefinitely quoting similar texts where Jesus calls His disciples to humble and gentle service which excludes any use of sanguinary violence (John 10:15-16, *et al.*).

As the preceding pages should have proved clearly enough, this is certainly how the apostles understood their mission. They had the very definite feeling that Christ's non-violent weakness pledged them and obliged them to live themselves in the same spiritual attitude. 'And walk in love, as Christ also hath loved us, and hath given himself for us an offering and a sacrifice to God . . .' (Eph. 5:2; II Cor. 8:9). 'Let this mind be in you, which was also in Christ Jesus: who made himself of no reputation, and took upon him the form of a servant . . . and became obedient unto death . . .' (Phil. 2:5-8). 'Christ also suffered for you, leaving you an example, that ye should follow his steps . . . who, when he was reviled, reviled not again; when he suffered, he threatened not . . .' (I Peter 2:21-23).[58] On the other hand, not a single text can be quoted, in which either Christ or the apostles envisaged a reversal of this rule, any sort of dispensation, any authorisation however provisional or occasional, to employ violence. From one end to the other it is always the same note that is sounded.

With fine poetic power Paul has described the weakness to which he has held firm, in his life and his ministry, through faithfulness to the crucified Christ: 'God hath made of us the last of men, as it were condemned to death. . . . We are fools for Christ's sake . . . despised . . . buffeted . . . being reviled, we bless; being persecuted, we suffer it; being defamed, we entreat: we are made as the filth of the world, the off-scourings of all men . . .' (I Cor. 4:9-13). 'We are troubled, but not in despair; persecuted, but not forsaken; cast down, but not destroyed; always bearing about in the body the dying of the Lord Jesus, that the life also of Jesus might be made manifest in our body . . .' (II Cor. 4:8-11; 9:13). Because of this perpetual miracle of grace Paul glorifies in *weakness* (II Cor. 11:30), for he has learnt that the power of God is fulfilled in the Christian's weakness: 'Most gladly therefore will I rather glory in my infirmities, that the power of Christ may rest upon me. Therefore I take pleasure in infirmities, in reproaches, in persecutions, in calumnies, in distresses for Christ's sake; for when I am weak, then am I strong!' (II Cor. 12:9-10).

Imitation of Jesus Christ? Or the effort to live a life of obedience in harmony with the Gospel? It does not matter much; these two attitudes are doubtless both there at once. But the essential thing is that the Christian is a being called to follow Christ on the road of the Cross. 'In the Cross, where Christ's life found its most complete expression lies the secret of all Christian *action*.'[59] The weakness of the Christian means that he lays himself completely open to God's power, gives it free access to his heart for a witness which shall be truly to the glory of God alone.

It is often said that this is an unrealisable 'ideal.' But the New Testament's teaching on marriage can also be considered as unrealisable, yet the Church has never ceased to preach it faithfully. Moreover, the assertion that non-violence is unrealisable seems a little hasty, for surely the Church records countless lives of Christians who have been truly non-violent—even if, of course, they were not saints who had reached moral perfection—and there are doubtless thousands of Christian martyrs whose very names are forgotten because they disappeared anonymously in the arenas, the prisons, the galleys, and who were none the less non-violent. Nor is it so easy to reject the witness of Gandhi; after him, who can say any longer that non-violence is impossible for political man?

God gives what He commands. This testimony of non-violence is not an 'ideal' which will appear at the end of our 'efforts.' Here, as everywhere else, the life of *obedience* to which we are *called* is *given* to us by *grace*. This weakness, which I called a demand implied in the Gospel, is really a magnificent promise made to anyone who believes in Jesus Christ. If the branch remains attached to the vine, it too will bear the rare and delicate fruit (John 15). Besides, to live in Christ and keep His commandments is surely one and the same thing. In other words, the triumphant life of Christ crucified and resurrected springs forth of its own accord in the heart of anyone who joins himself to Christ by faith. We are not asked to practise non-violence and imitate Christ's weakness, so much as to remain in His communion. But He has proclaimed to us that if we remain in it and keep His words, He gives us the grace to live by His example, because He comes Himself to live in our being and to obey for us. Then our daily existence is genuinely a witness, because it tells of His love and sings of His power.

But the man who can say 'Christ lives in me' is the man who 'has been crucified with Christ' (Gal. 2:20). To 'know Christ and the power of his resurrection,' one must first 'know the fellowship of his sufferings, being made conformable to his death' (Phil. 3:10). 'Now if we be dead with Christ, we believe that we shall also live with him' (Rom. 6:8). In other words our obedience as Christians, which is at once asked of us and promised to us, can be genuine obedience only if we live here and now in the communion of the crucified Saviour. Then it can be the fruit of the Holy Spirit. 'But the fruit of the Spirit is love, joy, peace, long-suffering, gentleness, goodness, faith, meekness, temperance' (Gal. 5:22). In short, the Christian faith expresses itself on the moral plane by non-violence. This is at once the demand and the grace of the Good News.

It is sometimes said that countless Christians have kept this *inner* spiritual attitude while taking part in war. But surely the Gospel demands harmony between our inner attitude and our outward behaviour? This is probably why Jesus, as if to preserve us in advance from spiritual unawareness, uses equivalent expressions alternately: dwell in me, keep my words, keep my commandments (John 15:7; 14:23; 15:10; I John 2:3-6; 3:22-24). Piety cannot be dissociated from morality. Man's love for God is proved true by his love for his neighbour, according to the 'new Commandment' which Jesus has given us: 'That ye love one another as I have loved you' (John 13:34).

To return to our original question: can a Christian take part in war? Is our participation in the general killing a glorification of the name of Jesus Christ, a clear positive witness rendered to our Saviour, an evident and indisputable expression of our loyal and living obedience to our Lord, a preaching of the Son of God crucified and resurrected for the salvation of all men, a fruit of the Holy Spirit within us? I find it impossible to answer these questions with anything but a categorical 'No.' And in pronouncing that 'No,' I believe I can hear the whole New Testament singing with me, as in a majestic Bach chorale, the glory of the Crucified and His martyred disciples.

Chapter 6

SOME OBJECTIONS

AT this point I would pause to answer certain objections which I am putting in the mouth of an imaginary critic. In the next part of the book I shall consider in detail the only one which raises a serious problem, that of Christian obedience to the State. The other objections, though they have been made or implied by reputable theologians, seem to me more or less trivial and easily disposed of.

1. Moralism

'Jesus is not a moralist. He did not come to bring the world a table of new values, saying "this is good, this is bad"; His aim was to go beyond the categories of good and evil, to replace the letter by the spirit, obedience to the law by Communion with the Father.'

Now of course it is false to lay all the stress on the outward act, on rules of conduct, ignoring the intention behind the act. But that is no reason for ignoring the act itself, which after all expresses an intention and cannot be dissociated from it. As Conord puts the point:[60] 'There are no Christian principles in the abstract sense . . . on which you could build a co-ordinated system . . . for it is concrete obedience to the living God which makes the Christian. But negatively there are regulatory, critical principles which reject, after the manner of the prophets, "all that is evil in the sight of the Lord" . . . and there are also positive principles, if they are considered as guides for the Christian . . . to help him make his personal decisions.'

Jesus does not abolish the law; He fulfils it (Matt. 5:17). Yes, the Gospel abolishes the Law as a means of salvation, but preserves it as the norm of obedience for the regenerate Christian (Gal. 5:22). If it is being a moralist to say that a Christian should not kill or steal or slander or deceive his wife, we are presumably all moralists! The Church today seems far more in danger of devitalising the Gospel than of becoming excessively moralistic.

If our imaginary critic should say that I am putting men back under the law instead of under grace, I would answer: grace can be conceived only as a dialogue between the Gospel of forgiveness in Christ and the condemnation brought upon us by the law; if there is no more law, there is no more grace either.

Martin Dibelius writes:[61] 'The so-called commandments of the Gospel are therefore not commandments as the Jews knew them, observances which everyone must fulfil in the same manner, preparing for them punctually, applying them exactly and laboriously; they are present *examples* making concrete the eternal demand of God. They show man what is God's demand now and for him; this demand is not for all men and for all times, but for him in his actual situation.' There is a weak point, however, in this superficially attractive formulation: if one cannot generalise from 'do good to your enemies' because it is a particular example, a special case, the same will surely apply to 'be subject unto the higher powers.' The choice seems rather arbitrary between those of the New Testament's moral demands which 'of course don't apply to all Christians in all ages'—a convenient way of pigeon-holing them—and those which are to be kept as essential and permanent, so that the Christian must go on obeying them today. And if, to avoid such a contradiction, it is asserted that Romans 13, as well as the Sermon on the Mount, made a real demand only on those to whom it was addressed, then we are plunged into complete moral agnosticism.

An excess of 'moralism' is doubtless a deformation of Christianity, but without a minimum of it one could hardly make a distinction, for instance, between marriage and concubinage. Some of those who accuse pacifists of being too moralistic are themselves very inconsistent: they maintain that there is no Christian morality outside personal faith and the Holy Spirit's immediate inspiration, valid for the individual only at a particular time and place; they also maintain that the morality of the Gospel has nothing at all to do with the State or the *political* activities of the citizen. But what of the Christian's attitude as a citizen, of that part of the morality of the Gospel which is concerned with the Christian's *political* obedience? If all Christian morality is Christological, yet politics are not affected by the Gospels, what happens to this very concrete sector of Christian life? Our theologians are again reduced to a moral agnosticism more in keeping with the sickness of our times than with the proud language of the New Testament.

Karl Barth strangely introduces the notoriously ambiguous concept of 'liberty' when attacking pacifists' 'moral absolutism': 'they are not free men,' he says,[62] 'because of their refusal on principle to take part in war.' But is there nothing a Christian must refuse to do on principle in all circumstances? If a Christian says, 'I would *never* rape a woman,' does this limit his liberty in any real sense? The conscientious objector who is prepared to go to prison rather than abandon his convictions may be nearer than most, I should have thought, to true Christian freedom: resolute obedience to God as He has spoken in the Gospel.

2. Casuistry

'But if you are so anxious to avoid defiling yourself by having anything to do with war, you will become entangled in a casuistry reminiscent of the Pharisees. Where do you draw the line between what is permissible and what is not? Should no Christian become an army chaplain, or a stretcher-bearer? Should he pay his taxes, or travel on the railways?'

But the Christian who submits to military law has the same difficulty in drawing the line, the same problems of conscience. Surely he is bound to feel a constant tension between the witness of the Cross and his military obedience. If all the army's demands and orders are necessarily Christ's demands and orders for him without the shadow of a doubt, his conscience may be at rest; but if so, his faith too has gone to sleep. A husband torn between wife and mistress still has problems of conscience; not so the husband who has gone off with his mistress. A soldier for whom obedience to Jesus Christ in the army raises no difficulties has left his true Lord and gone off with the god Mars.

In fact, of course, there is exactly the same sort of problem for the Christian who goes into the army and the Christian conscientious objector. The former, if he truly believes in Jesus Christ, will constantly be asking himself painfully: 'can I glorify Christ while I do that? Shall I not be separated from Jesus by this mission I have just been charged with? Can I really shoot hostages I know to be innocent? Organise a field brothel for my battalion? Torture this prisoner from whom my chiefs want to extract important secrets? Release my bombs on this village which I can see is full of civilians?' If this is casuistry, then there is no escape from it for anyone who takes Christ seriously as his Lord. Whether soldier or conscientious objector, he will inevitably have to face agonising problems of conscience.

I cannot here consider all these problems in detail; but I would beg the Church of Christ not to go on preaching, unless sure such a proposition is true, that you can remain in the Saviour's communion with a tommy-gun in your hand.

3. Compromise

'But listen, a Christian cannot avoid making compromises. You will have to, just like the rest.'

A compromise is an agreement whereby adversaries make concessions to each other. In the case we are concerned with, the adversaries are on the one side the Gospel, and on the other a certain politico-philosophic conception which justifies and even glorifies military service. By talking of compromise, you are implicitly acknowledging the fundamental antagonism between the two sides. But if there is such an antagonism, can we imagine Jesus being ready to make an agreement with his adversary? Does He not demand a total obedience from us, even to 'hating' others and our own life? Can there be an agreement between Christ and Belial (II Cor. 6:14-15), between Christ and Mammon (Matt. 6:24)?

Moreover, the idea of compromise implies that of justification: consciences have been reassured by the agreement made, a standard has been justifiably modified or altered. But what compromise was possible between the Gospel and Nazism? The least concession made by the representatives of Christianity to the Hitlerian ideology was bound to be a deformation, a betrayal of the Gospel. Why should not the same apply for the philosophy of military service? Either it fits properly into the Christian ethic, in which case there is neither compromise nor problem, or it is a 'foreign body' in relation to the Gospel, a demand which does not flow naturally from the Christian ethic, in which case any compromise can only be a corruption of the Gospel.

4. Responsibility

'It is impossible for you,' writes Jean Brice,[63] 'not to take your share in the sin of the world. The fact of carrying a sword or not will make little difference to your responsibility. . . . What is the point in cutting off your hand to keep you from striking, if you do not cut off your tongue to keep you from lying?'

This objection is based on a confusion between two very different ideas: on the one hand, the responsibility we bear and share with all men for the factual situation which exists in the world, and in particular for the starting of wars; on the other hand, the responsibility we are personally involved in with every act we perform.

Let us call the former type of responsibility metaphysical and collective, the latter ethical and personal. The former charges me before God with having sinned, the latter adjures me in the name of God not to sin. The former calls me to repentance, the latter to obedience. The fallacy in Brice's statement is therefore obvious.

For according to the former definition everyone can agree: yes, we have all taken our part in the sin of the world, we all bear part of the responsibility for the starting of wars; and if any Christian pacifist ever imagined that in refusing military service he had redeemed his responsibility for a war, claiming to be innocent of the disaster, then one may say straight out that he was wrong. Even in prison the conscientious objector bears a part before God, probably equal to anyone else's, in the collective responsibility for the situation which has led to war or will lead to it. In this sense, but in this sense only, Brice is right that 'the fact of carrying a sword or not will make little difference to our responsibility.' Whatever we do, we are all guilty of the war, which is the fruit of all the sins of the whole of humanity.

But in the other sense, from the point of view of ethical and personal responsibility, Brice's words are a mere quibble, amounting only to this: since I am already in sin up to the neck, there is no reason not to commit that particular sin too. 'What is the point in refraining from sleeping with this pretty girl, since I have already looked at her lustfully?' The quotation above would seem to justify this argument equally well. When the apostle writes, after the Sermon on the Mount: 'Whosoever hateth his brother is a murderer' (I John 3:15), he is exposing the hypocritical self-righteousness of those who believe themselves pure because they have not committed blameworthy *acts*; but he certainly does not mean, any more than Jesus did, that since I have hated my brother, I may just as well kill him.

'But you cannot help participating in the sin of war: by merely paying taxes, walking on strategic roads, by eating and by breathing you are still participating in the crime you claim to repudiate.'

'Really?' would be my answer. 'And what about Jesus Christ? Did He not pay taxes which served to maintain either the Roman army of occupation or the Temple police—who were to arrest and torture Him? Did He not walk on roads which helped the domination of the foreigner? Did He not cure possible soldiers? Did His words not bring comfort to the morale of a population ready to revolt against the occupying power? Did He not buy food and so fall in with the war economy of His time? Did He not breathe under the protection of the army? Did He thereby participate in the crime of war? Here is Christ convicted of sin!'

That is what comes of trying to prove too much: you fail to prove anything; by being too clever you talk nonsense. Jesus paid taxes and walked on roads; if by so doing He did not participate in social and international crime, then neither did I. It is not by my taxes and my use of the roads, but by my sin, selfishness, national pride, lack of civil spirit, by my fears, that I participate like anyone else in the sin of war. But just because of my responsibility for war's coming, it certainly does not mean that once it is started I must work to make it as murderous as possible. Because I have a part in its causes I am not obliged to take part in its execution. If by carelessness I set fire to my house, I do not therefore have to make sure that the whole house burns down.

The martyrs of the first centuries, the Huguenots of the sixteenth, did not believe themselves freed from responsibility for the situation of their time; but the sense of their common guilt in the sins of their respective peoples did not stop them from saying a categorical 'no,' which cost them their lives, when men tried to constrain them to an act they saw as a denial of their faith in Jesus Christ. In saying this 'no,' they may have felt just as much sinners as the rest, but for them it was a question of obedience: solidarity with our country should not be confused with solidarity in our country's crimes.

There are two ways of washing our hands of a crime. There are those who when Christ has been crucified insist they had nothing to do with it; they are indeed absurdly naïve. But there are also those who, when the question comes up of committing this crime in a concrete situation, withdraw behind so-called human solidarity in sin and deliberately crucify the Saviour 'with a good conscience.' Certainly we have all crucified Him, but that is no sort of reason for doing so again. By taking up arms, am I crucifying Christ or not? That is the only question, and it is futile to attempt arguments from collective responsibility.

5. Lack of 'Realism'

'You ignore the concrete reality of the world you are living in; you deny the positive character of the political order; you leave out of account all the bonds tying you to the human society of which you are a part.'

There is a serious warning here. Many Christian pacifists have too easily resolved, or rather by-passed, the problem, ignoring in their reasoning the positive and compelling reality of the State with its indisputable demands. By denying one of the terms of the contradiction, one of the poles of tension the Christian is involved in merely by living in the world, they have imagined they were solving the problem of war; instead, they were just evading it. Jesus Christ is the Lord of governments as well as of the Church; the Christian is both a member of the Church and a dutiful citizen. In forgetting this double context, some Christian objectors have invalidated their testimony, at least from the theological point of view. But it by no means follows that any Christian refusing military service *must* adopt such a theological position.

Traditional Christian 'militarists,' however, have also ignored the concrete reality of the world we live in. They use abstractions like 'national self-defence,' which nowadays seems more like national suicide, and 'the just war,' which is exceedingly difficult to envisage in terms of modern war; but in any case they would also suppress the fundamental tension inherent in the Christian life, because at least in case of war they normalise the Church's surrender to the State, the Christian's subordination to the citizen. Instead of withdrawing piously into their ivory tower, as some pacifists have done, they charge into battle with religious fervour: like the Inquisitors, they claim to be carrying out God's judgment! They reject the sixth commandment and the Sermon on the Mount, and when mobilisation is ordered they can use Romans 13 as an excuse for putting the rest of the New Testament into cold storage 'for the duration.' By emancipating themselves from the morality of the Gospel, from the need to obey Jesus Christ, they show the pride of setting themselves above the human condition.

6. The State

'But if the State requires you for military service, are you not called to obey it by our Lord Himself?'

Here at last is a pertinent objection. If it points to a geniune demand from the Gospel, we shall have to consider how far it will modify or amend the call to non-violence which otherwise seems to be enjoined on us so powerfully.

PART III

THE CHRISTIAN'S OBEDIENCE TO THE STATE

Here, then, is the antithesis we must consider in the next chapters.
'Yes, of course, the Christian must be non-violent *in his private life*,'
I shall be told, 'but as the State must secure respect for order and
justice by compulsion, and as the Christian is also an obedient
citizen, he is called on to support the State, and to use violence, if
need be, in helping it to defend the nation against its enemies. In
short, the Christian must also obey the State.'

Chapter 1

THE CHRISTIAN'S ATTITUDE TO THE STATE

I HAVE used the word 'State' only with some hesitation. For one thing, the word is not in the Bible, and it is always dangerous to introduce into theology not only a word, but an idea with that word, an idea which is foreign to Biblical thought. It may also be ambiguous, since there is little enough in common between the Israelite theocracy, the pagan Roman Empire, the Christian theocracy the men of the Reformation dreamed of, and the modern State, secularised and more or less totalitarian.

There is, however, a common denominator behind these widely varying forms of political organisation: there have always been authorities who exercised the civil power over a given territory. It is in this sense, then, that I have reluctantly decided to use the word State; but we must take good care here not to introduce into theology the pagan virus of a deified City.

1. *The Evidence of the New Testament*

The first striking thing, when we approach the problem of the Christian's obedience to the political authorities, is the very small number of texts which can serve as a basis for such a study. That in itself is significant.

(*a*) In the Gospels we find an allusion to the kings who 'exercised authority' over their peoples (Mark 10:42), two ambiguous texts about the payment of tribute to the Romans (Mark 12:13-17; Matt. 17:24-27), and the equally ambiguous answer which Jesus gave Pilate on the power He had received from on high (John 19:11). And that is all. For we have already seen that if in certain parables Jesus presents kings who exact tribute and punish, no normative conclusions can be drawn from such people, who are described as they are, not as they should be. I shall be returning to these four Gospel texts later on.

(*b*) The evidence to be found in the Acts is extremely vague. It is true that in it the apostles always keep a very respectful attitude towards the civil authorities, whether the Sanhedrin of Jerusalem

(Acts 4:9; 7:2; 23:5) or the Roman authorities (Acts 24:3, 10). Sometimes Paul does not hesitate to appeal to the latter for protection against the mob attacking him (Acts 23:17; 25:10-12). He proudly invokes his status as Roman citizen, one privileged under the law, to avoid unjust punishment (Acts 16:37; 21:39; 22:25). But elsewhere the apostles do not seem to have been unduly concerned to respect these authorities' orders. Peter and John openly flout the Sanhedrin, who had forbidden them to preach the Gospel (Acts 4:29, 33; 5:42). They even go so far as to proclaim frankly before the Sanhedrin that they will go on preaching Christ's name (Acts 4:19-20). Paul for his part seems to have maintained a very unrestrained attitude towards the local and Roman authorities he was continually coming up against in his missionary tours; and we should not forget that he was very often in prison. But apart from the proud answer of Peter and John, 'We ought to obey God rather than men' (Acts 5:29), there is no precise indication in the Acts to throw light on our problem of the Christian's attitude to the State.

Let us note, however, that the proconsul Gallio refuses, as representative of the State, to pronounce on religious questions, so long as no crime has been committed against the public order (Acts 18:14-15). This text appears to fit in well with the traditional theory of the separation of the two orders. But why should the theologian consider Gallio's attitude as *normative*, when the Acts show us several other representatives of the political authorities whose attitude does not fit in with that theory nearly so well? Let us see we do not choose in the Scriptures anything which corresponds to our preconceived ideas, while discreetly leaving on one side anything which contradicts them or simply does not corroborate them. All one can say is that the author of the Acts *may* have seen Gallio's attitude as a model of political wisdom. But it is equally possible that we in the twentieth century find it excellent because it agrees with our ideas, whereas it is reported here in a purely objective way without any apparent hint of approval. Calvin, for instance, actually blames the proconsul for having stopped Paul making a defence, for speaking in mockery and disdain of God's law, and for not 'maintaining the pure service of God' by upholding the truth Paul was proclaiming. For 'there is no greater absurdity than to leave the service of God to men's appetites.'[64] In fact Calvin deplores Gallio's religious neutrality, which nowadays we tend to admire. So we must be careful how we use this text, and not try to make it the basis for any sort of theory of the State.

(*c*) It is in the Epistles that we find the most definite texts on the Christian's obedience to the political authorities, in particular the only one which is truly explicit and apparently categorical: Romans 13. This will serve as a basis for my whole study, and so I shall not linger on it here.

In the first Epistle to Timothy Paul asks that prayers be made 'for kings and for all that are in authority, that we may lead a quiet and peaceable life in all godliness and honesty. . . . For God . . . will have all men to be saved, and to come into the knowledge of the truth' (2:2). Barth, it is well known, has tried to find in this text the theological foundations of Law and the State—which must maintain the order indispensable to human society and thus allow the Church to preach the Gospel. Calvin had already expressed the idea in his own theological perspective: 'The magistrates are ordered of God for the guarding and preservation both of religion and public peace and honesty.'[65]

Paul also tells Titus to remind believers 'to be subject to the magistrates and the authorities, to obey, to be ready to every good work . . . (Titus 3:1). Even if the word 'obey' goes with 'the magistrates,' which is not certain, it would merely confirm that there is a general duty of obedience to the authorities. Let us look more closely at what is implied in such a duty.

In the First Epistle of Peter (2:13-17) there is a text which seems to be a commentary on Romans 13, and which does not otherwise bring in anything new: 'Submit yourself to every authority established among men, for the Lord's sake: whether it be to the king as supreme; or unto governors, as unto them that are sent by him for the punishment of evil-doers and the praise of them that do well. . . . Honour the king.' Calvin interprets 'sent by him' as 'sent by God,' though without justifying this interpretation; but even if we accept it, we still have only a new confirmation of the general duty of submission to the State; nothing about *how far* a Christian should submit.[66]

(*d*) The allusions to the Roman State in Revelations are strikingly different from those in the Epistles. The Roman Empire is represented rather unflatteringly as a beast with ten horns and ten crowns, to whom 'the dragon gave his power and his seat and great authority.' This beast has 'a mouth speaking great things and blasphemies,' he 'makes war with the saints,' but 'all that dwell upon the earth adore him . . .' (Rev. 13, see also 17:8-18). Obviously the atmosphere here is quite different: the Roman Empire's persecution of Christians had reached its climax. The author of Revelation therefore sees the State as a reality essentially hostile to the Church and the kingdom of Christ, the 'incarnation of the devil.'[67] 'For the (Christian) community realised that it was confronted by a State which claimed absolute power; so it could only consider that State as delivered over to demons.'[68]

This passage scarcely suggests that the Roman State received its power from God. 'It was given unto him,' says verse 7, 'to make war with the saints, and to overcome them; and power was given him over all tribes, and tongues, and nations.' The context expressly reveals that this power and authority comes to 'the beast' from the dragon (v. 2); verse 6 speaks of his blasphemies, and verse 8 of the pagan worship of him. If despite all this the State's authority is taken as coming from God, it is only a *de facto* authority granted by God's mysterious providence, not a *de jure* one legitimising the State's activities. The three other times 'it was given unto him' is used in verses 5 to 7, and the general use of this phrase in Johannine writings[69] makes it impossible to take the phrase at the beginning of verse 7 as meaning a *de jure* authority explicitly given by God.

So there are very few New Testament texts which might serve as basis for a theology of the State. Doubtless it was so delicate and dangerous a subject, both for the readers and for the writers of the documents of primitive Christianity, that the latter did not dare express themselves freely. We should remember that in Palestine, and in most of the countries referred to in the New Testament, men were living in an atmosphere of great bitterness and resentment because of the Roman occupation. This was odiously cruel and universally detested. The tragic dilemma between resistance and collaboration is latent everywhere in the Gospels[70] as in other books of the New Testament. So because there are few texts on the 'political' question,[71] we should not conclude that the Christians of the primitive Church were not concerned with it. It was certainly an important and painful question for them, especially as 'the primitive community was confronted by a State which set itself up in a religious sense, not merely an earthly and human one.'[72]

It seems very likely that the texts favourable to the political authorities, particularly those in the epistles which so strongly recommend obedience to the magistrates and to the king—that is, to Caesar—were written precisely in reaction against a tendency among Christians of that time to reject and despise those authorities. 'It can be seen from several passages,' says Calvin, 'that the apostles had great difficulty in keeping the people submissive and obedient to the magistrates and principalities. For we all have a craving to rule, so nobody of his own accord becomes the subject of somebody else. Many people thought that the publication of the Gospel brought such liberty for themselves that everyone could free himself from slavery. Moreover, because they saw that the principalities and powers of the world were contrary to Christ, they easily came to think that these did not deserve to be honoured. For all the magistrates of that time were adversaries of Christ, and abused their authority.'[73] Further on Calvin explains why Peter strangely puts 'the king' in the very last place of those who should be honoured (I Peter 2:17): 'Yet he names the Emperor: all the more because this kind of domination was more odious than all the others, and the others were included in it.'[74] In these four texts, in fact, Paul and Peter were reacting against the anarchist tendencies of the Christians they were addressing; and this must be taken into account in order to appreciate properly the significance of their recommendations.

The Gospels, like the Epistles, were intended for wide diffusion through public reading during services; and so their writers may well have taken care to put in nothing that might displease the police authorities of the time, who were always on the look-out for possible rebellion.[75] When they spoke of the State, then, they might insist on Christians' positive duties towards it, and pass over in silence the complaints they had against it. This is probably why the writers of the New Testament do not accuse Pilate of the crime of Christ's death; why the author of the Acts lays the blame at the door of 'the Jews', as if they alone were responsible for the difficulties the apostles met with, and to present the Romans as loyal protectors of those preaching the Gospel. It is not by chance that Acts ends with words which sound somewhat one-sided: Paul preaching at Rome 'in all freedom, no man forbidding him.'

Only Revelations shows us the State in a frankly gloomy and pejorative light. But it does so in a very mysterious language, which would therefore be inaccessible to the profane; it is also a book which was clearly not intended for wide diffusion. Yet it probably gives us a better picture of the first Christians' real attitude towards the empire and Caesar than do the recommendations of the Epistles, which may be slightly over-officious. Opposition to the worship of the Emperor and to the Roman State's religious pretensions exists throughout the New Testament: it appears in many discreet or indirect allusions revealing 'a line which, from indifference towards the State, must lead to an attitude consciously rejecting it.'[76]

Of course we must be content with the few texts we have, and take them as they are. But just because they are so few I believe we should look at them in the context I have just described. They have been juggled with too often, used too often as a repository for general laws, where in fact there are only admonitions to prudence and solemn warnings—very circumstantial and couched in a language where words are most carefully weighed. Even in Rom. 13 I find it mistaken to look for a calm, systematic summary of the relationship between Church and State.

2. Texts on the State in the Gospels

In the light of all this, what guidance on our problem can be found in the four texts from the Gospels?

(a) 'Render to Caesar the things that are Caesar's, and to God the things that are God's' (Mark 12:13-17). Here is certainly one of the texts in the Gospels most often quoted both by theologians and profane authors. It is also one of the least understood, for it is usually quoted carelessly, out of context and in the wrong sense, making Jesus say things alien to His thinking. Some writers do not seem to have realised that for Jesus and His contemporaries Caesar was the equivalent of what Hitler was for Frenchmen, say, in 1943— and even worse. Almost all of them triumphantly bring up Jesus' words to justify their own doctrine which puts Church and State in different spheres. The profane authors are happy, with the authority of Jesus Himself, to relegate the Church to a vague 'care of souls'; while the theologians are happy to invoke that authority in justification of their surrender to the State's demands and of their anxiety to avoid any conflict with the political authorities. Unfortunately the commonly accepted interpretation is altogether unsound.

Before examining the text itself, we must ask whether this famous phrase is an answer in the realm of *principles* which can serve as a basis for a doctrine of the State. Did Jesus mean, in a general and permanent way, that the believer has duties to fulfil towards the State besides his duties to God? Plainly He did not, and we must anyhow give up the idea of interpreting His words as a clear affirmation of principle. His answer is rather a sort of riddle, for these reasons:

1. The question asked by the Herodians and the Pharisees is a trap: if Jesus falls into it, it could discredit Him for good. Mark

specifies that they came to him 'to catch him in his words.' The parallel with Luke is also explicit: 'They . . . sent forth spies, which should feign themselves just men, that they might take hold of his words, that so they might deliver him unto the power and authority of the governor' (Luke 20:20). If Jesus answers, 'Yes, the tribute to Caesar must be paid,' the Pharisees, very patriotic and with a great popular following (since the vast majority of the people are anti-Roman), will at once say: 'He can't possibly be the Messiah; he tells you to obey the Gentile foreign tyrant'—which may well be fatal for His ministry. But if He answers, 'No, the tribute to Caesar should not be paid,' the Herodians, unashamed *collaborateurs*, will quickly have Him arrested as preaching subversive ideas which Pilate obviously cannot tolerate—and everybody will be rid of Him. It is a cunning and formidable trap. 'And they marvelled at him,' Mark concludes the episode. 'And they could not take hold of his words before the people,' comments Luke; 'and they marvelled at his answer, and held their peace.' So His answer is more complex than is generally believed: He avoids both 'yes' and 'no,' each of which would have meant falling into the trap. It is therefore not a statement of principle either acknowleding or disputing the legitimacy of the Roman tribute.

2. There is only one other text in the Gospels which can throw a little light on this one. During the trial of Jesus, the following charge is made against Him before Pilate: 'We found this fellow perverting the nation, and forbidding to give tribute to Caesar, saying that He himself is Christ, a king.' (Luke 23:2). There is no proof that this charge refers to the text we are considering here, but it seems probable. In any case, if those accusing Him before the governor are alluding to another statement by Jesus, it can hardly be supposed that He would have spoken then about the tribute question quite differently from the way He does here. The Jews, in fact, when accusing Him to Pilate, dishonestly give His words, 'Render unto Caesar . . .', the meaning 'do not pay tribute'; and they could not have done so if such an interpretation had been obviously absurd. So at least that statement can be taken in contradictory senses.

3. There are a great many other texts showing Jesus' enemies trying to trap Him with cunning questions. Usually He answers by asking *them* something. Besides showing, no doubt, that it is He, the King, who has the right to ask questions, He is putting them in a corner, forcing them to give the answer they have come to get from Him.

In Matthew, for instance, there are twelve other occasions when the priests or the Pharisees ask Him questions: only twice does He answer clearly; three times His answer is ambiguous; and seven times He retorts with another question. Plainly He does not care to be cross-examined, as can be seen again in His trial. In the present text Jesus also begins by asking questions back, and His final answer can really be taken as a new and decisive question to the Herodians and the Pharisees. Indeed, if it called for an answer from them, this would explain Luke's 'and they held their peace.' The alleged statement of principle turns into another question, leaving the Jews to draw their own deductions in applying His words to the payment of tribute.

4. Jesus' answer is also ambiguous in its logic. 'It is easy to see that the parallel is deliberately ironical,' writes Dibelius.[77] For 'what on earth' (literally) are the things which are *not* God's, and could therefore be reserved for Caesar? 'The silver is mine, and the gold is mine, saith the Lord of hosts,' proclaims Haggai (2:8). So there is no question of a division into separate and independent spheres, as when you cut a slice of cake, and the slice is now a separate and independent entity from the rest of the cake. Jesus' words assume quite a different image: two concentric circles, with the smaller, that of Caesar, remaining an integral part of the larger, that of God, from which nothing is subtracted. So His words cannot be applied at all easily to the particular problem of the tribute.

To sum up, when the Jews come to ask Jesus whether it is 'lawful' to pay tribute to Caesar, yes or no, He refuses to give either answer, and His words are ambiguous. To appreciate their full significance let us now look at the text itself.

Verse 13: 'The Pharisees and the Herodians.' At first sight the association of these two parties seems strange, but they differ less in their practical attitude (both do in fact pay the tribute) than in their ideas on the Messiah. Their question is more concerned with how the Messiah would regard Rome than with the immediate problem of paying tribute. The Herodians would have been pleased to recognise the Messiah among the kings of the Herodian dynasty, who would somehow collaborate with Rome; whereas the Pharisees cannot imagine a Messiah respecting the Roman domination, and in that they have almost the whole of popular sentiment behind them. What both parties want here as in most other cases, is to force Jesus out of His reserve on the subject. They are not so much saying 'Ought we to pay?' as, 'You claim to be the Messiah, so tell us

whether we ought to pay.' The question of the tribute is only a pretext to unmask Him in His Messianic pretensions. This explains
why they flatter Him with phrases like 'we know that . . . thou carest
for no man'—though the contempt of these Jewish aristocrats for
the upstart from Nazareth is barely concealed in their obsequious-
ness. They hope He will be flattered, and provoked, into making
some rash anti-Roman statement which will be His undoing.

Verse 14: 'Is it lawful to give tribute to Caesar, or not? Shall we
give, or shall we not give?' All Jews faced the problem of the Roman
tribute, and it was insoluble. Caesar was even more a religious enemy
for them than a national enemy; he was the real anti-Christ, preventing the manifestation of the Messiah. To pay the tribute was a grave
infidelity towards the God of the Promise, as if you had given up
waiting for your Messiah. Monnier relates that new coinage was
struck under Bar Kokaba, and Roman currency declared invalid.[78]
It was against the Roman tribute that Judas of Galilee revolted.
Yet anyone who did rebel against the tribute was bound to be
crushed; so the problem remained insoluble. Caesar was master of
Palestine, and the Torah surely called for obedience to the authorities
whatever they were. Yet Israel's deliverance must be expected. Wait
till the Messiah gives the signal for insurrection—was that all you
had to do? The Pharisees said 'yes,' but the Herodians retreated
before this masked nationalism. So if Jesus approves their prudent
reserve, the patriot crowd will see clearly that He is not the Messiah.
If He encourages the nationalist sentiments of the Pharisees, He
will be faced as Messiah with having to head the movement of revolt
against Rome, or else be called a cowardly and impotent Messiah—
or be at once denounced and arrested. Both parties are equally keen
to extract an admission from Him that He is not the Messiah, and
both think they have as good as got such an admission

Verse 15: 'But He, knowing their hypocrisy . . .' This is not only
in laying a cruel trap for Him, but also in trying to attack His claim
to be the Messiah while apparently submitting to His judgment a
difficult problem of conscience. Perhaps too they are showing even
graver hypocrisy, swallowing a camel and straining at a gnat. For
they pretend to be tormenting themselves lest by paying tribute they
delay the Messiah's coming; yet when He is there before them, they
refuse to believe in Him.

'. . . said unto them, why tempt ye me?' The word 'tempt' ($\pi\epsilon\iota\rho\acute{a}\zeta\omega$)
has a double sense of 'laying a trap'—'putting to the test,' and also
'leading into temptation.' For here again Jesus is tempted, even by His

enemies' words, to declare Himself as the King whom Israel is awaiting. But His Kingdom is not of this world; He will not head a revolutionary movement to liberate the fatherland; He does not believe in violence.

'. . . Bring me a penny, that I may see it.' Here is the whole point of the story. Jesus at once puts the question on the level of practical realities, limiting and simplifying the problem. There are no abstractions concerned here, but only this coin. He will answer not in generalisations but through the concrete reality embodied in the material object He has asked them for: a denarius (or penny, our nearest equivalent). Rather mischievously, indeed, He catches them in disobedience to Rabbinic observances; for here is one of them carrying on his person this idolatrous and abhorred money, against all the rules of 'purity.'

By getting them to produce a denarius, Jesus is pointing out the facts, without raising the problem of whether Rome has a right to be occupying Jerusalem. His serene assurance shows only that He does not regard Caesar as His personal enemy. Caesar is not the anti-Christ, but holds *de facto* authority over the country. That is all.

Moreover, in asking to see this coin, Jesus is showing both Pharisees and Herodians that they have already answered their own question, since they carry on them this impure money, symbol of the Roman domination. But He does not blame them for it, since Caesar is not the direct adversary of the Messiah. By their earthly and nationalist idea of the Messianic kingdom, the Jews will always see Caesar as anti-Christ. Their obsession with Caesar's hated reign almost hypnotises them, and gives them an inferiority complex towards Rome. Jesus, however, the true sovereign of the world, though His kingdom is not of this world, can smile quietly, sure of His own power, and point to the sign of Caesar's ephemeral rule.

Verse 16: 'And they brought it.' With some shame, no doubt, at holding between their fingers this sullied object, and uneasiness at being taken unawares by their formidable adversary. How is He going to use it?

'Whose is this image. . . ?' For the peoples of antiquity the effigy on a coin was the sign of who owned the coin. So instead of giving any decision as to whether or not the Roman tribute is lawful, Jesus merely says: 'You have accepted the domination of the Romans, since you have traded with them, and apparently you have some of their currency on you. Draw your own conclusions. Caesar demands this coin, which belongs to him; so return it to him. It makes absolutely no difference to the Messiah's kingdom.'

But the use of the word 'image' ($\epsilon\grave{\iota}\kappa\acute{\omega}\nu$) may well be deliberate, evoking another, complementary image; recalling the verse in Genesis, 'God created man in his image' (1:27), where the word used in the Greek text is the same. Jesus is then implying: 'This coin is in Caesar's image, so return it to him; but remember that you yourselves are in God's image. The whole of your personalities must be consecrated to His service.'

The image of God? Since the Fall no man has carried it fully within him except the Son of Man. He, Jesus, is the image of the invisible God (II Cor. 4:4; Col. 1:15). So He is inviting His questioners, and us too, to recognise that He is the only genuine image of God. Why, then, do they refuse to understand this, and draw the consequences by believing in Him?

'. . . and this superscription?' My Messianic interpretation of the debate is confirmed by the fact that Jesus mentions the inscription going with Tiberius' effigy: 'Tiberius Caesar, son of the divine Augustus, supreme pontiff.' The parallel He wishes to establish between the coin and Himself is obvious. Why bring in this inscription, so infuriating for the Jews, unless to suggest that He, God's only Son, is the true Supreme Pontiff? The Roman emperor proudly claims to be son of a god and the world's high priest, but his rights extend only to this little coin. 'Don't you realise that I, the true Son of God and High Priest, have all the rights over you all?'

'And they said unto him, Caesar's.' For the second time Jesus has made them utter the accursed name. By reminding them of the inscription on the coin, so much of an insult to them, He brings out still more sharply the contrast between Caesar and the Messiah, and the deadlock both parties have landed themselves in by their political conception of the Messiah, the Pharisees wanting Him anti-Roman and the Herodians pro-Roman.

Jesus, however, destroys this opposition, showing them they should acknowledge Him as Messiah despite Caesar's crushing power and this little coin with its idolatrous effigy and scandalous inscription. For both are in a sense signs, however grotesque, of His royalty, no less than the Temple at Jerusalem and its High Priest. The Jews are wasting their time defending their Temple against Caesar. Jesus knows that He is proclaimed by one as much as by the other; and both are equally powerless before Him. Caesar's representative in Palestine may have the illusion of being able to destroy Him (John 19:10). But all Caesar's power has really been given him by God; and through Pontius Pilate he will unwittingly play an important part in bringing about the Redemption. God uses a Caesar in sovereign fashion. For the divinity claimed by Tiberius is only vanity; Christ alone is the Son of God, the true King.

'Render to Caesar the things that are Caesar's, and to God the things that are God's.' 'This coin you are showing me bears Caesar's effigy? Then you must give it back to him, if he demands it, because it belongs to him. But give back to God what you owe Him: all of yourself created in His image, straining towards Him by the faith in His only Son who bears His mark and perfect image.' Let us note once more that Jesus is not passing any judgment on the lawfulness of the Roman tribute; He is speaking only of this particular coin. It represents the things that are Caesar's, not a foreign tyrant's right to exact a tribute. In other words, Jesus recognises Caesar as having the right to the coin but not to the tribute. This is what disconcerts His questions and breaks their trap. His concrete answer to their abstract question gives no handle to their malice: from this formidable Rabbinical duel Jesus emerges as victor.

If He is not pronouncing here on the principle of the tribute, He is clearly still further from pronouncing on the principle of the obedience due to the *de facto* political authority. 'Nothing was more remote from His thought than to establish a principle from which the domains of God and of Caesar would be exactly delimited for the rest of time.'[79] As Martin Dibelius expresses it, 'the story is completely misunderstood when statutory relations between Church and State are deduced from it. There is a conflict between the occupying power and national piety, but instead of entering this conflict, Jesus formulates another: God and the world. As surely as the money bears the emperor's image, so surely is it of the world and belongs to the powers of this world, to the emperor. . . . So when Jesus says, Give the Emperor what belongs to him (not "what comes to him by virtue of a divine order") and give God what is His, it is an ironical parallel—which would not be noticed straight away. Jesus had no intention of putting the emperor's rights and God's on the same level. The emperor's rights flow from the order of this world, and Jesus makes no judgment on them. He seems to be saying: give the same thing to God as to the emperor. But what He means in reality is: above all give God what is His, perhaps in conflict with everything else. The people who in pretended piety ask "Do you support the national resistance?" receive no reply. Instead they are reminded that their "piety" is chiefly concerned with nationalist claims, which may be necessary and may be harmful, but are anyhow of the world. Jesus gives no more decision on them than He does on the social system. All who wish to talk about them and make judgments on them should first notice the question He asks as soon as He is approached on a national problem: are God's demands satisfied?'[80]

So those who deduce a theory of the State from this text have a series of gaps throughout their argument which they do not attempt to bridge. They talk of the rightful State, but Caesar was a hated foreign tyrant (like Hitler in occupied France). They talk of the obedience due to the State, but only the tribute was in question. They start from the idea that Jesus sanctioned the payment of a tribute, but this is just what He did not do. Most incredible of all, they use this text to justify both the national payment of tribute to a foreign occupying power and the national army which defends its country by arms against the foreigner. For them Jesus was sanctioning both collaboration (by payment of tribute) and resistance (by armed combat). Patently, in fact, they are trying to justify preconceived ideas, without even bothering about consistency, rather than seeing what the text actually says.

Some readers will perhaps be disappointed and disconcerted by the strictly Messianic interpretation I give to this famous text. 'Is it no more than that?' they may ask, feeling that I have unduly minimised the importance of Jesus' words. But a terrible trap had been set for Him, and He easily escaped from it. Moreover, He was a Jewish Rabbi who had to adapt Himself to the kind of religious discussions His contemporaries were used to, even if this may upset us a little because our historical perspectives are distorted or inadequate: there are other Rabbinical discussions reported in the Gospels which are strictly duels of oratory.[81] But I would add for the benefit of such readers that it is wonderful to see how the Master succeeded in using a vicious trap to proclaim implicitly that He was the Messiah, and in confronting His hearers with an essentially spiritual question, which applies equally to us today: that of our faith in Him.

It is indeed disconcerting, however, to find so many writers misusing this text to justify their theory of a division of spheres between the State and God. But the Church after Constantine was rash enough to introduce the Roman idea of the City and the Empire into its theology; and probably this is the way in which the very name of Caesar, execrated by the Christians of the first three centuries, became the symbol of an inherently good and benevolent

State. How many 'Christian sovereigns' have been proud to be called Caesar! Louis XIV, coveting the title of Caesar, accorded to Leopold I of Austria, even had himself represented on a statue in the costume of a Roman Emperor! The whole of Christian tradition has been so distorted by such an attitude that for centuries Christians have persistently interpreted this text in a way which would have seemed stupefying and monstrous to the apostles and the writers of the New Testament. We must not make Jesus say what He not only did not say but could not possibly have said.

(*a*) H. Roux, for instance, claims that by His answer Jesus 'gives a Christian content to obeying the authorities of this world' (*L'Évangile du Royaume*, p. 267). G. Dehn, on the other hand, writes justly: 'I do not think it can be said (here) that Jesus is specially considering the State' (*Le Fils du Dieu*, p. 209).

(*b*) The episode of the State (Matt. 17:24-27) is the replica of the preceding, but the tribute here is being collected by the Jewish authorities for the upkeep of the Temple and the priestly administration at Jerusalem: this time it is a national and religious tribute. But although Jesus declares it to be lawful, that is all that can be deduced from His attitude and language in this passage. A new threat is hanging over Him, a new trap has been laid: does He respect the Law of Moses? This Temple tribute is expressly prescribed in the Law (Exo. 30:12). So He is confronted by an embarrassing dilemma: not to pay would be to violate the Law openly, and also show Himself no patriot; worse, to show Himself a bad Jew, for it is well known how sacred the Temple of Jerusalem was in the eyes of the Jews. If He refuses to pay, He will offend the people's deepest feelings, will scandalise them in a way that may gravely compromise His authority. Moreover, He has always conformed before to the Law's demands, and there is no reason why He should depart here from His usual line of conduct.

But if He pays the tribute, He will act so much as an ordinary citizen that it will be like letting these tax-collectors strip Him of His claim to be the Messiah. Besides, He, Jesus, is the real Temple of God, while the Temple of Jerusalem has been to some extent superseded since He started His ministry; so if He pays the Temple tribute, He will be putting the accent on the sign, when the reality this sign announces is already present—stressing the provisional (Matt. 24:2) at the expense of the permanent.

He decides nevertheless to pay this tribute, but does so in a very detached manner, no doubt wishing to underline that as Son of God

He could dispense with a custom which has been nullified by His own coming. But He submits to it so as not to give 'offence.' The whole point of the story clearly lies in this word, and it must be interpreted in the light of Biblical teaching on 'offence.' Anyhow Jesus is here proclaiming 'the double principle of liberty and charity':[82] the Christian is free from subjection to any, as Luther was to say, but submits voluntarily to all by reason of his love and respect for them.

From this mysterious episode no teaching can be deduced on the Christian's relations with the State. The question of the religious tribute belongs more, in Jesus' eyes, to the chapter on 'Christian charity' than to the chapter on 'rights of the State.' True, he pays the tribute, pays it for Peter as well (since it was often jointly paid by two people so that they could pay more easily). But He has not paid it from His own purse, but with the aid of nature, showing such casualness that nobody can seriously take His attitude to justify the principle of the tribute, let alone any principle concerning the State. Also, His exclamation, 'then are the children free,' sounds fairly anarchist or Anabaptist, whatever Calvin may say about it. All we can say here with certainty is that this is a Messianic text, not one where the problem of the State comes up at all.

(c) '. . . they which are accounted to rule over the Gentiles exercise lordship over them; and their great ones exercise authority upon them . . .' (Mark 10:42). 'Jesus remarks on the fact without discussing its lawfulness,' says Roux.[83] This is obvious. The same might be said of Jesus' question in the preceding episode: 'Of whom do the kings of the earth take custom or tribute? Of their own children, or of strangers?' (Matt. 17:25). There too He was speaking of kings as they are, not as they ought to be. I even think that implicitly, though very discreetly, Jesus is here deploring this tyranny of the great ones of the earth: for He demands of His disciples an attitude diametrically opposite to that of the tyrants. 'The Church of Jesus Christ has nothing to do with those who govern the people and oppress them . . . the spirit of domination and tyranny and the spirit of love and sacrifice are mutually exclusive.'[84] The two verbs used by Jesus stress the pride of these kings, and Mark's text even has a note of sarcasm concerning them: 'those which are accounted to rule . . .' or 'imagine themselves to rule . . .'[85] But of course if Jesus criticises them, it is because of their spirit of proud domination, not their being kings. Once again Jesus simply points out that there are kings, that they rule over peoples and make those peoples pay tribute. 'And very necessary too,' it may be said, 'if human society is not to disintegrate.' No doubt; but this is to bring in ideas, reasonable though they may be, which are not implied in the text.

(*d*) "Thou couldest have no power at all against me, except it were given thee from above.' Jesus makes this reply to Pilate who has just said to Him: 'Knowest thou not that I have power to crucify thee and have power to release thee?' (John 19:10-11). What exactly is this power or authority (Greek ἐξουσία) which Pilate has received from above, that is, from God? Is it an occasional, *de facto* power, as one might speak of the power of a lion which attacks you and may kill you or (to use an example given by Karl Barth) of the Tower of Siloam (Luke 13:1-5)? Or is it a *de jure* power foreseen in God's plan and properly integrated into the order He has fixed for the world? If the former, our text offers no justification of the political authorities; but if the latter, here is a text at last which might give a Scriptural basis for the theory of the divine right of such authorities and of the State. Only I find it very difficult to see how this latter hypothesis can be maintained.

Calvin first sets out the former interpretation: 'The world is governed by God's will; whatever the machinations of the wicked, they will not be able to lift their little finger to stop God's secret power governing from above.'[86] This explanation is undoubtedly in agreement with the general thinking of the whole of the Bible. 'But,' he goes on, 'those who restrict this passage to the position and office of magistrate have a sounder opinion in my judgment.' He does not, however, give very convincing reason for this judgment: 'For by these words Jesus Christ rebukes Pilate's mad arrogance in setting himself up on high, as if his power had not been from God. . . . But Pilate was not made judge without His providence.' This fits in very well with the hypothesis that Jesus was speaking only of a *de facto* power which had indeed been given Pilate by divine providence.

Karl Barth devotes several pages to this text,[87] but without giving any precise answer to the question I have raised. He interprets the text in the light of the theory of political demonic powers, according to which the political authorities are dominated unawares, through God's express will, by angelic powers which are yet often in revolt against God. The power of the State, embodied in Pilate, would thus be theologically founded in law. But does our text really imply this doctrine? Simply because the Greek translation of Jesus' statement uses the word ἐξουσία (authority), must we say that Jesus saw in Pilate one of these 'authorities' legitimately ruled by angelic powers?

In other words, did Jesus recognise Pilate here as having a *de jure* power?

The word ἐξουσία is used several times in the Gospels,[88] in texts where one cannot find the smallest beginnings of a theory of political 'demons.' On all but one occasion it is applied to Jesus' own power or authority, and the exception, 'this . . . is the power of darkness,' which He says when being arrested (Luke 22:53), can hardly refer to a *de jure* power. These are the only texts in the Gospels, to my knowledge, where ἐξουσία is used in the singular; and in the Epistles, where Paul refers to 'angelic' powers, it is always in the plural. Because the singular is used almost exclusively of Jews, I believe that in our text Pilate's power should be interpreted by reference not to any angelic powers he might represent, but merely to his proud opposition to Jesus' power. In any case we obviously cannot define Pilate's power too exactly from this text.

But even if there is more than mere coincidence in the use of ἐξουσία, surely in contrast with Jesus' power Pilate's power represents the world, not the State. The State has not been referred to in this chapter, while the world is expressly mentioned (John 18:36-37), and is often contrasted with Jesus in the Johannine writings. All that John may have meant was that Pilate is the occasional and passive instrument of the divine providence, which uses him to bring about the Justification; it would be very hard to read more into the verse than this. I agree, in fact, with F. J. Leenhardt's conclusion: after analysing the text in detail, he writes: 'It treats of the Roman magistrate's *de facto* power, not the political government's inherent authority.'[89] I wonder, incidentally, how those who think this text shows Jesus approving Pilate's political authority, can avoid thinking that He must also have approved of foreign occupations.

So the result of our enquiry is negative: the Gospels, the Acts, and Revelations contain no texts which imply a definite doctrine of the State or might serve as a basis for one. Traditional Protestant theology must have built up its extravagant theory about the State on a tendentious interpretation of three texts in the Epistles; these texts I shall now discuss.

3. Submission to the Political Authorities

'Let every soul be subject unto the higher powers,' Paul writes to the Romans, and a little later: 'Wherefore ye must needs be subject, not only for wrath but also for conscience sake' (Rom. 13:1, 5). To Titus he writes: 'Put them in mind to be subject to the magistrates and to the powers, to obey . . .' (3:1). Peter uses a still stronger phrase: 'Submit yourselves to every ordinance of man for the Lord's sake, whether it be to the king . . . or unto governors . . .' (I Peter 2:13). What exactly is entailed by this submission to which Christians are clearly called?

First, it means that the political authorities, and in general all the authorities which exist within human society (like masters and husbands, for instance) have a real and positive value in the eyes of God, and therefore in the eyes of a Christian. God takes them seriously, and somehow integrates them into His plan. This is why we must be 'subject' for the Lord's sake. It implies that we too accept and take seriously the authorities who are placed above us; it implies a readiness to obey them. This is why slaves are called to submit to their masters (Titus. 2:9; Eph. 6:5; Col. 3:22; I Peter 2:18), wives to their husbands (I Cor. 14:34; Eph. 5:22; Col. 3:18; I Tim. 2:11; Titus 2:5; I Peter 3:1), and citizens to their kings and governors. Also, the young should submit to their elders (Eph. 6:1; Col. 3:20; I Tim. 3:4; I Peter 5:5), and the faithful to their spiritual leaders (I Thes. 5:12; Heb. 13:17).

We must therefore respect, be ready to obey, these higher powers or authorities—'higher' meaning 'those placed above us.' Render therefore to all their dues . . . honour to whom honour,' writes Paul (Rom. 13:7); and Peter specifies the hardest thing for a Christian: 'Honour the King'—that is to say, Caesar (I Peter 2:17). Now Peter and Paul probably became martyrs at the hands of this 'King,' who they say should be honoured, and these 'authorities set up by God' to whom they say submission is due. Christian dialectic has to reckon with this, and submission must not be confused with passive obedience. Calvin translates 'be subject' in Romans 13 by 'voluntarily endure and support the power and domination of the magistrates.'[90] Karl Barth finds even finer shades of meaning: 'It is not a matter of being the subject of a person but of respecting a person in the position he occupies.'[91] And elsewhere: 'The apostle's thought does *not* mean that Christians must obey the civil power and its functionaries *like subjects*, must say yes and amen to everything they do; it means rather that they must all simply give to the State, according to Romans 13:6-7, what it asks of them to ensure and maintain the proper functioning of the city and allow it to fulfil its tasks.'[92]

The spiritual content of this submission implies three profound attitudes: first, intercessory prayer for those in authority over us, that they may be faithful and just in carrying out their task—hence

Paul's exhortation in I Timothy 2:2 to pray 'for kings and for all them that are in authority.' Second, the *witness* of our faith rendered to these 'masters,' that is, a true ministry of the Word by which we must help them to learn their real vocation as chiefs according to God's Word. For they are very often ignorant of this, and only the Church knows, thanks to the Scriptures, how human authorities should carry out their function; only the Church can reveal to them the spirit in which they must work.[93] Finally, it implies suffering, precisely because these authorities are not naturally just. This is true for slaves particularly (I Peter 2:18-20), but it is also true for all who are called to be submissive. As citizens, Christians can scarcely avoid suffering at the hands of the State, especially if they are faithful to their proper vocation. They must endure these persecutions, and not rebel against them. Yet this is not resignation, since they are also called to prayer and to witness. But 'where disciples of Jesus Christ are concerned, their vocation of submissiveness and meekness is bound to lead them on a road of suffering.'

It is very important to note that our three exhortations to submit to the political authorities come into the whole apostolic teaching on mutual submission (Eph. 5:21) and submission towards whoever exercises an authority among men. It is all too easy to detach these three texts from their setting, and then claim that they call for a more or less *unconditional* obedience to the State. But in that setting the question is not primarily of obedience, but of love, suffering, meekness. Submission certainly implied obedience, and with reason: we should remember the actual situation, at the time of the apostles for wives, children, slaves, and citizens. But as it happens, all these texts avoid insisting on the passive obedience which the respective 'masters' were likely to demand from those who were 'subject' to them, often because they literally belonged to them. On the contrary, the texts insist on the personal dignity of those who are placed under the rule of their superiors. They do not by any means urge the 'subjects' to revolt, nor even to criticism; but communicate to them the feeling of their own value as Children of God redeemed by the Christ. This is particularly clear in the Epistle to Philemon and in almost everything in the Epistles which treats of slaves. But it is true also, I believe, of all these texts we have been considering.

The call to submission is thus addressed to people who are in fact oppressed and persecuted. These are the people who are asked to pray, to suffer, to witness, by their meekness and their faith. They are expressly not asked to obey absolutely everything their masters command, for the accent is put elsewhere: before these masters who oppress or may oppress them, they are asked to be true men and women, children of God aware of their personal dignity but refusing deliberately, from love for God and for their masters, worthy or unworthy, to defend themselves, to rebel, or even to escape from the subjection in which they have been placed. Because of the example of Jesus Christ (I Peter 2:21), whose whole life and whose death as well have been the perfect realisation of that submission (Luke 2:51; Phil. 2:8), because of that example, and dwelling in His communion, Christians are called to suffer. But they are never called to inflict suffering; which shows already that these who would justify military service by these three texts are exploiting the texts in a sense they do not have.

(b) Each of these texts on 'submission' must be interpreted in the light of its context; and in all three cases the context speaks of non-violent love of our neighbour and our enemies. The exhortation to submission is thus part of a call to believers to offer the unconditional love I have described earlier. Submission to the political authorities is an integral part of loving our neighbour: not a different chapter, a different question, but one of the aspects of the charity to which every believer in Jesus Christ is called.

The vital text to Romans 13 is immediately preceded by admonitions of brotherly charity: 'Bless them which persecute you; bless, and curse not. . . . Recompense to no man evil for evil . . . avenge not yourselves. . . . If thine enemy hunger, feed him. . . . Overcome evil with good.' And immediately *after* the passage on magistrates, we have 'Owe no man anything, but to love one another. . . . Thou shalt not kill. . . . Thou shalt love thy neighbour as thyself. . . . Love worketh no ill to his neighbour. . . .'

Titus 3:1 is preceded by exhortations to moderation, patience, charity, submission, then to piety and good works. Immediately after calling for submission to magistrates, Paul adds a call to be pacific (literally: not taking part in fights), gentle, full of meekness towards all men. For we ourselves also were sometimes foolish, disobedient . . . living in malice and envy, hateful, and hating one another. But after that the kindness and love of God our Saviour toward man appeared.'

It is the same with I Peter 2:13. 'Dearly beloved,' says the apostle just before, 'I beseech you as strangers and pilgrims, abstain from fleshly lusts which war against the soul; having your conversation honest among the Gentiles: that, whereas they speak against you as evil-doers, they may by your good works, which they shall behold, glorify God in the day of visitation.' Then, after the verses on the political authorities, he goes on, speaking specially to Christian slaves: 'For this is thankworthy, if a man for conscience toward God endure grief, suffering wrongfully. For what glory is it, if when ye be buffeted for your faults, ye shall take it patiently! But if when ye do well and suffer for it, ye take it patiently, this is acceptable with God. For even hereunto were ye called: because Christ also suffered for us, leaving us an example, that ye should follow His steps: . . . who when He was reviled, reviled not again; when He suffered He threatened not. . . .' Finally, after exhorting wives to submit to their husbands and husbands to respect their wives, he ends the whole teaching with these words: 'Be ye all of one mind, having compassion one of another, love as brethren, be pitiful, be courteous, not rendering evil for evil, or railing for railing: but contrariwise blessing. . . .' The same note sounds all the time.

So these three texts on the political authorities should surely be interpreted by reference not to any doctrine of the State but to the brotherly charity to which believers are called and to which in fact the context of these verses is devoted. When theologians see a text which mentions the State, they so often seem to exclaim: 'Ah, now that the State is concerned, it's a different chapter of theology!' All of a sudden, because the shadow of the State has appeared, some divinity (we can guess which, but in any case not the God of Jesus Christ) must be bidding them take off their shoes, 'for the place where thou standest is holy ground.' Whereupon these verses are carefully cut out or removed from their context, as if the matter under consideration were something completely different. Understandably enough, some people even manage to deduce that on occasions you must kill your neighbour; probably they have quite forgotten what the context was dealing with.

But why, in fact, do they always treat anything to do with the State as part of a separate body of teaching? Why do they start by serving this other master, and afterwards do the best they can to follow the rest of the Christian ethic? Submission to the political authorities is a question concerned with brotherly charity as well as with the doctrine of the State; yet it is always fitted into the 'State' chapter, never the 'Charity' chapter. Yet in the latter, which is at least as legitimate as the former, it is much easier to see what the Christian can grant and what he must *refuse* to the State—because you do not start from the assumption that the State is a very important master.

Let it not be thought that I am cunningly undermining the Christian doctrine of the State, which in fact I shall soon be trying to set out. But there is a line to be drawn somewhere, and frankly I am afraid of State idolatry. Through always giving it 'the better part,' we tend to make texts say that it must always be obeyed—although these texts do not ask servants, wives and children to show such an *unconditional* obedience towards those they must also submit to. On the contrary, several of these texts, specially those addressed to slaves, presuppose that on certain points they must have had to refuse obedience to their masters because of their fidelity to Christ. This is why they suffer 'for conscience towards God' (I Peter 2:19; 3:14). The New Testament teaches us clearly that the authority of the State is on the same level as that of master, husbands, and fathers—so let us be vigilant.

4. The Significance of the State for the Christian

Why must Christians be submissive to the political authorities? Considering what those authorities were then, and what they still are today in most countries, one might have thought that believers would consider the State as a reality, doubtless inevitable, but neutral from the point of view of their faith, and towards which they would have felt no sort of voluntary obligation. Plainly, the apostles fought against this tendency, and made great efforts to show the faithful that the State has a positive significance in God's eyes. By continuing our study of Romans 13 (to which Titus 3:1 and I Peter 2:13-17 add practically nothing), we shall be able to discover the apostles' thought on the subject, thanks to the very explcit nature of the text and the fact that its words have clearly been weighed with care.

Paul is writing to *the Romans*. We may suppose that he is careful in his language from fear of the Roman police, and also that Rome's Christian community was probably attracted by an attitude of anarchy, or anyhow was very contemptuous of the State, as so often happens with minorities in big capital cities when they are barely tolerated. 'It may be an exaggeration to say that the only purpose of the instructions in Romans 13 is to restrain a tendency towards political rebellion; but this is certainly one of its purposes.'[94] Through Aquila and Priscilla (Acts 18:2) Paul had long known how much Rome's Jewish community, and therefore also its Church, were agitated by the political question. Moreover, we should remember that this Epistle was written in 57, seven years *before* the first great persecution.

We cannot, however, think that Paul is here using insincere flattery towards the Empire. He may not express the whole of his thought, but what he does demands all our attention. G. Dehn recognises that there is 'a contradiction between what is expressed in the Epistle to the Romans and the thought of the rest of the New Testament authors.'[95] So the interpretation we give to Romans 13 must be modified in the light of the rest of the evidence from the New Testament, especially as in verse 1, the most strongly affirmative towards the State, 'the idea that every authority exists by God's command is not a theory of Paul's but a traditional Judaeo-Hellenic one.'[96] In these first verses of the Chapter, as Dibelius goes on to say, 'there is no trace of a specifically Christian motivation,' and nobody would know from them that a Christian apostle is here exhorting a Christian community.'[97] Paul has adopted this Jewish formula, and given it a Christian and eschatological significance; but other New Testament passages on the State should be checked against the formula itself. There is an important difference here, for traditional Christian theology has built a doctrine of the State on the basis of a text which *in its formulation* is not specifically Christian—'and should not be overrated,' Dibelius insists. 'St. Paul,' he concludes, 'completely lacks any decisive thought for a future study on the duty of Christians to take their responsibilities in the world.'[98]

Let us also listen to the warning of a great Christian philosopher: 'These words (of the apostle's) have exercised a fatal effect: they have usually served to express a servility and opportunism towards the State, and a justification of the forms of power, which had nothing to do with Christianity. In fact, these words have no religious sense at all; they have a purely historic and relative character, determined by the situation of Christians within the Roman Empire. Paul was afraid Christianity might be turning into an anarchist and revolutionary sect. . . .'[99] This text was intended to divert the Christians of Rome from the mad temptation of resort to arms; it has been exploited much too often to justify the use of arms in general. Let us look at the text in detail.

Verse 1: '. . . For there is no power but of God . . .' Literally: 'It is impossible that an authority exists without God having set it up.' The very principle of authority being exercised among men is thus of divine origin, and sanctioned by God. To stop men living in anarchy and chaos, God wished there to be 'chiefs' among them, invested with a real power, so as to give order to human society—so that there should be a society at all. God shows His love towards humanity, by preserving it in this way from the self-destruction to which it would surely be brought by the wickedness and sin of human beings if He did not to some degree stem the ravages of evil by means of these authorities. But it is the authority of God Himself which has been delegated, as it were, to these 'chiefs' or the father of a family, so that they may exercise it only 'for the time being,' that is, while awaiting the Kingdom of God. This is why the Church must constantly remind the chiefs of the gravity and significance of the authority they are entrusted with; while to the men who are subject to them it must repeat that they honour God by respecting their chiefs' authority. Since His Ascension Christ has become the King of kings, that is, the supreme chief of all the authorities which exist among men, and even more than that. So whoever is a chief among men is really in Christ's service, even if he does not realise it. For the Lord is not only the Head of the Church, its Bridegroom; He is also the Sovereign of the whole world. In this way a dangerous dualism is avoided, to which a revolutionary anarchism among Christians would inevitably have led. C. Dehn writes with reason: 'If the apostle had not written Romans 13, the communities would have been in danger of withdrawing from the world into the obscurity of a private society for spiritual improvement; or else, at the other extreme, impelled by their claims concerning the world, they might suddenly have burst forth as a warrior community, religious and revolutionary, the champions of a better world. But this would have meant the secularisation of the Church and its message.'[100]

'. . . the powers that be are ordained of God.' Paul passes here from the principle to the concrete situation, and makes a value judgment on the Imperial Rome of before A.D. 64.[101] For even if all authority comes from God on principle, it does not follow that all *de facto* authorities are equally 'ordained' by Him. The verb Paul uses here means: 'to establish someone in a position, to give him the authority and responsibility inherent in that position.'[102] Such an 'ordaining' from God is not a right which can be claimed by any and every authority. But by an appraisal of the existing circumstances made in the faith, Paul declares that these present authorities have been ordained, established by God. It often happens that men usurp this authority which is willed by God, and use it arbitrarily for their own profit like a stolen tool: thus does Paul foreshadow the passing of the Rome of Romans 13 into the Rome of Revelations. In any case, even when the authority is usurped or 'demonised,' dominated by heavenly powers in full revolt against God, it still merits our respect and 'submission' because it remains a sign of Christ's sovereignty and God's Judgment. But on the other hand, the State cannot claim to possess an absolute and permanent value, since day after day, as it were, by grace, it must receive from God Himself its dignity as a State ordained by God. For the Beast is embryonic in every State.

Verse 2: 'Whosoever therefore resisteth the power, resisteth the ordinance of God . . .' Here Paul is obviously denouncing and fighting a tendency to rebellion and systematic opposition to the State. He is stressing that his previous qualification has not opened the door to anarchy. For God wishes there to be an order in society; and Christians, from love of their brethren, must do all they can to uphold that order and fight against the disorder which would stop them all from living a human life. They must always recognise the positive value and divine origin of authority, even if the men actually embodying the authority are unworthy. Calvin says: 'It is not in us to cure the ills caused by an unjust tyrant, but the only thing left is to implore God's aid, in whose hand are the hearts of kings and the changes of kingdoms.'[103] Meanwhile our part is 'to obey and to suffer.' 'If the State opposes God,' writes Karl Barth, 'respect still remains due to it, but the readiness to serve it can only be passive and limited.'[104] If the Church's liberty is compromised by the State, the Christian should resist with respect, and is rendering a service to the State by reminding it of its true function. But to revolt against the State would be almost to revolt against God's providence. Not that taking the State's authority seriously implies in any way that the Christian should *obey* it in all circumstances; for there are cases where it is better to obey God than men (Acts 5:29). But the believer is then opposing some specific demand of the State's, not its general authority, which he always recognises as willed and created by God. I think there is unanimous agreement on this point among Biblical scholars and theologians. There is still, however, the controversial question of whether the State, by imposing military service on Christians, is commanding something against God's Will.

'. . . . And they that resist shall receive to themselves damnation.' For to revolt against authority as such is to fight against both the State and God. Anyone who does so may become liable to judgment from both at once; the condemnation he faces from the State is even a sign of the condemnation by which God rebukes our attitude.

Verse 3: 'For rulers are not a terror to good works, but to the evil. . . .' In these verses Paul must be thinking of Christians whose conversion to Christ was in danger of degenerating into licentiousness; otherwise it is hard to see why he should go so far as to remind them of the sanctions they are exposing themselves to. Perhaps some of them had already 'made fools of themselves'; hence his stern and prosaic call to order. The honour of God, Christian witness, and the Christian community itself, are all threatened and compromised by evil actions. To love your neighbour also means: not to commit evil actions which may be punishable by the magistrate; it means, in a very down-to-earth sense, being a 'good citizen,' a man who has no 'trouble with the police.' So now this verse is reminding us of one of the essential aims of the State: to preserve the world from social chaos. Any State, as soon as it has a real authority, fulfils this function, perhaps unawares. 'There cannot be a tyranny which does not to some degree serve to maintain human society.'[105]

'Wilt thou then not be afraid of the power? Do that which is good, and thou shalt have praise of the same.' Rome's small Christian community must have lived in daily fear of the civil authorities. Paul knows of this fear, so he tells them that if they wish to be as free as possible from State interference, they must put into practice the ethic of Romans 12.[106] The most corrupt authority will almost always approve of 'good conduct' in the believers. I shall be returning later to the vital question of this 'good' which Christians must do, and shall then try to see what is the norm for it. Here Paul is speaking on the level of common sense: you will be 'respectable' in the eyes of the local police if you do 'what is correct and just in the city,'[107] if you practise the (non-violent) love with which the context is concerned: this is indeed self-evident. Normally there should be no conflict between State and Church, if Christians practise a true brotherly charity towards all, and also, of course, if the State on its side does not try to force them out of this meekness and love. But there was probably no question of this at the time Paul was writing. The whole passage 'presupposes that the authority knows what is good and bad, and acts accordingly, thus accomplishing the will of God. The problem of an unjust government does not seem to be raised here.'[108]

Verse 4: 'For he is the minister of God to thee for good.' Leaving aside the definition of 'good' for the moment, let us look at the term 'minister' ($\delta\iota\acute{\alpha}\kappa\text{ovos}$). Whether they know it or not, the magistrates are in God's service. If they rule over other men, it is not for themselves, but on behalf of God, before whom they are responsible. It is understood that this 'ministry' of the men of the State comes into the extra-ecclesiastical sphere constituted by the existing reign of Christ; for that goes beyond the limited domain of the Church. Believer or unbeliever, the magistrate is a servant of God. He must be vigilant for the 'good' in society; and clearly it is God who in the last resort appreciates and determines what is good (I am here touching on one of the crucial points of this whole book). Anyhow, what is clear from this Verse is that the State was made for man, not man for the State. Our text therefore condemns the Macchiavelian and totalitarian régimes of all varieties which sacrifice the individual not only to a collective, but also to the State. According to the Scriptures the State exists to serve man.

'But if thou do that which is evil, be afraid; for he beareth not the sword in vain . . .' The sword is symbol of the constraint to which the Roman State resorted in order to ensure public order. Paul refers to the law of his time to warn Christians that there will be positive sanctions, perhaps very serious punishments, if they do wrong.

'. . . For he is the minister of God to execute vengeance and punish him that doeth evil.' Thus the magistrate must not punish at random. He must punish those who do evil; for which, once again, he cannot himself fix the norm: that belongs to God. Literally, he must 'pursue in justice in view of (God's) anger' those who do evil. Stapfer translates: 'To avenge God and show His wrath.' As we have seen, the State's punishment manifests God's anger; it is the sign of His punishment. Paul did not imagine a lay State in the sense of one morally independent of God. Quite the contrary: by this verse he seems to be trying to mark the limits of the State's undisputed authority; for God has charged it to punish *evil* and approve those who do *good* (I Peter 2:14). The State has not received unlimited authority from God.

On the punishment the magistrate administers, there is a point which must be clearly made if we are not to fall into a theological error as formidable in its consequences as, alas, it is frequent: the connection between the State's punishment and God's Judgment. A good, amplified translation of this verse would seem to be that given by F. J. Leenhardt: 'The authority is in God's service to avenge Him and show His wrath to anyone who practises evil.'[109] Now, 'wrath' in the New Testament is always an eschatological idea relating to the Last Judgment (Rom. 12:19). The punishments inflicted by the State are not, therefore, in Paul's thought, a sort of anticipatory *execution* of the Last Judgment, but they *are* a *sign* of that judgment: not at all the same thing. For a punishment inflicted by men is a sign of wrath precisely when God uses them without their knowledge— whereas, when they claim to be themselves the instrument of the divine wrath, they fall into incredible pride and cynicism.

So those who claim, in making war, to be the instruments of God's judgment, or in Calvin's words, 'the executors of his ire',[110] are placing themselves on ground which is alien to the New Testament: they are in flagrant contradiction with all the parables of the Judgment, especially that of the wheat and the tares (Matt. 13:24-20).[111]

O. Cullman, I believe, is contradicting his own linear idea of time when he writes on this subject: 'When the State appears as dispenser of justice, it does so only as servant of God, to whom vengeance belongs. It is incumbent on this servant to *accomplish* the divine vengeance and to *execute* the righteous judgment of God's wrath. . . .'[112] But it is only by the faith, and thus within the Church, that God's judgment can be considered as in a sense already accomplished; the 'actualisation' of God's justice by the State is inconceivable, for the State is completely ignorant of the work accomplished once for all by Jesus Christ. The Church may, then, and in fact should, see the State's punishment as a sign of *God's* future judgment; but the State can never claim that it is already executing part of that judgment.[113] It is, of course, even more ridiculous to make this claim in the case of war: in 1915 was it the French or the German army which was executing the judgment of God; or was God using both armies to punish both countries at the same time? But in that case we are again faced with providence, no longer with the specific mission of the State, servant of God!

'Wherefore ye must needs be subject, not only for wrath but also for conscience sake.' 'This last word,' explains Leenhardt, 'evokes the positive participation, the voluntary adhesion, which the Christian gives to the order emanating from the authority following the judgment which assures him that the authority commands as minister of God.'[114] Paradoxical as it may seem, the witness of Christians in the world consists in this voluntary submission towards those on whom God has conferred an authority over them. It is thus that they love their neighbour, and God at the same time. It is their way of proclaiming the sovereignty of Jesus Christ. This is why they must absolutely avoid causing a scandal by getting involved in dishonesty which would bring them before the courts and perhaps into prison. Such faults cannot help gravely compromising the Church's witness, and they are also a sign that the community of brothers has in one way or another been broken. This is why all these verses form part of the teaching on brotherly charity; they are right in place in their context. We must always love our neighbour to the end. 'Dearly beloved, avenge not yourselves, but rather give place unto wrath,' wrote Paul, and added: 'Love worketh no ill to his neighbour' (Rom. 12:19; 13:10).

Verse 6: 'For this cause pay ye tribute also: for they are God's ministers, attending continually upon this very thing.' Here is Paul frankly sanctioning the tribute! It is true that he is addressing the Romans, who for their part had no reason not to pay it. It is for him an aspect of submission to the political authorities, since it is according them the indispensable means of carrying out their mission. And again he is proclaiming that the magistrates are ministers of God, thus stressing for the third time that the State's domain is not neutral as regards the Gospel.

Verse 7: 'Render therefore to all their dues: tribute to whom tribute is due; fear to whom fear; honour to whom honour.' Note that there is no question of loving the State; only the totalitarian State demands a devotion bordering on love. That is the very way in which it is pagan, because it is arrogating rights it does not have, and misunderstanding its true vocation, which is to be the servant of God, and only that. So there is no question of loving the State, nor worshipping the Emperor who embodies it, but only of showing it 'a simple, responsible and resolute attitude.' What we owe it is the tribute, respect, and honour. With the word 'fear' Paul has a play on words which is probably deliberate: the φόβος is at once the fear of punishment (since the magistrate punishes!) and the deferential fear, or respect, towards the superior who should be honoured. It is because the State is the delegate and minister of God that we must fear it rather as we fear God Himself. 'We owe all our superiors, in so far as they rule over us, whatever they are, the same sort of reverence as we see in David . . . so that we may learn not to criticise the people we have to obey.'[115] A Christian may not hate, nor despise, nor worship, the political authority of his country.

It seems unnecessary here to go further into the text of I Peter 2, which adds nothing to the recommendations supplied by Romans 13[116] or of Titus 2:1, to which I shall be returning. I Timothy 2:1-7, on the other hand, is very important for the eschatological orientation which it gives to the problems of the State. Paul is there exhorting Christians to pray for the political authorities that they may faithfully carry out their mission, which is 'to ensure external peace and tranquillity',[117] so that the Church can pursue its own mission in peace: that of evangelising the world. 'For God wishes that all men should be saved and come to a knowledge of his truth.' Karl Barth has shown, in a manner which I find unanswerable, how the State is charged unawares with the mission of ensuring protection for the preaching of the Gospel.[118] I shall therefore not press this aspect of the problem of the State, especially as it has no direct relevance to the problem of war.

5. The 'Demonisation' of the State

Several years later Rome burned. Most of the New Testament writings, being after the fire, have lost the optimistic attitude to the Empire seen in the Epistle to the Romans. The almost complete silence of the Epistles is eloquent, since the question of the relations between Christians and the Roman State was certainly crucial for them. The three other texts quoted above, the only ones which expressly mention the political authorities, are already more reserved than Romans 13; they no longer contain the definite statement that these authorities are willed and 'ordained' by God—although the author of I Peter is writing from Rome and seems to be inspired by Paul's Epistle to the Romans.[119] One has only to compare the two texts to note the change of atmosphere. For another thing the Epistle of Peter alludes too often to the persecutions Christians have endured for anyone to be under any illusions about the actual situation the author is evoking. Finally, we have seen that Revelations shows us the Christians' real attitude towards the Empire: they saw it as the instrument and the embodiment of the devil.[120]

How is the apparently contradictory evidence to be reconciled? It has been justly remarked[121] that behind the civil authorities they came into contact with, the New Testament authors saw supernatural *powers*, like guardian angels exercising an all-powerful control and domination over States and their chiefs. These angels had revolted against God, and thereafter led governments to defy Him and persecute the Church of Jesus Christ. Even in modern times it often looks as if States were dominated by demonic powers, the Hitlerian adventure being a typical confirmation and a terrifying demonstration of this. Karl Barth explains that 'the State, set up by God according to Romans 13 as protector of the law, may become the

State dominated by the Dragon, demanding the worship of Caesar, fighting with the saints, blaspheming God, the Beast of the Abyss from Revelations 13, ruling the whole world. It is just the angelic power which *can* be perverted so far as to become a demonic power.'[122] 'When the State goes beyond its limits,' adds Cullman, '. . . the Christian sees it as escaping from the sovereignty of Christ, the demonic power getting loose, the Beast appearing.'[123] This explanation helps to reconcile the apparent contradiction in these different parts of the New Testament.

But most of the texts referring to these heavenly powers which rule the authorities[124] present them precisely as hostile to Christ; this is a fact, I think, which has not been enough stressed. So if these texts do concern the State, it must be admitted that most of them show it to us in a pessimistic and pejorative light, in an atmosphere far removed from the serene collaboration between Church and State which is too often, and wrongly, seen in Romans 13. For 'let every soul be subject to the higher powers . . . which come from God' must surely be interpreted in the light of all these texts which talk of the political demonic powers; and this will modify its meaning.

Here are what the texts say: these authorities, powers, or dominions have been created in Christ, by Him, and for Him (Col. 1:16); but ignoring God's wisdom, it is they who have crucified the Lord (I Cor. 2:8, see Luke 22:53). However, Christ has triumphed over them by the Cross, and has despoiled them (Col. 2:15). Since His resurrection He is the chief of them (Col. 2:10). He is enthroned above them (Eph. 1:21). Since that day they have been subject to Him (I Peter 2:22), but the Church by its preaching must reveal to them the wisdom of God (Eph. 6:12); for in their revolt they continue to fight against the Christians (Rom. 8:38-39, see Luke 12:11), who must arm themselves with all the arms of God to strive against them (Eph. 6-12). But they will be finally destroyed (or reduced to impotence) in the day of Christ (I Cor. 2:6; 15:24). It will be admitted that there is no question in all this of collaboration between Church and State, but rather of a pitiless spiritual battle which often leads the Christians to martyrdom (Rev. 13:7).

The Constantinian heresy comes up here in the way the State's 'demonisation' is shown as a somewhat *exceptional* occurrence, when clearly it was always the case in New Testament times. Jesus was crucified by a coalition of Romans and Jews. The Roman emperors had themselves deified and worshipped. They all 'went past the limits' envisaged by God for a just state. Nor are our good western democracies of today really 'just States' respecting their proper calling. It is amazing how many theologians say in such conditional terms, '*whenever* the State deifies itself . . . *whenever* it demands a declaration that Caesar is the Lord. . . .'[125]—as if this were not always more or less the case! As if 'for reasons of State' were not in the last resort their permanent self-justification.

'It seems,' writes F. J. Leenhardt, 'that the existence of any State is bound to mean an authority imposing its power almost without discussion. . . . It is in the essence of a State to be totalitarian. . . .'[126] K. Barth acknowledges that, if one cannot say that the Swiss State is like the Beast of the Abyss, 'one *can* say it today of more than one other State.'[127] He is alluding, of course, to totalitarian governments, but are the others 'just' in the eyes of God? What optimism! G. Dehn is nearer reality when he writes: 'The authority is constantly in danger; it faces a strong demonic temptation; the danger of succumbing exists at every instant.'[128]

The fact is that since Constantine Christians have tended to think if a State no longer *persecutes* the Church, that is a sure sign of its being a just State. Contrary to the testimony of the New Testament, they have a prejudice in favour of the State, which goes to the point of passive and unconditional obedience to it. But because the State does not persecute the Church, can one really conclude that the State is faithful and has not been 'demonised'? Is it not equally possible that the State is well and truly demonised, but does not persecute the Church which grants it all it wants, and is in haste to satisfy all its whims, like a mistress afraid to lose the favours of her rich, protective lover? The fact that a State does or does not persecute the Church could never be a sufficient criterion in itself for judging whether that State is 'just' before God. There is no more a 'just State' than there is a 'just war'; all that scholasticism is irreconcilable with the Bible's message.[129]

'We wrestle against principalities, against powers, against the rulers of the darkness of this world, against spiritual wickedness in high places,' wrote Paul (Eph. 6:12); and we know now that these authorities he speaks of are the political authorities. The first Christians actually lived within this terrible struggle: almost all the New Testament heroes were imprisoned, tortured, or condemned to death. But have these words still a significance for us today? For centuries we Christians have denied it, turning upside down the Gospel message: 'We must strictly obey the principalities and

powers, and must serve them faithfully. . . .' In Protestant theology
Romans 13 has eclipsed Ephesians 6:12: it is surely obvious that our
traditional perspective is distorted.[130] What tribute have the Churches
paid, then, to enjoy such a peace? Might it by any chance be in their
submission to military service?

Chapter 2

THE LIMITS OF OBEDIENCE TO THE STATE

1. *Legitimacy and Significance of Disobedience*

IN theory everybody agrees that the Christian does not owe the State an absolute, unconditional obedience. 'In relation to the State,' writes Cullman, for example,[131] 'the Christian will always put an ultimate question mark, and will remain vigilant and critical. . . .' In theory all the theologians recognise that 'in certain cases' the believer has no other solution than to resist the State and even refuse to obey it. Most of the time, however, it is no more than a conventional tag, a mental qualification, to relieve their consciences. For they very rarely give precise guidance on the exact conditions where the Christian has the duty of disobeying the State. Everybody 'sensibly' obeys the State, the average patriotic Protestant's reactions to conscientious objection reveal all the elements, alien to the Gospel, which have obtained 'the freedom of the city' in the Church. F. J. Leenhardt is quite right to denounce the attitude of Christians who 'of their own free will or from resignation, submit to the public authority because it commands . . . without examining whether it has a right to command or is commanding what is right. . . .' 'What is this fatalism,' he protests a little later, 'which leads to saying that one *ought* to do something because one cannot help it? Is the authority's legitimacy to be found in its power to compel obedience by force? Are there regions in the Christian life so far outside the Holy Spirit's control that one can live in them with a good conscience, according to a law totally different from the faith?'[132]

In theory, then, everybody agrees that the Christian's obedience to the State is not unlimited. There are three reasons for this: first, Christianity can scarcely deny the glorious martyrs of its past, those who preferred death rather than submit to the demands of the political authorities of their time—but today, of course, our States ask nothing contrary to the Gospel! Secondly, it can scarcely leave out of account the proud reply of the apostles who said that one must obey God rather than men—but today, of course, one is always assured of obeying God by obeying the State! Finally, the postulate of unconditional obedience to the State can scarcely be reconciled with the doctrine of God's sovereignty, which is essential for the Reform Churches; it would mean the co-existence of two absolute sovereigns, so in theory the priority is given to God—but today, of course, to disobey the State is to revolt against God Himself and the order He has established.[133]

So it is only in exceptional cases that the Christian must resist the State. 'As members of the State,' A. Vinet wrote, 'we must submit with good grace to certain restrictions on our personal liberty. . . . But we can by no means sacrifice our conscience to it.'[134] Calvin himself had demanded 'that all obey (the magistrate) so far as he does not command anything against God.'[135] Certainly by his disobedience the Christian is rendering the State an important service, showing it that it has exceeded its rights and reminding it what is its true mission as a State. But for the Christian's witness in resisting the State to be a true preaching of the glory of Christ, its protest or disobedience must not deny the State's authority, but merely affirm the supreme authority of the living God, under Whose judgment the State is also placed.

The Christian's disobedience then becomes a paradoxical yet positive and essential form of its submission. It will never be a kind of anarchy, for however monstrous and perverted the State may be, it always remains for the believer a sign of the Last Judgment and of the Kingdom. His opposition will always remain 'respectful,' for even if the State makes a demonic use of its authority, that authority comes to it in the last resort from God Himself. Just as a Christian son will never fail in respect towards his father, however perverted, because this *is* his father, so the Christian citizen will not cease to honour the political authorities, even when he finds himself constrained to disobey them openly—because these are the authorities, and God wills the existence of political authorities. Doubtless it will often lead him to martyrdom, that is, to the witness of his faith; but this is how he will observe the fifth commandment and put in practice the instructions of Romans 13 when confronted by a State which wants to make him disobey his God. Because he is called to pray for the political authorities (I Tim. 2:2), he bears their responsibility with them, and can therefore never be released from his involvement with them; he honours them by the very act of respectful disobedience. I do not think the point needs further discussions, for probably all theologians would agree.

2. *Need for a Criterion of Judgment*

But how shall the Christian know when he has the right to disobey the State? This is a point on which disturbing confusion seems to reign among Christians, or even a surprising silence. 'A liberty of conscience which avoids moral anarchy, an obedience to State authority which stops short of acquiescence in evil—that represents an ideal hard to define or to realise.'[136] True enough; and many theologians do not even raise the question, while some allude to it in such veiled terms that one cannot help thinking they must prefer ambiguity: they talk of the Church's struggle, its resistance to the totalitarian State, but without specifying *what* refusal of obedience this resistance implies.

What must the Christian do who receives an order from the State he finds fundamentally immoral? Traditional theology gives the State 'the benefit of the doubt': that is, if in doubt, obey. This seems at least partly based, it is true, on the apostolic texts which talk of submission to the authorities. But only partly, for there will almost always be doubt, and therefore almost always obedience. The most appalling crimes, from the Inquisition to Auschwitz, have been committed on this principle that in case of doubt you must trust the authority which has taken responsibility for the order. Luther said that 'when subjects are uncertain as to the rightness of their prince (who begins a war they think unjust), they may follow him without compromising the salvation of their souls, so long as despite all their efforts they have not succeeded in being sufficiently well informed. . . .'[137] But obviously, as those who hesitate to obey are bound to be threatened with prison, being put to death, or other State reprisals, only quite exceptional personalities will *not* discover some doubts! So it practically comes down to saying that the State must always be obeyed.

For F. J. Leenhardt, the main criterion is that *order* reigns. That idea is very widespread in Christian circles: the Churches have often been the defenders of order. 'Order is the end God wills when He clothes some in authority and enjoins obedience on others. Disobedience to the established authority engenders disorder, while order is the necessary consequence of an authority being exercised . . order is a sort of good in itself, a preliminary to the true good which the State must pursue. It is the good resulting from the authority's very existence.'[138] Leenhardt acknowledges, of course, that the *status quo* is 'sometimes a stability prejudicial to justice'—an established disorder, one might call it. 'We must be vigilant against this dangerous distortion, but disorder is no improvement. . . . Inasmuch as it commands, authority is a creator of order.'

If 'order' means the opposite of the social chaos which results when the political authority is powerless or absent, then 'even if what the authority decides is not good, at least its giving commands is good.' But is such an abstract and negative definition really tenable, a definition so stripped of all concern for ethics? If order is a situation (or action) conforming to what God wills, one can see at once that there are forms of order which are disorders in God's eyes (for example in totalitarian states), while there are forms of disorder which may not be so in God's eyes (for example, resistance to monstrous injustices). So Leenhardt's statement that 'inasmuch as it commands, authority is a creator of order,' must have this simple qualification, 'depending what it commands.' When Hitler gave his armies the order to invade Poland, when he organised the extermination of the Jews, did he create order? Did not such 'orders' destroy God's order? So we are brought back to our problem: what is the criterion by which the Christian can judge the State's orders, to decide whether they contribute to the *true* order, and are worthy to be obeyed?

3. The State's Mission as Criterion

Leenhardt then suggests that the mission God has confided to the State contains the necessary criterion. 'All the duties the State imposes are not necessarily legitimate. We have said that authority should in certain conditions be submitted to a critical judgment. Since the State has a mission, the Christian has the means and the obligation to test the State's decisions by that mission. This is by no means to authorise individual discussions with all manner of officials, but to indicate the nature and limits of necessary obedience. For *this qualification being expressly made*,[139] it is in fact for obedience that the Christian must decide when the State, in the legitimate exercise of its responsibilities, commands him to do something which he cannot approve from his Christian point of view. We are aware of the gravity of such a point of view, and the abuses it could give rise to with lazy consciences. Our opinion should not be quoted to dispense Christians from the obligations to witness and perhaps to resistance. Even when such witness brings one into conflict with the authorities, it should be borne, if the conflict is due to a weakness on the part of the authorities, who are thus unfaithful to their mission. Our remarks are intended to show that resistance to authority and disobedience should be decided on by the Christian only after examining what is not his duty as a Christian but the authority's duty.'

For Leenhardt, then, Christians have the right and even the obligation to disobey the State, but only when it commands them to do something contrary to *its* mission, when its order ceases to be 'the legitimate exercise of its responsibilities' as a State. In short, the *ethical* significance of orders given by the State does not matter, provided they tend to realise the aim it is pursuing, which constitutes its 'mission'. Nor does it matter what *ethical* significance my obedience will have, or if in the sphere of Christian *private* life it is a false witness, provided I am sure the State in giving me this order is not being unfaithful to its mission.'[140]

'The Christian magistrate,' Leenhardt goes on, 'must accept this divorce, implied by the very nature of authority. His scruples must not lead him to refuse to act as is required of him by the exercise of authority which God has established; they should impel him to act only in such a way that he remains faithful to his mission.'

This whole conception is open to a great many objections. It must surely lead to a dangerous division in the Christian's personality, yet Leenhardt remarks elsewhere that 'it is inadmissible to divide the Christian life in two.'[141] When the Christian magistrate is in conflict between his private fidelity as a Christian and his duty as a magistrate, why must it necessarily be this second demand which will have priority over the first? Strange that Leenhardt has not thought to give a theological basis for such a choice, since it is far from obvious that a very human assessment of the State's duty must prevail over the clear and express guidance of Scripture in what concerns the Christian's so-called private life. In this priority, in fact, you can see the idolatry of the City.

Moreover, his conception seems to imply that the end justifies the means. If the State's mission is the only criterion by which I can judge the legitimacy of the orders it gives me, then I should not make any judgment on the means it is using to carry out its mission. For example, if I believe that the State must make it impossible for criminals to harm society, must I therefore refrain from judging the definition it gives of 'criminal' and the means (tortures, etc.) it uses against them? It is obvious that to look exclusively at the end regardless of the means can lead directly to every kind of abuse. The State, of course, will always justify its ultimate end: even when it is brutally 'eliminating traitors and enemies of the people,' it will always find it easy to show that it wishes to ensure order and save the nation. Another example would be the public licensing of brothels 'in the interests of public health.' The real problems of conscience arise for us not only over the official objectives given by the State, but also, and far more, over the means it uses and commands us to use. That is another reason why the criterion Leenhardt suggests seems to me inadequate.

There is one more thing: if we take the State's mission as a criterion of the orders it gives, even supposing that we can define this mission in a way that is neither abstract nor arbitrary, then we are bound in the end to make the State its own standard, which leads at once to totalitarian ideas. It is a short step, for instance, from Leenhardt's position to the Nazi formula that 'the task we have to accomplish is so important for our race that all moral considerations must give way before it.' Leenhardt realised this so well that he sought the criterion of the State and its mission in the idea of good. That mission, therefore, cannot serve as a criterion for the Christian's obedience, since it needs itself a criterion founded on Scripture.

4. Religious Criteria

Some suggest a religious criterion to mark the limits of the Christian's obedience to the State. According to them, the Christian does not have to make a value judgment, from an ethical point of view, on the orders which the State addresses to him; but he can refuse his obedience when the State takes up a blameworthy religious position. Eberhard, for instance, writes: 'When the civil authority, by abuse of its power, tries to impose on us a form of worship of God, a creed, whatever it may be, that is contrary to the Revelation, then it must be rejected.'[142] But there are surely actions which imply a denial of the Gospel, whether or not they are part of an explicit pagan mystique. What will the Christian do, for instance, when convinced that by putting on military uniform he is worshipping the god Mars and thereby denying Jesus Christ?

Cullman demands of the Christian 'an unshakable resistance as soon as the State makes a god of itself.'[143] But what does he think is the legitimate Christian resistance to the deified State? He gives no clear answer to this question. 'One must render to Caesar only that which is his';[144] but what exactly does this mean? 'When the State demands a declaration that Caesar is lord, the Church in its preaching will courageously oppose it and designate it as a member of the Kingdom of Christ which has broken away from its subjection'[145];

must we conclude from this that the only means of fighting allowed to the Church is preaching *by word*? Or does that 'opposition' imply concrete refusals of obedience as well—and if so, which? Why talk of 'unshakable resistance,' if in the last resort it is only verbal opposition? Also, how do we judge when a State has begun to make a god of itself? Are not all States more or less deified?

Karl Barth foresees the possibility that the State opposes God: 'Even if, in this case too, respect remains due to it, (the Christian) can only be at its service in a passive and therefore limited way. In no case can it mean that the Church and its members must give their approval and their free consent to the intentions and enterprises of the State power, if these, instead of being designed to protect the preaching of the Justification, tend to injure it. Even then Christians must not refuse the State *anything* of what comes to it necessarily as delegate of public law, as power of order. . . .'[146] For Barth, then, the Christian's obedience ceases only as soon as the State interferes with the freedom of preaching the Gospel.[147] In that case, Christians cannot 'make such enterprises their own . . . nor themselves assume responsibility for them.' Although he does not explicitly speak of refusing obedience, it is what Barth's veiled words seem to suggest. But he does not appear to have foreseen two objections. First, at what stage can it be considered that the State is interfering with the freedom of preaching: what are the minimum conditions of freedom of speech which the Church must claim as normal, and beyond which you can speak of interferences?[148] As soon as you try to draw a definite line, you once more become completely arbitrary. Secondly, can a strictly religious criterion be enough here? Are there not instances where the State, chivalrous as it may be towards the Church, nevertheless gives orders so monstrous, so contrary to God's will *from an ethical point of view*, that one must still refuse to obey it, even at the cost of one's life?

To give only a few examples: a woman in a totalitarian country finds out that her husband is in a resistance movement, and the State requires the denunciation of 'traitors'; she herself risks the death penalty if she does not inform on her husband: must she obey? A German woman with a non-Aryan husband is required by the Nazis to get a divorce from her husband: must she obey? A policeman is ordered to strip a woman naked to interrogate her and extract confessions from her by burning her breasts with a cigarette: must he obey? A doctor in a concentration camp is ordered to sterilise a thousand Polish prisoners by cauterisation; he knows most

of them will die from the operation, but he also knows that if he
refuses, he will be tortured to death: must he obey? A German
captain in occupied France is shot himself for refusing to shoot
hostages he knows to be innocent: was he wrong? One could go on
indefinitely, with other examples nearer home and of more recent
vintage; but it is easier to see from such extreme cases the absurd
inadequacy of solely 'religious' criteria for deciding when disobedience is a positive duty.

In none of these cases was anything like 'freedom of preaching'
involved: as Reinhold Niebuhr wrote in 1936, 'A Church which
refrains from any criticism of the State on a moral plane, and in the
last resort allows itself only a religious criticism of the State's religious pretensions, will end up logically in the same painful situation as
the German Church is placed in today.'[149] And if it be admitted that
in such cases the Christian must of course disobey the State, then
we are still looking for a criterion in cases where it is not so obvious.
If the Christian must sometimes obey God rather than men, he must
have a criterion of judgment to tell him when the State is demanding
something contrary to God's will in all spheres including the moral
one. It is true that Peter and John were forbidden to *preach* the
Gospel, but this represents only an infinitesimal minority among
the cases where the Christian must be afraid of denying his Lord if
he obeys the State.

Luther seems to have felt that there was a real problem here: 'No
one is obliged to commit an injustice,' he writes; 'in this case he
must obey God, who requires justice, rather than men, according
to Acts 5:29.'[150] But he does not give any criterion of justice for the
civil order! O. Cullmann is one of the few modern theologians to
admit that '. . . within the sphere assigned to it the State (sometimes)
ceases to be founded on law, and reverses the ideas of justice and
injustice.' But he adds at once: 'The New Testament nowhere provides for such a case, and envisages only cases where the State
relapses into its demonic folly, exceeding its limits by imposing the
worship of the Emperor. . . . (The New Testament) supplies us with
no criterion of judgment by which we could tell in all cases whether a
State exercising its proper functions is remaining within God's plan
or not.'[151] What caution! So the Church of Jesus Christ has absolutely nothing to tell believers faced with problems of conscience such
as I have evoked, but leaves them entirely to their own resources:
this seems to be yet another sign of a Church which is no longer
faithful and has given up the struggle.[152]

5. *In Search of a Moral Criterion*

I turn, therefore, towards those who have sought a criterion at once theological and moral for the State's demands. Calvin was one, and the La Rochelle Confession of Faith is explicit: 'God has put the sword in the hands of the magistrates to curb the sins committed not only against the second table of God's commandments, but also against the first.' This is why the political authorities must be obeyed, 'even when they are unfaithful, provided God's sovereign empire remains intact.'[153] His catechism of 1537 says: 'There is always one thing to be excepted in obeying superiors, and that is that it does not draw us away from obeying Him before Whose edicts the commandments of every king must yield. . . . If the men set up over us command something against Him, one must do none of it, nor consider it.' The Scottish Church, for its part, 'has always thought that its loyalty (to the State) was conditional, depending on how the State pursued the moral ends for which God founded it. In past centuries it has sanctioned, and even provoked revolts; and it still reserves the right to criticise the State's policies in the sphere of morals.'[154] In recent times the report of the Oxford Œcumenical Conference proclaimed in its turn the Church's 'duty to be loyal and obedient towards the State, disobedience becoming a duty only if obedience is clearly contrary to God's commandments.'[155] Finally, in the truly Calvinist tradition, I would quote the Theses of Pomeyrol: 'The Church recalls to its members that every Christian owes obedience to the State, it being understood that such obedience is ordered by and subordinate to the absolute obedience to God alone; God's Word exercises its command and control over all obedience rendered to men.'[156] These texts admit that Christian citizens may legitimately make a value judgment of an ethical order on the State's commands, and may also refuse to obey when that judgment is negative.

Calvin has a particularly lucid passage on this point, although he has not himself drawn all the consequences from it. 'But in the obedience which we have been taught is due to our superiors, there must always be an exception, or rather a rule which is to be kept above all things. It is that such an obedience never deflects us from obeying Him beneath whose will it is proper that all the desires of kings be contained, and that all their commandments yield to His ordinance, and that all their haughtiness be humbled and abased before His majesty. . . . If those who have pre-eminence over us come to command something against Him, we should set it at nought; nor in doing so have any regard for all the dignity of their superiority, which has no injury done to it, when it is made to submit and set below God's power, which alone is real at the cost of the rest. . . . Truly we are then rendering to God such obedience as He asks, when we suffer all things rather than turn aside from His holy word.'[157]

And again: 'Whatever title men have, therefore, we must never hear them (command) without making this exception, that they should by no means turn us aside from rendering obedience to God.'[158] For Calvin the criterion is thus God's will, His ordinance, His holy word. For him God's authority remains effectively sovereign, and the State has no right to deflect us from the obedience we owe to Him. 'If laws are imposed on us, though they be unjust, we must still bear them; but if they detract from obedience to God . . . let us not be afraid to transgress them or to anger men.'[159] The Lord must be served first, that should be self-evident for anyone who recognises the authority of the Scriptures and the sovereignty of the God of Jesus Christ.

Alexandre Vinet has expressed the same idea with his undisputed authority: 'Take care, for the laws themselves are sometimes rebellious, rebellious against the eternal law of right, the supreme law of God. Placed between these two laws, a citizen may remember that he is a man, and also a believer. And then, having to choose between his fellows and his Master, between man and God, he will decide in favour of Him by whom kings reign, legislators make laws, and magistrates administer justice. . . . He is ready to be a rebellious citizen in the society of men so as to be a loyal and faithful citizen in the society of the chosen. . . . An unjust law must be respected by me, despite its injustice, when it harms my interests alone. . . . But an immoral law, an irreligious law, a law which would make me do what my conscience and God's law condemn, if I cannot get it revoked, I must challenge it! This principle, far from being subversive, is the principle of life of any society. It is the struggle of good against evil.'[160]

If I adopt Calvin's viewpoint, because I find it right in principle, that does not mean I am unaware of the difficulties as soon as you try to apply it in concrete situations. For is the individual, in the last resort, to be sole judge of what is contrary to God's will? If God's Word is the criterion of the obedience we owe the State, what is the criterion of God's Word? People may find anything they want somewhere in the Bible, so as to justify or condemn anything in its name.

These are certainly major difficulties, and we shall later be considering whether a sound and definite criterion of judgment for the State's orders can be drawn from the Scriptures. But at the point we have reached, this assertion can be made in any case: the orders given by the State always remain beneath God's judgment and His Word; and a Christian has not only the *right* but the *obligation* to disobey, whenever he has the conviction, founded in the faith, and if possible confirmed by the authority of some brethren, that by obeying the State he would be disobeying God and denying Jesus Christ. And as the Holy Spirit cannot speak in a manner contrary to the Scriptures, it is in the Word that he will have to seek the elements of his inner conviction. The ideal, of course, would be for the Church to make this judgment[161]; but alas, most of the statements I have just quoted are in a tragic minority, so it must usually be made by a Christian in isolation, and often without warning. It is by his conscience, illuminated as much as possible by the Scriptures, that he will have to decide whether he must obey or not. There may, even so, be signposts or landmarks in the Bible which will help him in his anguished heart-searching; to this possibility I shall return.

6. Legitimacy of Governments

The vast majority of those who support the traditional doctrine consider that submission to the State implies undisputed obedience in anything concerned with the necessities of society; the quotations I have given are explicit enough on this subject. These authors take good care not to raise the question of the legitimacy of governments; most of them do not even mention the distinction between *de facto* and *de jure* authorities; they close their eyes to the obvious fact that very often power is exercised by two superimposed authorities fighting against each other, both demanding the obedience of citizens —as was the case in Palestine in Jesus' time. They seem to ignore revolutionary movements and civil wars on the one hand, and military occupations on the other; while naturally they do not make the slightest reference to colonisation. For most of those we have consulted, the *de facto* political authority is also the *de jure* authority, which obviously simplifies the problem, and enables them to demand of Christians an unqualified obedience to 'Caesar', whom they childishly identify with the State. But it is dishonourable to evade this difficult problem.

If you believe that the authority, the magistrate referred to in the New Testament, is the *de facto* political authority whatever it may be, as soon as it effectively exercises power over the country, then no doubt it demands from Christians an undisputed authority. But that would implicitly condemn any participation by Christians in a revolutionary or merely anti-governmental movement, as being a serious revolt against the order set up by God Himself; it would also condemn all the Christians who have in any way taken part in resistance movements, not to mention Christian soldiers who are momentarily encircled by the enemy in a country where the enemy has become the undisputed master, and who yet continue the battle; and the Christian prisoners of war who try to escape and rejoin their country's forces. All these have disobeyed the authority exercising the *de facto* power over the territory they are in.

If, however, the idea of a *de jure* authority, the legitimate government, is brought in, then obviously there are bound to be cases where Christians will be recommended to disobey the 'de facto' government for motions not necessarily religious. According to the traditional position, in France during the war only Christians who strictly obeyed the Vichy government were respecting the authority 'established by God'; and the resistance were 'resisting the order established by God' (Rom. 13:2). But nobody today would go quite as far as that!

'Obedience must be rendered to all superiors,' Calvin declared, 'because if they are raised in authority and honour, it is not by mere chance but by God's providence. For we are none of us . . . to enquire too curiously by what right princes rule, it should be enough for us that we see them in power. . . . The Romans undoubtedly entered Asia and conquered these countries more from selfish interests than for a rightful cause; and the emperors who ruled over them thereafter had seized the monarchy by violence and tyrannical force. St. Peter therefore stops all this from being brought up for debate, because subjects must obey their superiors without contradiction: especially as their being in authority has not come about without God having raised them to this high degree.'[162] It is not surprising that Calvin goes on to exclude any right to disobey princes and kings; but on this point our present patriots are obliged to disavow him. There are, alas, situations where one is indeed obliged to 'bring up these things for debate' and 'criticise' those who rule over us.

But how are we to make the judgment on the State which is clearly necessary? The religious criteria suggested by Cullmann and Barth are often inapplicable, as we have seen. French Christians did not disobey the Vichy government because it 'deified itself' more than any other government does, or interfered with the freedom of preaching; their motives for disobedience were far more emotional or moral, and if religious motives were sometimes invoked, they were certainly no more than pretexts. The Christians in the Resistance disobeyed the *de facto* government of the day from their personal conception of '*la Patrie*', of the right political and economic order; and also perhaps because they felt that the government they were rising against had corrupted and overturned the order of God indispensable to a civilised society. In any case, it is not my concern here to judge or to praise them; I am merely showing the inadequacy of the traditional theological position. If you want explicitly to maintain that in certain cases a Christian has a right to resist a bad government, you are bound to need motives of a moral order as a basis for that right. If the individual, confronted by the tragic problem of collaboration with a government whose demands and pretensions are morally monstrous, is not to be left to decide arbitrarily from his own emotional or philosophical reactions, we must seek an ethical criterion in this sphere too, by which he can make a value judgment founded on objective reasons. We are brought back, then, to the same conclusion: there is an order of God which the State must respect, and the Christian must not help it to defy that order.[163]

7. *The Christian's Disobedience*

What, then, must faithful Christians do when the State would constrain them to commit an act they consider a denial of Jesus Christ? Their submission to the State can then only be a false witness. I think most believers will follow me when I sum up this chapter by answering these questions as follows:[164]

1. When the State in its activities and its orders does not violate God's order, the Church will take an attitude of benevolent submission towards it, implying scrupulous obedience of the State's orders by Christians.

2. But when the State violates God's order on one point or another, the Church would be unfaithful to its own ministry and its responsibility towards the State, if it did not clearly *protest*, reminding the State that it is the servant of God for men's good, not to aggravate their discontent or their disorder. This protest can be embodied in definite and significant acts. However, Christians must patiently endure without rebellion the injustices of which they may themselves be the victims at the hands of the State.

3. When the State, not content with violating God's order, tries

to make Christians take a personal part in such violation, the Church and Christians must respectfully but openly disobey that demand by the State. This is the price of their fidelity to Jesus Christ.

But what is God's order which the State may violate? What is the criterion of 'good' which the State is charged by God to ensure in society? This is what we must now investigate.

POLITICAL MORALITY AND GOSPEL MORALITY

1. The State's Mission

WHAT is the task which God in His plan has confided to the political authorities, of whom the Scriptures tell us that they are His servants? The Scriptures themselves contain no explicit answer to this question, so I find it very rash to try to construct a *theology of the State*; there can only be a theology of obedience and disobedience to the State.

(*a*) *The State's Dual Task.* Most theologians agree that in God's plan the State has a dual function: to protect and maintain religion and morality on the one hand, and on the other to protect and ensure social order. Luther and Calvin, living in the Constantinian illusion of a Christian world, worked out, each in his own way, a theocratic conception of the State, according to which the prince is the protector of religion and good morals, as much as of society itself. Anglicanism is equally founded on this conception.

The secularisation of the modern world showed its inadequacy and Karl Barth has recently tried to modernise it. According to him, the State's mission, whether conscious or not, is by ensuring social order to enable the Church to carry out *its* task of preaching the Gospel. 'It is because the Church's liberty can only be guaranteed by the City that the Church on its side must guarantee the City's existence by praying for it.'[165] This theory rests on the text of I Timothy 2:2-4, where Paul asks that prayers be made 'for kings, and for all that are in authority; that we may lead a quiet and peaceable life in all godliness and honesty. For this is good and acceptable in the sight of God our Saviour; who will have all men to be saved, and to come unto the knowledge of the truth.'

There is little need to linger on this first function of the State's, for in the sphere of the protection accorded by the political authorities to the free preaching of the Gospel, the conflicts of conscience arising for Christians are relatively simple: they will sometimes refuse to obey the State for religious reasons, whether it tries to make them worship another God than that of the Scriptures, or to make them take an active part in interference with the freedom of preaching. In both cases all theologians seem to approve of Christians' disobedience faced by what is really an abuse of power by the civil authority. It is in relation to the State's second function, the maintenance of social order, that troubling problems of conscience arise for believers concerned to be faithful to Jesus Christ: it is here the Christian needs as clear as possible a criterion to know if he should or should not obey the State in a particular case.

This 'political' task of the State's has itself a dual aspect: negatively it consists in preserving society from chaos and self-destruction by checking the anarchic and corrupting forces produced by men's sin, if need be through physical constraint. In this sense the State limits the damage caused by the power of sin: without it, society, left to its own resources, could not long continue. By 'punishing transgressors,' it allows the community to survive despite the mortal gangrene it is infected with: in a word, it enables society to live.

Let us note in passing that all this would need qualifying before it became beyond dispute; and many theologians too easily take the point as proved. For example, G. Deluz writes: 'The State makes order reign in society; this order is relative, but thanks to it the world remains more or less policed and inhabitable: men cannot tear themselves to pieces at will and abandon themselves to the laws of the jungle. . . .'[166] But even if the State certainly does on occasions have this function through its police and courts, there are other occasions where through its armies it actually organises mutual massacre, expressly commands men to tear each other to pieces, and imposes the laws of the jungle on them in all their inhuman rigour: this is what is called 'war,' which is also the work of the State. It would be hard, after all, to imagine a form of chaos more murderous and destructive than war.

Yes, I believe it is part of the State's mission to stop men tearing each other to pieces according to the laws of the jungle; but this means that resort to war seems to me contrary to the State's true task. Whereas the traditionalists ought to have the courage, the honesty, or simply the lucidity, to say: 'The State's mission is sometimes to stop men tearing each other to pieces according to the laws of the jungle, sometimes to urge them and constrain them to do so under its iron authority.' But if they did this, one could still ask where to draw the line between the chaos the State forbids and the chaos it organises.

It is not only in the international field that the State often shows itself incapable of carrying out this first, negative side of its mission; within the nation too, alas, it is sometimes a creator of disorder. 'Often,' confesses the Oxford Conference report, 'the State, which should have been able to stop the progressive disintegration (of society), has not done so, and has sometimes even helped to quicken the pace of that disintegration.'[167] When theologians repeat the formula, 'The State makes order reign in society,' they generally omit to add that this 'order' is very often, and in a sense always, an 'established disorder'—which is worse than a 'relative order' (in Deluz' euphemism). There is even some truth in the Marxist theory that the State is an instrument of oppression used by the ruling class to exploit the other classes: which might indeed apply to the Soviet State itself.

The Constantinian heresy is apparent in this easy optimism concerning the State, this stubborn refusal to see it as anything but beneficent protector of order, this readiness to idealise it and even deify it.[168] True, God has charged it with stopping disorder; but as it is also quite often a creator of disorder, the Christian must be very careful and clear-headed in considering the submission he owes it.

It is amazing that defenders of militarism like R. Niebuhr persist in accusing conscientious objectors of optimism, when it is *their* position which is optimistic about human nature (in the opposite way to Rousseau), insisting on the individual's sinfulness but believing in the State's 'natural goodness.' Well, we see man's sinfulness in the Cross, but despite some washed hands, the State took part in this crime as much as the individual did. Men are so naturally wicked, we are told, that only the truncheon and its equivalents can keep them in a decent existence. Perhaps so; but why pass over in silence that the men who hold the truncheons are also naturally wicked, as if by some permanent miracle of providence *these men* were all inspired with goodness. The State has been so much idealised in traditional Protestant theology that you would imagine as long as it did not interfere in so-called 'religious' questions, it was worthy of absolute confidence—and blind obedience![169]

All this being said, I still agree with the theologians when they define the negative aspect of the State's mission, from the Christian point of view, as the duty, confided to it by God, *of stopping men destroying each other*.[170] It is highly debatable, however, to say the least, whether the State will succeed in carrying out that duty by itself destroying a certain number of men. Is that what God expects of it? It is a little like asking whether the State will succeed in suppressing the crime of clandestine prostitution by itself organising brothels. In both cases, you can hardly expect to stop a crime by practising it yourself. Evil is not overcome with evil, said Paul (Rom. 12:21), and his words are not concerned only with the order of redemption.

But the State's strictly political function has also a positive side: that of establishing an adequate social and political order, which notably will offer a definition of 'criminal' by contrast with that order, [171] and as we have seen, will even enable the Church to fulfil its own mission. The real difficulty is where to find the norm for this social order, how to know whether a particular measure—such as the 'elimination' of lunatics—helps to ensure that order, or rather to destroy it. We are brought back, in fact, to the vital question: what is the order God wishes for civil society?

(b) *God's order for the City.* It is hard to give this question a clear and precise answer. For many it seems that God's order is the social *status quo*, that what exists is what God wants; but of course this position is untenable. Its premises are contrary to the indications of the Scriptures, notably to the doctrines of God's sovereignty and the corruption of the human race. For others, the nationalists, the social order desired by God is that which best ensures the national interest: anything the State does in the interests of the nation is *ipso facto* good. But again there is no criterion as to the nation's true interests: how do we know whether the elimination of lunatics contributes to them or not? Also, the idea of the nation needs a theological basis, and this is far harder to find than some appear to think. The nationalist conception of the political order implies that the nation is its own norm, which is theologically inadmissible.

Some, therefore, look for a general principle transcending the nation as the norm of God's order for the world of politics: one school talks of law, another of justice, another of liberty; and others invoke 'the defence of the human personality'. But all these abstractions are open to the same unanswerable objection: their definition cannot help being quite arbitrary; and it seems impossible to base them even partially on the testimony of the Scriptures, which includes no sort of pointer to a so-called 'Christian-type social order'.

The only satisfactory answer would be to produce from the Scriptures a relatively precise ethical criterion for judging the moral value of the State's laws and demands in the sphere of social and political life, which would thus enable the Christian to decide whether he should obey them or not. We shall be considering whether this is possible; but it must be noted that the vast majority of theologians do not go so far: those who defend the traditional position even expressly refuse to do so. The Christian 'militarists' are content to justify their position in these sort of terms: 'The State judges it good to ensure the nation's defence by arms; it mobilises me; I have only to obey without trying to find out whether the State is right or wrong in using such means to arrive at its ends.' But is the State really its own authority where its behaviour and demands are concerned?[172]

2. The Traditional Doctrine

The traditional doctrine is based on the following set of propositions: God has charged the Church with the duty of preaching the Gospel, and the State with the duty of ensuring the political order; the Christian is both member of the Church and citizen of the nation; as the former he must obey God by conforming to the Gospel ethic as it emerges from the New Testament; as the latter he must obey God by conforming to the political ethic of which the State is the judge and which is not to be disputed from the Christian point of view, unless the State tries to impose a religious belief or interfere with the freedom of Christian preaching. In short, the Christian glorifies God equally by respecting the Gospel morality in his private life, and by respecting his country's laws in his political life. Most theological attempts to justify Christians in military service seem to fall within this framework, which has a certain attractiveness. Clear distinctions are generally popular, and this division of the Christian's life into two parts appears to safeguard personal 'godliness' while granting the State all it unfortunately needs to maintain society's material life. But it will probably be obvious to the reader by now that there are grave objections to this 'clear distinction'.

(a) *The division of the two spheres.* First, it postulates that the respective spheres of Church and State can be exactly defined. There is, plainly, a profound difference between the special task of the Church, to proclaim Christ's salvation to the world by the Holy Spirit, and that of the State, to watch over the maintenance of human society's physical life by physical means. One may indeed speak of an order of redemption and an order of conservation: these distinctions correspond to scriptural realities, and are more or less implied in the Bible's message.

But I very much doubt whether a strict boundary line can be drawn between the two spheres, for these reasons. First, there is only one Lord, Jesus Christ, who is Lord both of the Church and of the State; given the complexity of human life, the Christian will sometimes inevitably be placed in difficult concrete situations where his Master makes demands on him in both capacities. To satisfy the *whole* of his Master's personal demands, he must synthesise them rather than ignore one aspect or the other, and such a synthesis will necessarily straddle the theoretical dividing line between the two 'spheres of influence'.

Nor can the Christian Church be relegated to one of these spheres: it would simplify a lot, but it isn't possible. For the Church is very much a natural, as well as a spiritual community, and as such it is also situated—very concretely, alas—in the world of fallen creation.[173] And all this is true *a fortiori* of the Christian, who is never part-time citizen and part-time member of the Church, but always both at the same time, so that he can never draw an exact line between these two aspects of his obedience.

(b) *The Dual Morality*. The traditional doctrine also postulates a dual Christian morality, which has had incalculable and disastrous consequences in the Church's history.[174] We know how deeply Catholic faith and theology have been influenced by the distinction between common Christian morality and Gospel counsels of perfection. The whole Roman ethic rests on this dual morality: the one down-to-earth and easy, for ordinary Christians; the other sublime and ambitious, for the clergy and those who in general are aiming at saintliness. We know how this theory is applied to our present problem: ordinary Christians are entitled to take part in war, because too much cannot be asked of them, but monks and priests are dispensed from military service, which is excessively contrary to the Gospel ideal; at least this was the case in France till the end of the last century. And when the Church wished to be rid of its adversaries, it had them destroyed by the 'secular arm' of the soldiers and police, because its clergy were not permitted to defile their hands with blood; whereas this was permitted to ordinary Christians, those to whom God will be more indulgent, because they were spiritually less ambitious.

It was Luther's glory to denounce frankly the error of this dual morality, and to face all Christians with the ethical and religious demands which are exactly the same for all, whether clergy or laymen. But by a tragic irony of fate it was also Luther who introduced into the Reform Churches another dual morality, by opposing the Christian's duties to those of the citizen:[175] the distinction of the two moralities has simply been shifted into traditional Protestant theology—the profession of soldiering had to be justified, of course! —so that the same Luther, who hymned human kindness better than anyone, could also call his brethren to massacre each other in language of extreme ferocity.

Traditionalist theologians all admit in one form or other this splitting of Christian morality. They all postulate that the New Testament's recommendations are addressed to the Church and not to the State, to the member of the Church and not the citizen. Their theories vary, but the fundamental position remains the same. Some, for example, claim that the morality of Jesus was only meant to be put into practice within the community of His disciples, as if Jesus could have imagined a spiritual life independent of life itself. Others insinuate that the ethic of the Sermon on the Mount is strictly individualist and has no concern at all with men's social relations.[176] Some suggest that the Gospel exhortations to non-violence and love of one's enemies should not be taken too literally,[177] and others distinguish between prophets and citizens, the former alone being called to refuse any compromise between the Gospel ideal and the harsh necessities of social life.[178] Some distinguish between the absolute and the relative,[179] going so far as to insinuate that after all Christ himself only realised very relatively the absolute ideal He had preached;[180] and others have discovered most conveniently that several of the moral demands of the New Testament, and especially of the Sermon on the Mount, were *not yet* valid for the Christians of our time, but will only be so in the distant future—as if it were not today that someone may smite us on the cheek and take our coat! Enthusiastic over their discovery, they do not hesitate to see a distinction within the Gospel morality, between what is valid for today and what will only be required of us tomorrow. By common accord they transfer to eschatology the verses implying the condemnation of military service! Others, finally, introduce the idea of particular vocations, and would explain that all Christians have not been called to the same vocation: there are ordinary vocations, and prophetic or exceptional ones, like those, for instance, of conscientious objectors.[181]

But all these theories introduce into Christian theology an important idea which is open to the most obvious objections, although the vast majority of people 'go along with it' more or less unconsciously: the idea of a dual Christian morality. This is inadmissible for four reasons:

1. Even the idea has no basis whatever in the New Testament. It is true the apostles speak of little children who must be fed with milk, while there are also adults who can support a more solid diet (I Cor. 3:2; Heb. 5:11-14; I Peter 2:2). It is true that Paul knows there are in the Churches those who are 'weak' in the faith and the 'perfect' who have reached a great knowledge of the Gospel and a greater moral liberty (Rom. 14:1-7; I Cor. 8; Philip. 3:15-16). But it is clear from these passages themselves that the ethical norms and moral demands of the Gospel remain exactly the same for these different categories of Christians, between whom there is anyhow no exact distinction.

It is true there were very varied ministries within the apostolic churches; but although their ecclesiastical functions could be very different, they were all called, it is clear, to the same obedience in the moral sphere: the various exhortations addressed to this or that category of ministers (deacons, bishops, etc.), are morally valid for all Christians indiscriminately, so that what the Scriptures require of bishops, for instance, on the moral plane, is exactly the same as what they require of all Christians (I Tim. 3, etc.).

It is true that the apostles were addressing Christians who occupied very different situations in society (husbands, wives, masters, slaves, children, parents, etc.); but it is impossible to discover in these various exhortations addressed to different sorts of people the slightest trace of a moral differentiation according to their respective social conditions.[182] They are all called to glorify Christ by a moral obedience, the essential norms of which remain the same for all.

2. We have a certain number of exhortations addressed by the apostles to Christians with a particular function to fill in society, whether because they are called to command others, or because they are called to be submissive to the former category. These exhortations are definitely on the plane of the order of conservation, they concern these Christians' social life, not their Church life. They are in perfect agreement with the body of Gospel recommendations. Neither husbands nor slaves, for instance, are ever asked to behave in a way that cannot be reconciled with Gospel morality. On the contrary, it is obvious that it is in their social relations that Christians are called to put into practice the non-violence of the Gospel.

If there were really two moralities, the texts concerned with the order of conservation would show different emphasis, a change of tone, different requirements from those you find, for instance, in the Sermon on the Mount. But this is just not the case. There is a fundamental harmony between the exhortations on the family and the city, and those scattered throughout the New Testament on the Christian's obedience in his church life—or rather, his whole life. In the New Testament, in fact, there is no duality between the good which concerns civil society and the good which concerns the Christian's so-called 'private' life: one's difficulty in finding adequate terms is in itself significant. No, there is only a single Christian morality, only a single good in the eyes of the God of Jesus Christ; and the ultimate norm of that good is that it glorifies God in *Jesus Christ*. There is no good which denies Jesus Christ, contradicts Him, or even leaves Him out of account.[183]

3. Christians cannot have a split personality. It would be superfluous to say this, if so very many of them did not implicitly accept such 'schizophrenia', finding it quite normal to kill and lie when the State requires it, or seems to require it, while protesting virtuously that they would never perform such acts in their 'private life'. This schizophrenia is surely, in the last resort, the most serious consequence of the Constantinian heresy. The true Christian life implies a tension between different aspects of man's personality, not its disintegration.

4. The idea of a dual morality would mean that Christians were constantly on the wrack between contradictory duties: that God asks me as French citizen to kill the soldiers who invade my country, and at the same time as member of the Church to welcome them by proclaiming the Gospel to them.[184] This is plainly impossible, I can only choose, according to my lights and my courage, to be either death-giver or life-giver; I must give up being either soldier or witness of Jesus Christ.

F. J. Leenhardt is highly unconvincing in his claim that 'this division of soul is not in itself reprehensible.' 'One must remember,' he says, 'that it is the inevitable lot of the Christian who is faithful to the double duty imposed on him by being both citizen of God's kingdom and of a kingdom here below. . . . The Christian agrees in some measure to disobey God from love for His brethren, so as to love them as God would have them loved, since the only way of loving them is by in some way disobeying God, just so as to obey Him.'[185] This casuistry, which tells us we are obeying God when we are disobeying Him, is most alarming; and, of course, completely

alien to the language of the New Testament. Where, too, does Leenhardt get his strange postulate that it is impossible to avoid disobeying God? The whole question is whether two contradictory
orders can both be from God.

The only example Leenhardt invokes to justify his thesis, boomerangs: Jesus was not 'obliged to choose between the duty of obeying God's law by respecting the Sabbath and the duty of healing a
man.' One only has to read the text attentively to see that the healing
of the man with the withered hand was in contradiction, not with
the actual commandment on the Sabbath, but with the rigid and
un-Scriptural interpretation of it which was given by the Rabbinic
tradition. By performing this act of healing, Jesus was not violating
but fulfilling the Sabbath. Who would dare claim He was 'disobeying
God' by healing somebody on the Sabbath day?

If God asks me to glorify Him by my witness as member of the
Church and also by my submission to the State, He would surely
have Himself provided for a minimum of consistency and unity between the two spheres of my obedience. How can He be asking me as
citizen to do the opposite of what He would have me do as member of
the Church, when He knows that I am always both citizen *and*
member of the Church. It would make Him a very incompetent or
incapable Master whose orders are so contradictory that the
Christian is left to choose which to obey according to his own lights.
So I prefer to think that the idea of a dual morality is an invention
of men which fundamentally perverts the Gospel. Political and
Gospel morality cannot be independent of one another to the point
of being contradictory; they can only be concentric.

For we must indeed escape from the deadlock which is the end
of so many discussions on war. Here, for instance, is an imaginary
dialogue given by G. H. MacGregor between himself and William
Temple, then Archbishop of Canterbury:[186]

Temple: In matters concerning relations between countries, the
  Church must be content to align itself with the State, reverting to
  a sub-Christian ethic.
MacGregor: It would be more legitimate to conclude that the Church
  must refuse to collaborate with the State, where the State refuses
  to apply an ethic to which the Church is bound.
Temple: Love is not applicable to nations; that is why Christians,
  when they act as members of their nation, are not bound by the
  law of love.

MacGregor: If nations cannot or will not behave like Christians, then Christians cannot conform to what the nation does.

In my judgment Temple is right to say that Christian love cannot be expected of a nation, but wrong to believe that Christians can sometimes be released from the law of love; and MacGregor is wrong to hope that nations as such can live the Gospel morality, because this presupposes faith in Jesus Christ, but right to affirm that Christians must not conform indiscriminately to all their country does, especially if it does something contrary to the Christian ethic.

Maurice Voge has seen the difficulty very clearly: 'There is an interval, a time-lag, between simple "morality" and political morality, a tension between these two which tend to diverge but are naturally bound together. . . . When we confuse these moralities, which ought to be distinguished, we run away from the difficult problems of the incarnation into a symbolic witness and give political man the impression of evading reality. We are no help to him: this is the confusion of clericalism. If we separate these two moralities, we go outside the Gospel, which does not admit two moralities, and rejoin the "realists" . . .—from whom the politician has nothing to learn, since they are his imitators—or the abstentionists, who leave his hands free.'[187] And finally, here is Visser t'Hooft: 'It is clear that a Church which is aware that its Lord is the Lord of the State cannot accept the fundamental dualism between the spiritual and political spheres, a total separation, that is, between Christian life within the Church and Christian life within the State.'[188]

(c) *The State's Moral Autonomy.* The traditional doctrine implies a third postulate: that the State in God's plan enjoys complete moral autonomy. It can do what it likes in the sphere of moral and social life, and can thus compel citizens, whether Christian or not, to any moral or immoral orders it thinks fit—although the words 'moral' and 'immoral' seem to have little meaning here. It seems as if in the eyes of many theologians the classical idea of morality cannot be applied to the State, the behaviour and demands of which are on a different plane than that of an actual ethic. For these writers the State would seem to be moving, with God's tacit agreement, in an a-moral world; the only political rule they can imagine for it is that of effectiveness. Here again the traditional conception puts the State back into paganism.[189]

Heering's work contains a detailed and pertinent study of the philosophic history of this a-Christian and a-moral State in its relationship with the Christian ethic. Ch. Westphal has bluntly expressed the postulate of the State's moral autonomy in this comment: 'The just exercise of power presupposes that the State is sovereign in its own function.'[190] But the postulate is covertly present in most studies dealing with this question, and it forms part of the traditional doctrine: 'The nature of the world opposes any attempt to govern the world according to Christian principles,' wrote Luther;[191] and Barth[192] repeats: 'The State as State is wholly ignorant of the Spirit, of love, of forgiveness.' Cullmann too, as we have seen, accords the State full powers on the moral plane.[193] Admittedly Luther says that the government's laws and orders must be useful for the people and consonant with equity.[194] But he does not say what the norm is for such usefulness and equity. Apparently the prince himself is sole judge of this.

Protestant theology seems to have been more influenced in this by Luther than by Calvin, doubtless because the progressive secularisation of the modern world has favoured the Machiavelian moral dualism, to the detriment of the theocratic claims of Calvin, for whom God alone should have ruled over the *whole* life of the people of Geneva. From insisting that the State is a servant of God, the theologians have come to suppose that it has received full powers from God Himself for everything that concerns the material life of society. Its power in social matters thus appears almost beyond dispute.

Luther and his followers rejected the infallibility of the Pope, but seem almost to have brought in a new infallibility, doubtless without realising it, that of the political authorities: for traditional Protestant thought has the tacit postulate that in political matters the State can do no wrong. Christ's supreme sovereignty is placed above both the authority of the Scriptures and that of the State; but the State's authority never has to submit to that of the Scriptures! These two subordinate authorities are independent of each other, each depending *directly* on God; and it is merely a matter of form to remind the State that it is a servant of God, according to Romans 13; this being said, it is left full liberty of action. In fact, it supplants the Scriptures in a large part of life: as soon as the State speaks, Jesus Christ has only to keep quiet.

The postulate of the State's moral autonomy must be rejected I believe, for four reasons:

1. I find it inconceivable that the State, established by God for His service, should be independent in its behaviour of Scriptural

Revelation. For after all, as the Report of the Oxford Conference puts it very well, 'every political action (of the State) presents the inescapable alternative of being an instrument of God's compassionate law, or of hindering it.'[195] 'We believe,' the Report says later, 'that God is the source of all justice; consequently we do not consider the State as supreme source of the law but as its guarantor. It is not the master, in fact, but far more the servant of justice. . . . The Church will serve the nation and the State by proclaiming that God's will is the supreme norm to which all human wills must submit and conform their conduct. . . . Hence the (Church's) obligation to criticise the State when it leaves the norms of justice expressed in God's Word. . . .'[196] 'The Church should remind its members that the principle of the State's or the nation's unconditional authority, whether in peacetime or wartime, is incompatible with its faith in Jesus Christ as its only Saviour, and that consequently this principle can never be the final norm for judgments or acts.'[197] And Berdiaeff states firmly: 'What must be denied is the sovereignty of the State, which has only a functional and subordinate importance . . . no sovereignty of an earthly power can be reconciled with Christianity. . . .'[198]

2. By freeing the State from the obligation of submitting to the authority of the Scriptures, you at once give it the right to choose *the means* it may find most appropriate to reach its ends. But the principle that the end justifies the means is incompatible with the Gospel, as we have seen. By asking Christians to obey both the State, which works on this principle, and the Gospel, which absolutely excludes such a principle, you put them in an impossible situation—they were certainly not put there by God.

3. Most of the theologians I have read are very ready to acknowledge the State's right to use material constraint, and even physical violence, to impose the order it is charged to maintain in society: how often, and how complacently, they will quote the sword carried by the magistrate in Romans 13! But they are strangely silent on a difficulty which leaps to the eye: has the State the right to use *any* violence—including gas chambers and hydrogen bombs? Has it really the right to inflict the monstrous and refined tortures that modern culture seems to value so highly? Does the State's right of repression extend to mass genocide? It is staggering that so many serious authors have not even asked themselves this question,[199] and that others dismiss them with a sentence.[200]

I quite agree with K. Barth when he says that 'human law needs the guarantee of human force: if it did not, man would not be the sinner in need of divine justification.'[201] The use of force forbidden to the Church, is indispensable to the State; who would deny it? But that murder is an indispensable or inevitable aspect of the force used by the State seems, to say the least, debatable, so I cannot accept Barth's second statement here: 'The State, always threatened by force, from without and within, must be capable, if it is to continue as a State, of crushing force with force.' Do these last words mean that it can and should use *all means* to defend its existence? Is *everything* legitimate for the State?

F. J. Leenhardt settles the problem of military service in a page and a half. 'The Christian cannot abandon the State without defending it,' he writes, 'for it must safeguard the State's life, its very existence. . . . A refusal to use effective means would not be defending it sincerely.'[202] Does he mean the murderous weapons which modern States have at their disposal? Must theology end by justifying *all* the processes of modern war, all the sin of man in its infernal horror?

It is unthinkable that God's plan does not envisage a limit to the violence the State can use.[203] Without a shadow of doubt the State is in danger of abusing its power by excessively cruel repression. To me it seems obvious that this constraint, which is the State's arm, is only good, protective, and in accord with God's will, up to a certain limit, beyond which it becomes bad and destructive. Beyond a certain degree of violence, the State's constraint becomes a monstrous usurpation by which it ceases to contribute to the order of society and instead helps to contribute to society's disorder. One could multiply examples from the Bible and history showing that the State, when it abuses its power of constraint, creates a scandalous disorder: I simply cannot admit that the State is itself judge in this matter and party to the dispute; and to leave this judgment to human reason is to bring in natural theology again. If theologians are not to resign completely, they *must* tell the State what is the limit God imposes on it in the use it makes of constraint. So the State does not have moral autonomy.

4. Much has been said of the Church's prophetic mission: to remind the State, which is likely to forget or ignore these things, what its true vocation is and what are the limits of its authority; the Church must therefore *speak to* the State. But one cannot speak without language, and all language assumes a common measure. So the Church's prophetic ministry requires that there is a common measure between the State's activity and the truth on which the

Church depends itself and which it must reveal to the State. How could the Church speak to the State if it did not have Scriptural basis for a critical judgment on the political order (or disorder) brought about by the State? There is no conceivable prophetic ministry for the Church of Jesus Christ if the order of the State does not somehow depend on Scriptural revelation. So either all that has been said in these last years about this prophetic ministry is idle talk, a fantasy without any Scriptural foundation, without any chance of being applied in practice; or else, this ministry being considered as well-founded and realisable, the postulate of the State's moral autonomy is false: from this dilemma there is no escape.

(d) *The Traditional Doctrine has no Biblical Foundation.* There are only two texts which could be invoked to justify the division of Christian life into the duties of the member of the Church and those of the citizen. One, if you force it a bit, is Jesus' answer to Pilate: Thou couldest have no power at all against me, except it were given thee from above' (John 19:11)—but as we have seen, it is doubtful whether Jesus by these words acknowledged a *de jure* power of Pilate's. The other is Jesus' famous remark: 'Render unto Caesar the things which are Caesar's, and unto God the things which are God's' (Mark 12:17)—but we know that these words are being misunderstood when an attempt is made to extract from them any theory whatever about the State.

Some may be tempted to quote something else Jesus said to Pilate: 'If my kingdom were of this world, then would my servants fight, that I should not be delivered to the Jews . . .' (John 18:36). If Jesus had not had in view a kingdom of a spiritual order, they may say, He would have found it quite natural that His disciples should defend Him by arms; so He implicitly sanctioned war in the order of conservation, identified with 'the world.' But such an identification happens to be as childish as it is false. The term 'world' in the Gospel never designates the political order of conservation, but humanity fallen and rebellious in its hostility to Jesus. The 'world' enters the Church, alas, as well as the State; and in any case Jesus is Lord of the State as of the Church. The Bible even gives a hint that the Kingdom of God will be more a political than an ecclesiastical order. By saying, 'My Kingdom is not of this world,' Jesus did not mean, 'My Kingdom is not of a political order,' but 'My Kingdom is so far different from the kingdoms of this world that it does not hold sway over men by the physical *means* customary in the world.'

Moreover, did Jesus mean to say that if His kingdom had not

been what it is, His disciples would have *done well* to defend Him
by arms? That is far from obvious. It would make Him deliver a
value judgment which is not in the text. The Greek word translated
by 'fight', in fact, does not suggest war but wrestling contests. Here
again the text is often exploited in a sense it does not have. There is
nothing in Jesus' words to suggest that He thought His disciples,
while belonging to His Kingdom and complying with its spiritual
demands, should also belong to the kingdoms of the world in the
sense that He would have permitted them to do what He forbade
them in the framework of His own kingdom. Jesus is merely ex-
plaining here why He has let Himself be arrested by His enemies.
There is no trace of the traditional doctrine in this text.

As to the apostolic texts on submission to the political authorities,
we have seen that such submission comes within the framework of
general obedience by the member of the Church called to bear witness of his faith, in *all* the spheres of his daily life, by his peaceable
and non-violent love. The context in the three cases is all-important:
there is not the slightest hint of the political authorities being considered separately, or of a special rule being given for civil morality.
All these being excluded, there is not a single text which would imply
that in certain circumstances the Christian is exempt from the
obligation of respecting Gospel morality. The Gospel knows nothing
of the system of dispensations. The traditional doctrine, then, is in
any case anti-scriptural.

It is really only a tendentious theory. All those who follow it can
be criticised, in fact, for solving the problem by the very way they
present it. For as soon as you arbitrarily divide the Christian's life
into two clearly separated spheres, that of the Church and that of the
State—on a postulate without Biblical foundation, against all the
evidence, and before considering any other possibility—you are
bound to make the State a more or less absolute master in its own
sphere. By this 'pro-State' doctrine, our theologians hasten to grant
the State anything it may claim, with the rest of Christian ethic to be
organised afterwards as best they can. It is not a Scriptural requirement, but a justification *a posteriori* of the Concordat.

For the alliance between Church and State—implying, alas, as in
all alliances, reciprocal concessions between the two parties—is the
deep-rooted cause of the Constantinian heresy into which the Church
has fallen since the fourth century. This was the doctrine with which
theologians justified the Church's capitulation after the event. It had
been dazzled by Constantine's conversion to Christianity, and

blinded by the intoxication, historically understandable, of being at last confronted with a 'Christian State'. Grateful to be no longer persecuted, it offered that State all it could desire, and submitted to almost all its demands.

God had envisaged a dialogue between Church and State in which each would have kept its independence and dignity: 'Ye are the salt of the earth . . . the light of the world,' said Jesus to His disciples (Matt. 5:13-14). But in justifying the concordat, whether this was tacit or explicit, Constantinian theology transformed the dialogue into concubinage, thereby delivering its body, Christ's body, to the lusts of the State—when Christ was its only true husband.

In the Middle Ages the Church still tried to *ban* the use of the cross-bow, which then seemed an excessively murderous weapon. Today ('what a falling off was there!') it is satisfied with making vague verbal protests against nuclear and bacteriological weapons. But one cannot be surprised, of course: as soon as it capitulated on the principle, it could not help cheapening itself more and more by shutting its eyes to all the means the State might use, and by hurriedly collaborating in all the State's cruelties. It still grumbles a bit, washing its hands like Pilate, but it meekly *carries out* the will of the government.

For all these reasons, I believe that a theology claiming to be Christian must absolutely repudiate the traditional doctrine. A Christian doctrine of the State must be founded not on a postulate of reciprocal independence between political and Gospel morality, but on the declaration, deduced from the Scriptures, that there is a close relationship between these two moralities: that although perhaps not identical, they are nevertheless *concentric*; and that if one demands more than the other, they are still never contradictory. For there is only one Lord.

Chapter 4

THE CRITERION OF GOOD

1. What Is 'Good' for the City?

SEVERAL times already during this book I have been led to ask what is the 'good' which the State must respect and in view of which it is the *servant of God*: this fundamental problem must now be tackled. The State, as we have seen, could never be its own authority in the eyes of God; it is expressly submitted to a standard, for it is charged by God with the duty of punishing criminals (those who do the opposite of good) and of approving those that 'do well' (I Peter 2:14; Rom. 13:3-4). The magistrate is the servant of God 'for good'; but what good?

Most answers only seem to push the problem further back without solving it: various abstract ideas are suggested as 'good' without specifying the content of these abstractions. For instance, 'good' is said to be the State's normal fulfilment of its own function; or justice; or defence of the human personality: obviously this leads to the drawing of completely arbitrary lines or else complete uncertainty as soon as a practical question crops up, like the death penalty or the sterilisation of epileptics, for instance. I hope I have sufficiently shown already the inadequacy of the idea that the 'good' is for the State to respect the Church and leave it enough freedom for preaching the Gospel.

F. J. Leenhardt has had the rare merit of seeking a definition of 'good', starting from the Scriptures, which is valid both in the sphere of the State and also in that of the Christian's private life. 'The good,' he writes, 'for which the State is God's servant, is composed of two elements, like Christian love: on one side each person's rights, on the other the human community': on one side, 'the willingness to consider one's neighbour, to respect his personality, his person and his rights, and to respect them as all of us would wish them to be respected in ourselves. . . .'; and on the other side, 'to try to establish with one's neighbour the relationship which may be called fraternity, solidarity or communion, according to which way you look at it.'[204]

Here are ideas which he thinks can be used by Church theologians as well as by State jurists.

But how do you define your neighbour's person or rights? Am I qualified to do this myself, may I not define them differently from the way he does? Or is there an objective definition of these rights; and if so, where is it? In the Declaration of Human Rights in 1789? But then we are again in the field of natural law, and surely the Scriptures more than any human theories will tell us what are the fundamental rights of the human personality. If so, why does Leenhardt not give any clear analysis of these rights?

Moreover, it is hard to see how considering your neighbour's rights would help the believer placed in one of the dramatic situations I suggested in the chapter before last; or rather, it is all too easy to see that if he does respect those rights as he would his own, he would refuse every time to obey the legal authority, to denounce or torture or massacre. In fact, war itself would be impossible, for by killing others we are refusing them *the essential right to live* to which we cling ourselves. It is strange that Leenhardt later in his book rejects conscientious objection, not seeing that his theory leads directly to it.

The second criterion he invokes, that of human community, meets the same difficulty: how to define it? From the way he continues in the book, it would seem that only the national community counts for him. But why not the family, the race, and social class, the oecumenical Church—or humanity itself, which is, after all, referred to often enough in the New Testament in the phrase 'all nations'?[205] According to the community we happen to choose, we shall reach diametrically opposite conclusions. If we define good and love by reference to our country, we shall no doubt conclude that our country's armed forces are an indispensable aid to that good; if we define 'good' by its contribution to the international human community, we are bound to see all armed forces, including our own country's as bad, because they threaten to destroy the fraternity of man. Leenhardt is certainly right in saying that love and good are what contributes to the strengthening of the human community, but must the international community and the universal Church really be sacrificed to the national community?

There is another objection too: not all forms of human community or solidarity are good; from criminal gangs to profiteering monopolies there is a solidarity which is practised at the expense of society, and which is really the negation of love. Some religious, anti-religious or secret societies show a wonderful solidarity where their own members are concerned, but often to the detriment of non-members. The same applies, of course, to national solidarity in its relation to all mankind. The solidarity within a community is only good, then, if it works for the good of all communities, great and small: in the name of national solidarity, as we have seen all too often, you can destroy the family, human brotherhood, and much else besides. So the solidarity of Leenhardt's definition must work for a good transcending all the communities you can envisage: we still need a definition of good, and are left much where we were.

Karl Barth has also tried indirectly to find guidance from the Scriptures as to what the State should be and do from the Christian viewpoint: 'The State and its justice are a *parable*, an analogy with the Kingdom of God . . . to preserve the civil community from decline and ruin, it must be reminded again and again (by the Church) of the demands of the justice it is considered to *represent*. . . . To discriminate, judge, choose, on the political plane, always implies an initiative by the Church to *illuminate the relations* existing between the political order and the order of grace, to the detriment of anything which might obscure those relations. Among the various political possibilities of the moment, Christians will always be able to distinguish and choose those of which the realisation can be clearly seen as an analogy, a reflection of their faith. . . . The Christian community must demand that the State's form and substance within this perishable world should guide men towards the Kingdom of God and not deflect them from it. . . . It must demand that the grace of God, revealed from above and active here below, should be reflected in the body of external, relative and provisional measures taken by the civil community within the limits possible for this world.'[206]

Barth has seen the problem very well, it cannot be denied, and we must take both seriously and sympathetically the method he suggests for building the vital bridge between political and Gospel morality. Yet the various examples he goes on to give in applying his analogy principle, lead up to a description of the ideal State which has a strange resemblance to the existing form of government in Switzerland! It soon becomes clear that all these analogy judgments cannot help being rather arbitrary and abstract, with principles which can only be appreciated and compared by reducing very greatly both the grace of God and the activities of the State.

Another difficulty in this method of analogy is to find the right things to compare. In Barth's summary of principles he speaks of 'the Kingdom of God, so far as it is the object of the Church's faith

and preaching'; but the Kingdom of God is terribly indefinable in its
grandeur: who knows what it will be like and what it will be com-
parable to? (As has already been said, the parables concerning the
Kingdom are not ethically normative.) So Barth rapidly slides into
'the order of grace', which is obviously a more accessible term of
comparison; and in fact, all the examples he takes afterwards, seek
to define the analogous characteristics of the State by reference to
truths or affirmations from the order of redemption, whether it is
God's mercy or the Church's life.

Only, he has to justify military service, so he abruptly introduces
a different term of comparison: the wrath of God and His judgment.
Why compare the State at one time with God's mercy, at another
with His wrath, according to the political realities you want to justify?
Because wrath is implied in the grace, and cannot be dissociated
from it? But then why draw analogies, according to your needs,
now from grace alone, now from wrath alone? It is too easy.

Unable to justify war clearly from the Scriptures, Barth bodily
applies to it his principle of analogy: 'The settling of political conflicts by force . . . (including) defensive war undertaken against those
who threaten the legitimate State from outside, should be approved,
supported, and in some cases stimulated, by the Christian community. . . .'[207] This forthright conclusion is drawn from an analogy
with 'the wrath of God and His judgement,' but I wonder whether
he is equally in favour of hydrogen bombs 'to protect the State' because of their striking likeness to the hell-fire of Matthew 5:22 and
the lake of fire in Revelation 20:14.

As soon as you believe the State has the right to imitate God,[208]
there is no reason why it should not do anything—including tortures, massacres, etc. Barth does not raise the question of the means
to be used to obtain 'respect for the legitimate political order,' nor
that of the limits of the State's rights over the human person. He does
not seem concerned to reconcile this unexpected justification of war
with all he has said in earlier pages about respect for the human
person's essential rights; it is left to the reader to imagine as best he
can some synthesis between these various contradictory conclusions,
and try to guess when the State, because of the Incarnation, should
be 'at the service of men to protect his existence'[209] and when, because of the Judgment, it should massacre him. In short, the 'wrath'
of God justifies the wrath of the State in any form—and the armaments race, sanctified and 'stimulated' by the theologians, continues.

Admittedly Barth acknowledges himself that 'the passage and

transposition from one sphere to the other will certainly always be debatable and carry more or less conviction; all one can say in this sphere is far from being infallible. . . . Even by following the line we have tried to indicate, one will never be able to give an answer to everything.'[210] I quite agree. In any case, if the Christian soldier, with his machine-gun aimed at the women huddled in the church at Oradour, has to look for his Christian duty in the light of subtle 'analogies' with the father of the Prodigal Son on the one hand and the king who destroyed his enemies on the other, it will scarcely help him to answer his concrete personal problem. It is a criterion of judgment we need, not justifications, however attractive.

In our search for a political criterion of good, we meet two major difficulties. The first is that we are likely to look for it in human wisdom rather than in Scriptural revelation. The temptations of natural law, and therefore natural theology, remain terribly great. It sometimes seems as if theologians have instinctively looked for a criterion outside the Scriptures to avoid there being a conflict between the State and the Revelation. This is very understandable as soon as you start from the postulate that the State moves in a world *alien* to the Gospel. But by trying to avoid the difficulty you only make it worse, for the divorce between the State and the Gospel is thus rendered insoluble.

I refuse to have any part in natural theology, and this is why I reject *en bloc* all the abstractions suggested. If the State must protect justice or the human personality, we must find in the Scriptures the criterion for these concepts, since Jesus Christ is the Lord of the political authorities. Paul calls the magistrates to be servants of God; it is inconceivable that their Master left them absolutely no instructions, so that they were and are allowed to do anything—including destroying the universe by hydrogen bombs? Is there nothing in the Scriptures which enables the Church to say: 'Thus speaks the Almighty'?

The second difficulty is that we are likely to envisage two different 'goods' or criteria of good, one valid for the world of politics, the other for the Christian's private life. This is a disastrous temptation, because by such a subterfuge you relapse into the traditional doctrine, the falsity of which has been clearly enough shown. The testimony of the New Testament obliges us to reject the idea that what is good for the State might be bad for the Church, and *vice versa*.

It is, in fact, very noteworthy that our texts in the Epistles which mention the political authorities and specify that they are at the service of Good, come in contexts which are equally concerned with 'good' in terms of the general Gospel morality. They use the same words, good and bad ($\dot{a}\gamma a\theta\acute{o}\nu$ and $\kappa a\kappa\acute{o}\nu$), whether they are talking of political or so-called private life. So there is at least a close relationship between the political and the private 'good'. In Romans 13, the words 'good' and 'bad', which occur six times in the verses devoted to the magistrates, occur ten more times in the immediate context. In I Peter 2, the expressions 'evil-doers' and 'those that do well' (or their equivalent) are used indifferently whether the function of the magistrates or the witness of Christians is concerned: the 'good' in verses 15 and 20 is clearly the same as that in verse 14. Finally, in Titus 3, we find in abbreviated form the declaration of the unity of good; for no definite dividing line can be traced, among the various expressions in these verses, between those concerned with public life and those concerned with private life. And if we take the many New Testament texts exhorting Christians to do good, it is patent that neither the sentences themselves nor their contexts give any justification for the theory of a distinction between two 'goods'.[211]

Some may object that I am seeking a criterion of good which is too legalistic, too much in keeping with Pharasaic ideas, as if men's acts could be classed in categories of good and evil according to their external aspect. H. Roux does well to remind us that 'the idea of a good in itself, theoretical and abstract, is thoroughly alien to the Bible.'[212] Of course the good 'is what God is, does and wills.' But God's will is surely revealed in the Bible, and it is surely there that we must look for a criterion of good. I am well aware that in this whole enquiry I am constantly in danger of succumbing to the temptations of legalism; but the reader will doubtless agree that one must not succumb, either, to the temptations of illuminism (for the Holy Spirit cannot speak in a manner contrary to the Scriptures) and of a-moralism (for the whole Bible contradicts a position of moral indifference). We must go forward with care between these two abysses, and the salutary fear of legalism cannot stop us trying to find out what the apostles meant when they specified that the magistrates were charged with the duty of 'punishing *evil*-doers and approving those that do *well*.'

2. The Noachic Laws

It is just possible that the norm of good valid for States might be sought in the Noachic laws (Gen. 9:1-7). Given before the choice of Abraham, and therefore before the existence of the chosen people, these might serve as laws for the order of conservation. Indeed, some Jews today still consider they would serve for the Gentiles, should the age-old Jewish dream of religious supremacy over the world come to be realised. The Rabbinic tradition has long developed and amplified them to make seven precise commandments[213] strikingly similar to the Ten Commandments of Sinai, especially in their ban on impurity, killing, and stealing.

But how can a Christian theologian find his criterion in an Old Testament text as formulated in Rabbinic tradition? In any case these laws can be reduced to two essential commandments. one concerned with diet (from a point of view which seems more ritual than moral), and the other with the condemnation of murder as the crime of crimes: 'Whose sheddeth man's blood, by man shall his blood be shed, for in the image of God made he man.' Although this latter is clearly most important for our subject,[214] it will surely be conceded that these two points, diet and murder, are inadequate on their own to serve as criteria for political good! Moreover, these Noachic laws, unlike the Ten Commandments, find little echo in the New Testament: it cannot be said of them, as of the Law at Sinai, that the Gospel confirmed them: we are brought back to the Decalogue.

3. The Decalogue as Criterion of Good

Believing myself to be in the true Reform tradition which goes from Calvin to the Theses of Pomeyrol,[215] I think that the criterion of good for political life is to be found in the Ten Commandments of Sinai (Exod. 20).

It is worth recalling Calvin's teaching on this point. 'We confess,' he writes, 'that all our life should be ruled in accordance with the commandments of the holy Law, and that we should have no other rule for living well and justly, nor devise other good works to please Him, than those contained in it.'[216] 'For the social life of the community,' Chenevière explains, 'the Decalogue . . . is the sole indefeasible moral rule, by which the magistrate should be inspired when compelling men to live in relative honesty despite themselves.'[217] 'The law of the ten sentences,' continues Calvin, 'is an infallible rule. When we have that summary, we have the whole of God's will testified to us. And we must measure all individual laws by these ten commandments. They are the true touchstone with which to examine how each special law should be taken and stated.'[218] Only the Decalogue is 'the real and eternal rule of justice, ordered to all men in whatever country they may be and whatever time they may live in, if they wish to rule their lives in accordance with God's will.'[219] 'Thus,' explains Chenevière, in the case of conflict or hesitation, 'to find what is lawful for him, the Christian need not hesitate between the feeling of his conscience and the exact text of the Decalogue; it is to the Decalogue he must refer himself.'[220] In Calvin's thinking, of course, 'it is for the magistrate alone to see that the laws comply with the situation and with the supreme end which they must all pursue, the application, that is, of the rules of the Decalogue in social life.'[221] But even so the principle is there: God wills that the actual law should be submitted to the standards of the Decalogue. 'I approve a civil order,' Calvin writes elsewhere, 'which takes care that the true religion, which is contained in God's law, would not be publicly violated and defiled by an unpunished licence.[222] And Chenevière describes thus the relations between Church and State as the Reformer invisages them: 'Calvin does not ask magistrates to deliver dogmatic definitions or make consciences submit by force; the magistrate's role is limited to preserving the Decalogue in its role of moral law for the City. It is for the Church, not the State, to give a dogmatic content to the commandments, but it is for the State to protect them, to punish all those who might try publicly to undermine their authority, either by attacking them or by openly flouting them. . . . Consequently, men can think what they like, it is little concern of the State's; the State intervenes only when those thoughts are translated into external acts which may reflect on the authority of the Decalogue.'[223] The Church on its side 'while enjoying complete liberty in matters of preaching, administering the sacraments and ecclesiastical discipline, plays the part of benevolent moral counsellor to the State.'[224] The Church has no other power over the State to make it respect the Decalogue than the power of its word; but by its preaching it must indeed help the State to understand the Decalogue's implications.

There are, of course, qualifications to be made on this doctrine of Calvin's, notably regarding his aristocratic and theocratic conception of the magistrate, and (as we shall see later) his idea of a State which constrains people to live '*Chrétiennement*'. But in any case Calvin strikingly confirms my thesis: *the Decalogue is the criterion of good*.

Some may object that it is addressed exclusively to the people of Israel, since it begins with the words 'Hear, O Israel . . .' (Deut. 5:1). But the Church has always without the slightest hesitation considered this text as normative for itself also, giving the text a Christological interpretation. All the catechisms contain a study of the Ten Commandments, and the New Testament often refers to them (Luke 18:20; Rom. 13:9, etc.). Calvin showed definitely enough that it is the ceremonial and judiciary laws of the Old Testament which are particular to Israel, while the 'moral law', the Decalogue, is addressed to all mankind. Moreover, to claim that it concerns only the Israelites to the exclusion of all other people, is to postulate that God could have had in mind a different law for these peoples and for the Christian church—but which?

Anyhow, considering the close resemblance between the second table of the Decalogue and the various civil and penal codes revealed to us by the history of civilisation, from the code of Hammourabi[225] to the most modern codes, it can scarcely be maintained that the Decalogue was given by God to Moses for the exclusive use of Israel alone. When it says, for instance, 'thou shalt not kill . . . thou shalt not steal . . .', its political significance is exactly the same as in an Assyrian or Roman law, where exactly the same terms are used. Without here going into the problem raised by this striking concordance, we may surely conclude that the Decalogue remains valid for the Church, and through the Church for all the peoples it preaches to: in the last resort, that is, for all mankind. Israel has been the Light of the World, the Servant of the Almighty, above all because it has been charged with the mission of bringing to the world the knowledge of God's law (Isa. 42:1-7; John 4:22, Rom. 2:17-23; 3:2; 9:4-5).

There is equally little force in the objection that the Decalogue concerns only the Church, to the exclusion of the State and the sphere of the City; for each of the Ten Commandments, including those of the first table, have a direct and obvious reference to man's social life.[226] The last six commandments in particular are patently on the plane of the order of conservation *before* being relevant to the order of redemption. The family is an order of creation. Stealing, murder, false witness in court, are directly and first of all the concern of the State. The dual significance of the Decalogue is confirmed by the fact that it is addressed both to the people and to the individual.[227]

It is normative, in fact, for the orders of both redemption and conservation; and that is just why I see it as the standard of a 'good' which should be fundamentally the same for the Church and for the City! The Ten Commandments, in their New Testament and Christological interpretation, tell the Church what it means to 'love

God with all thy heart and thy neighbour as thyself'—which is realisably only in the faith in Jesus Christ; and they tell the State in their literal and direct interpretation what is meant by a 'civilised' political order, in which the human personality is respected. In this perspective the expressions of order, justice, liberty, rights of man, at last take on a clear meaning founded on the Scriptures. To be quite exact, let us say that the Decalogue is the *minimal norm* for the Christian's private obedience and only the essential *criterion* for his political obedience:[228] not the norm, that is, of what the State *should* do (this was Calvin's error), but the criterion of what the Christian *may* do in obeying the State.

This theory merely follows Calvin's Confession at la Rochelle and has Scriptural foundation; for there are several texts in the New Testament which seem to indicate that the Ten Commandments are the criterion of good and evil. In Mark 3:4 there is a parallel between evil and the act of killing; in Ephesians 4:28 between evil and the act of stealing; and in Romans 13:8-10 evil is disobedience of the commandments in the second table. In Romans 8 Paul repeats several times that the commandment is 'good' and it is of this that he says 'for the good that I would I do not' (see also I Tim. 1:8). For Paul, then, good is defined by the law, more strictly by the Ten Commandments (Rom. 8:7-8).

But there is another text in the Gospels which I find highly significant in this respect: when the rich young man asks Jesus what 'good' he must do to have eternal life, Jesus explicitly refers him back to the Ten Commandments (Matt. 19:16-17). The parallels admittedly do not mention 'what is good'; they apply the word 'good' to Jesus himself. Admittedly also, the text from Matthew is itself not certain, for some manuscripts follow the versions of Mark and Luke instead. But that is no reason to reject Matthew's version, which might well correspond to a definite tradition. And even if we must be careful, allowing for the text's uncertainty, we still have a text from the Gospels which expressly sees the Ten Commandments as the criterion of 'good.'

Of course there are no Biblical texts showing the Decalogue as the norm of the State's activities, for the good reason that neither the word 'State' nor the concept of it existed in Biblical times. Yet Isaiah says: 'The earth also is defiled under the inhabitants thereof; because they have transgressed the laws, changed the ordinance, broken the everlasting covenant. Therefore hath the curse devoured the earth . . .' (24:5).

This note is sounded to some extent through the Scriptures, and there are also texts showing that in God's eyes the Decalogue is valid for the king, as embodying the State, no less than for his subjects. I am thinking in particular of the passages concerning Saul at Endor (I Sam. 28), David in the episode of Carmel (I Sam. 25:33) and in the affair of Bath-sheba (II Sam. 11:27 and 12:9), Solomon and idolatry (I Kings, 9:4), Ahab and Naboth's vineyard (I Kings 21), and Herod and Herodias (Matt. 14:4). A whole monograph could be written on a great many obscurer texts, such as Exodus 2:12; I Samuel 24; Matthew 26:59; Acts 12:2 and 23; 23:3 and 5, etc.

Why then have Protestant theologians, including Barth, given up Calvin's idea that the Decalogue is the supreme indisputable standard for States and their laws? Today, indeed, they are more Lutheran than Calvinist on this point, since they leave the State a free hand provided it does not interfere with preaching.[229] Why do they no longer see the Decalogue as the criterion of the State's orders?

There are several reasons, I believe. Our civilisation has become more and more completely secularised, and this has no doubt been an excellent excuse for theologians to beat a retreat, to withdraw from a struggle which has become more and more difficult: how to recall God's commandments and their requirements to a State which more or less politely ignores God and which in any case no longer admits that it has to submit to a transcendent revealed authority?[230] The escape does not cover the theologians with glory, but it is an easy enough solution: since the State takes everything, you leave everything to it, clinging only to the right of publicly preaching the Gospel.

Probably a second reason was Calvin's error in thinking that the State could and should oblige citizens to put God's law into practice.[231] There is a particularly striking ambiguity in the sentence from a letter he wrote to the Queen of Navarre: '. . . princes should constrain their subjects to live like Christians.'[232] The Decalogue should indeed be the *criterion* of the State's laws and orders, but it can never be considered as a body of social *principles*, and should never have served as a pretext for establishing a puritan constraint as rigorous, and sometimes absurd, as that which reigned at Geneva in Calvin's time. The fourth Commandment, for instance, means that any man has the right to his Sabbath rest and should be able to worship God if he wishes and as he thinks fit; but Calvin was going a long way too far in having laws decreed obliging people to attend the sermon! The Decalogue marks the limits which must not be over-stepped, but it does not constitute, as Calvin wrongly thought, a starting-point for a Christian sociology. Unfortunately, on the pretext that he could not be followed all the way, his point of view was wholly given up even where he was right, and theologians fell into the opposite error: they lost sight of the fact that a Christian should obey a law only in so far as it does not violate the Decalogue or constrain others to violate it.

Chenevière gives us a third reason for Calvinists' *volte-face*: 'Through not having realised the Law's *social* function, apart from its strictly spiritual function, a great many writers have given the natural law a role and an importance quite different from what it was really given by Calvin in his political thinking.'[233] Thus, while the State became more and more arrogant and totalitarian, the theologians, having lost the sense of the Decalogue's political significance, preferred the theory of natural law inherited from Thomist scholasticism to Calvin's firm Scriptural doctrine. They thereby avoided all conflict with the State, but at the expense of betraying the Gospel.

Calvin's thought also contained a certain fluidity, one might call it an inner contradiction, which covertly contributed towards the later distortion of his doctrine. While proclaiming that the requirements of the Scriptural commandments were valid for all, he also thought that God's requirements were modified according to the situation or institution (marriage, royalty, etc.) men had been placed in by providence.[234] He does not seem to have tried to find a synthesis for these two contradictory views; and Calvinists, with their bias towards the latter, simply followed the line of least resistance by hurriedly returning to natural law and the Lutheran theory of the separation of the two spheres.

Finally, they may have realised very quickly that the principle of the Decalogue as a political criterion of good was incompatible with the justification of military service as Calvin himself had formulated it. For various reasons, they felt they could on no account give up the State's right to make war, so they simply passed over in silence, and then forgot, the principle which Calvin himself had affirmed so vigorously. There are conflicts which are merely evaded, however, by quietly suppressing one of the opposing factors.

So I believe that the Decalogue *is* the criterion of good we are seeking, by which we can *judge* the State's acts and orders. I believe it forms the link between Gospel and political morality though of course the latter derives, in the last resort, from the former. I

believe that thanks to this criterion we can preserve the necessary
moral monism; by it the two spheres of private and political life
(which, as we have seen, should be concentric, not independent of
each other) are fitted together: it is, so to speak, their common
denominator. Of course the morality of the Gospel (or of the Church)
demands infinitely more, both quantitatively and qualitatively,
than does (Christian) political morality; but the latter, which
demands a few things obdurately, cannot ask the opposite of what
the former calls for. The classification below may help to make this
clearer:

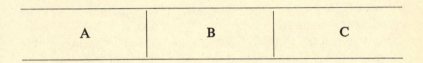

A	B	C

B represents proper respect for the Decalogue; A, the reign of
Machiavelianism and effectiveness, to the extent that it contradicts
the Decalogue. Gospel morality contains B as basis and minimum,
but continues in C up to the most absolute demands of the Gospel.
The State's activities are in A and in B (which is a maximum), but
not in C. Individual Gospel morality and Christian political morality
coincide in B. But the Christian can obey the State only in B and
not in A. The Constantinian heresy consists in denying that there is
a line between A and B, and so in placing the obedience of the
Christian as 'citizen' in A as well as in B. We still have to find out
whether military service comes in A or B.

Gospel morality is above all positive, proceeding from more or less
unlimited declarations: 'And as ye would that men should do unto
you, do ye also to them likewise'; political morality is more negative,
proceeding from prohibitions: 'Thou shalt not kill, thou shalt not
steal,' etc; but they do not contradict each other. It may not always
be easy to bring out in practice the agreement between the demands
of these two spheres of Christian morality; but in principle there is
still *harmony* between them. The Decalogue is an indispensable
control standard for both political and private morality.

Of course this does not at once resolve all problems; there will
always be border-line cases where making a decision is terribly
delicate and difficult. But there is one thing which *can* be said: if my
thesis is sound, it at last makes possible the Church's prophetic
ministry: in the name of the Decalogue the Church can appreciate

just when the State, servant of God for man's good, starts betraying its mission, becomes a demonic factor of disorder, and at once forfeits the right to Christians' obedience. The Church can protest against the State's abuses by reference not to an abstract conception of man, but to the Ten Commandments—which are concrete enough to be comprehensible to any State. Thanks to them the Church can make the indispensable critical judgment on the State's laws and demands—while leaving it a no less indispensable margin for liberty of action. By fighting—with spiritual arms, of course, including respectful disobedience—to make the State itself respect the Decalogue, the Church is rendering it the immense service of recalling to it what are the limits of the political order it is charged by God to establish and preserve.

Moreover, if the Church had a firm and definite teaching on this subject, each Christian would be helped a great deal when faced, in a concrete and perhaps tragic way, with the problem of obeying an apparently immoral order from the political authorities. Instead of being left to his own resources, he would have a relatively clear and definite standard to help him in the vital decision he then took. The hesitations and difficulties of assessment will not thereby have disappeared, but with this standard he should be able to avoid both arbitrary judgment and sheer surrender of his personal conscience. Nor need anyone fear that Christians would begin arguing about all the State's laws in the name of the Decalogue and thus living in anarchy; the sanctions the State has available are enough to discourage petty anarchists.

It should now be possible to define succinctly the political significance of the Decalogue. I would simply say that in the light of the Ten Commandments a political order will be just and humane, contributing to 'good', if it (1) does not make men put their trust in false gods (pagan ideologies); (2) does not demand of men the glorification of the State or of any creature (totalitarianism); (3) refrains from putting religion at the service of the State (compelling the Churches to obedience), or the State at the service of religion (clericalism); (4) protects man's work so that he does not become the slave or the victim of it (freedom of preaching); (5) respects and supports human authorities, in particular the family (as an essential cell); (6) respects and protects the life of man; (7) respects and protects the marriage bond; (8) respects and protects legally owned property (devaluations, confiscations, etc.); (9) respects and protects man's honour and reputation (courts and police); (10) does not use covetousness as a means of action (demagogy, nationalism, and imperialism).

In the various cases of conscience I have earlier imagined, the Christian summoned to obey an order he thinks may be immoral will be immensely helped in making his decision by this summary of the political implications of the Decalogue as criterion of good for the human society. He can then say to the State: 'You have no right to order me to do this thing, you are the servant of God for good and not for evil; you have no right to force me to help in doing what is evil, and what is more, it is my duty as Christian to recall you to your own duty by refusing to obey you; do with me what you will; but for me, since you are rebelling against God, it is more important to obey Him than men.'

Who will deny that in our amoral and dehumanised age God calls Christians to this essential witness: the refusal to sanction the contempt for and destruction of man which we are sorrowfully watching; and the refusal as far as possible to have any part in it? For 'the Son of Man came to seek and to save that which was lost' (Luke 19:10); and as Visser t'Hooft says, 'if man does not . . . discover in time that not everything is permissible, if he does not stop making a god of his own desires and relying on the voice of his blood, there will soon be no more politics, for there will be no more πόλις, no more city, no earthly order left. . . . Nothing, save the Word of God, can still give him a sense of the limits which must not be outstepped.'[235]

4. The Christian's Right to Political Disobedience

The Christian is thus by no means constrained by the Word to aid the State materially, without discrimination, in all its undertakings. On the contrary he has the express right and the duty of making a critical judgment on the orders he receives from it. In the light of the Decalogue he must try to find out whether these orders are directed towards good or evil; according to his findings, he will cheerfully obey or firmly and no less cheerfully disobey. Three possibilities may be envisaged:

(a) When the State betrays its proper mission, when it is indisputably increasing instead of limiting disorder, by violating the Ten Commandments itself, encouraging or even compelling citizens to violate them, it does not follow that I must also betray my proper mission of witness for Jesus Christ. The State's betrayal certainly does not give me the right to betray and deny my Master; and I should be betraying the State as well as Him by obeying the State; for it needs my witness as a Christian, even if it has no inkling of this, to 'call it or order'.

(*b*) When the State *fails* in its mission, it does not follow that I must fail in my personal witness: if, for instance, my government has failed (with other governments) to establish an international order, to organise a non-military defence of the country's territory, or to ensure social justice so as to avoid civil war, it certainly does not follow that I must obey it by letting myself be mobilised to participate in massacring my brethren. I am not respecting the State by helping it to plunge ever deeper into crime, by a submission which would merely be complicity in the crime on my part. Here again, the Decalogue must surely have more importance in my eyes than the demands of the State.

(*c*) When the State gives me an order on which it is hard for me to make an objective value judgment from the point of view of social necessities, in other words when I am not absolutely *sure* that the State is betraying its proper task by giving me that order, I should not obey—if I am absolutely convinced that by obeying I myself should be betraying Jesus Christ and expressly denying Him. 'The capital question for a Christian,' writes Oldham, 'is not how a society which is non-Christian or only partially Christian can resolve its problems, but how the Church, or the individual Christian, or a group of Christians, can in a given situation know and do God's will.'[236] For instance, I am given the order to turn a gun on hundreds of women and children shut up in a church; suppose I am not absolutely certain that the State has not the right to kill these people, but *am* absolutely certain that in massacring them I should be denying the Gospel and cutting myself off from Jesus Christ: where then is my Christian duty?

An exceptional case, it may be said; on the contrary, it is the whole problem of war in a nutshell: what happened at Oradour 'shows the logical end of all war. The curtain torn away, there is its true face.'[237] 'But if your efuse to fire, someone else will take your place, and these poor wretches will still be massacred.' But *my* problem is my own obedience, my own fidelity to Jesus Christ. Admittedly my individual conscience may be mistaken, even if founded on God's word, even if supported by the approval of other brethren; but this danger works both ways, and I shall be just as much in danger of making a mistake if I blindly obey my captain. The Christian life always implies such an element of risk, and in the last resort I must *risk* everything on the Gospel of Christ and on the Decalogue as the criterion of good.

Everybody admits that the modern world is threatened with death by its own inhumanity. Our so-called Christian civilisation might not have reached this pass had Christians been less docile about disobeying the Ten Commandments on the State's orders. And the Church might not be held in such contempt.

L

PART IV

THE SIXTH COMMANDMENT

Chapter 1

ITS SIGNIFICANCE

1. Murder in the Bible

(a) The place occupied by murder in the Old Testament is notorious, and many find it excessive: executions, slaughters, wars, succeed each other in a manner both nightmarish and disgusting. Murder undoubtedly plays a much larger part in its pages than does stealing, lying, lack of respect for parents, and even sexual offences. Yet it is not at all certain that murder was the most widespread or frequent of sins, so one is tempted to conclude that of all the transgressions from the second table of the Decalogue the Old Testament saw it as the most serious and odious. Some of these murders may have been committed with a good conscience by just men, who on occasions were even convinced that they were obeying God's express command, but this does not alter things at all: the writers of the Old Testament felt that murder, whether individual or collective, was a thing so serious in itself, having such repercussions, that they evidently refused to spare us any episode involving it, any detail however horrifying.

This impression is confirmed by the fact that the first sin committed after the Fall is the *murder* of Abel (Gen. 4), which can scarcely be mere coincidence: the elemental, the supreme crime is indeed murder—and this crime of Cain's is referred to twice more, in verses 23 and 25, so deep was the impression it made. Just before the flood God's anger against mankind is again because 'the earth was filled with violence,' which clearly means acts of murderous violence, since it is only against this crime that God puts Noah on guard when he leaves the Ark (Gen. 9:5-6). The extreme insistence on this one crime in the Noachic commandments is also striking: no other act is clearer evidence of man's unbelief, pride, and rebellion. This is also why, no doubt, the sixth commandment is placed at the top of the second table, opposite the first, as if these two were respectively the most important of each table—as indeed, for common sense as well, murder is the worst offence against another person that can be committed.

Passing to the New Testament, we find that the background to Jesus' life is also strangely full of killing. Soon after his birth Herod 'seeks to destroy Him' and 'slays all the children in Bethlehem' (Matt. 2:13 and 16). He begins His ministry at a time of brutal murders, including the violent deaths of the two false Messiahs (Luke 13:1; Acts 5:36-37). The shadow of death hovers over His own daily existence; it seems as if everybody would like to 'liquidate' Him: 'the Jews' (John mentions twenty-six times their intention of putting Him to death), Herod (Luke 13:31), the Pharisees (Matt. 12:14), the priests (Matt. 27:1), and finally Pilate (Matt. 27:26). Several times, as we have seen, His enemies try to capture Him in order to kill Him. These plots against His life are an oppressive refrain throughout the Gospels. In His teaching He constantly refers to His imminent death, whether simply foretelling it (Matt. 16:21), alluding to it indirectly in His parables (Matt. 21:38), or foreshadowing its spiritual significance (John 10:11; 12:24; Matt. 26:28). His friend John the Baptist is put to death, which seems to affect Him greatly (Matt. 14:10-13). His disciple Lazarus risks meeting the same fate (John 12:10). He Himself is condemned to death instead of a well-known 'robber' or assassin[238] (Mark 15:7; Acts 3:14), and is crucified as if by chance between two other such brigands (Mark 15:27): crucifixion itself was a form of punishment which the Romans introduced into Palestine in an attempt to stamp out the fanatical nationalist 'resistance' which was waging a continuous guerilla warfare against them.[239] There is no need to stress here the importance of the 'murder' of Jesus; but after His resurrection death again hangs over His disciples (Acts 5:33): Stephen is stoned to death (Acts 7:59) and James is beheaded. The greatest of the apostles, after having himself been a murderer (Acts 8:1; 9:1), is threatened with death from the day after his conversion (Acts 9:23), and this lasts the whole period of his ministry (Acts 23:12). According to tradition both he and Peter died martyrs' deaths at Rome, and how many others after them (Rev. 6:9)!

So if there is one commandment which was constantly being violated during the events which marked the birth of Christianity, it is the sixth. The Gospel was preached under the sign of murder, one might say; and it is dominated by that Cross which was the supreme murder. It is not by chance that the world has been saved on the occasion of that commandment being broken. Among those of the second table, it is indeed the commandment thrown into the sharpest relief.

Jesus warns His disciples that they will be hated and put to death on His account (John 15:18-20; 16:2; Matt. 10:20-21 and 28); but He protests in advance against the murderous rage which will be directed against Himself and them (Matt. 23:29-37); and when one of them succumbs to the contagion of this violence, Jesus severely rebukes him, reminding him of the inexorable law that violence breeds violence (Matt. 26:52). Satan, He says, is at work in every murder, for Satan 'was a murderer from the beginning' (John 8:44); and it is under his influence that murders and all that defiles man comes out of man's heart (Matt. 15:19). That is why Jesus confirms this commandment with all the others (Matt. 19:18), and even widens its meaning, since being angry with or insulting a person is likened by Him to murder (Matt. 5:21-22), as is merely not healing when you have the chance to do so (Mark 3:4).

Nor is there in the apostolic writings, any more than in the teaching of Jesus, the slightest trace of indulgence towards murder, which is expressly mentioned in the various lists of sins or crimes excluding from the Kingdom of Heaven those who commit them (Rom. 1:29; I Tim. 1:9; Rev. 9:21; 21:8; 22:15). One of the characteristics of the Beast is that it kills Christians (Rev. 13:15; 18:24; 19:2). The apostles also proclaimed the validity of the sixth commandment (Rom. 13:9; James 2:11); like Jesus they declare that the man who kills is possessed by Satan; like Him, they warn Christians on no account to render themselves guilty of this crime (I Peter 4:15), and even that anyone who hates his brother is a murderer (I John 3:15). The agreement between the Epistles and the Gospels is complete.

Throughout the New Testament, then, there is no truck with murder, no qualification or casuistry about it, no special dispensations for committing it. It seems almost unthinkable that a Christian who abides strictly by the message and affirmations of the New Testament can deliberately kill a man. 'For this is the message which ye heard from the beginning, that we should love one another. Not as Cain . . . who slew his brother' (I John 3:11).

(b) It may be objected that according to the New Testament God Himself caused men to die (Acts 5:5 and 10; 13:23); that Jesus in His parables represented Him as a king who destroys His enemies (Matt. 12:7, etc.); and that in Revelation, as in the parables describing the Last Judgment, it is specified that God causes His enemies to perish more or less terribly. So the deduction is that as God has killed, *we* have the right to kill.

But Jesus Himself never killed, either by natural means or by supernatural (John 8:11; Luke 9:55; Matt. 26:53); and *He* is our example, having been incarnated partly for this purpose (John 13:26; 13:15; Eph. 5:1-2; Phil. 2:5; I Peter 2:21; I John 2:6). It is by His own obedience to the Law that He is an example for us. And I would repeat that it is not for men to anticipate the Last Judgment, which will be the work of God alone (Rom. 13:19; I Peter 2:23; Rom. 14:10).

The apostles, it is true, saw the hand of God in the mysterious deaths of Herod and of Ananias and Sapphira; but the whole of the Bible declares that nothing happens on earth without God's will; it is He that causes life and death alike (Deut. 32:39; I Sam. 2:6). Not a sparrow 'shall fall to the ground without your Father,' said Jesus (Matt. 10:29); and Pilate could not put Him to death without the power having been given Him from above (John 19:11); it is impossible that anything should escape God's directing hand. So no normative character can be attributed to these deaths willed by God; if He 'willed' the death of His Son (Matt. 26:42), that certainly does not mean that men had the 'right' to crucify Him. For after all, God is God, and I am a sinner, a creature of God's: how shall I judge Him. If I suggest that 'God has also killed' I am condemning Him; so this objection is literally blasphemous.

In killing *above all*, man takes the place of his Creator. Perhaps the words italicised may cause surprise, so I will elaborate: it cannot be by chance that man's rebellion against God reached its climax in a murder, that of Golgotha; for we must give its full meaning to the terrifying refrain of the first apostolic preaching: 'Ye have taken and by wicked hands have crucified and slain . . . ye killed the Prince of life . . . by the name of Jesus of Nazareth whom ye crucified . . . Jesus whom ye slew and hanged on a tree . . . (Acts 2:23 and 36; 3:15; 4:10; 5:30; 7:52; 10:39; 13:38, etc.). As Jesus had to feel abandoned by God and become a symbol of God's curse (Matt. 27:46 and Gal. 3:13), so He had to suffer from *men* the worst of their faults against love. The horror of the crime of Calvary comes not only from the quality of its victim, but also from the act itself. Men had dared do what David himself would not do, raise a hand against 'the Lord's anointed' (I Sam. 24:6 and 7); this shows the bottomless abyss of human sin. It means, too, that in face of the Crucified we must discover the terrible seriousness of murder: God could not brand more clearly the act of killing. Yet traditional theology seems to have been inclined, whether intentionally or not, to minimise this vital fact: the Son of God was *killed*.

2. Does the Sixth Commandment Condemn Only Individual Murder?

Christian 'militarists' will tend to fall back on the following line of defence: 'The sixth commandment concerns individual murder, not war, nor even the death penalty pronounced in accordance with the country's laws. It is a fallacy to bring up the problem of war in connection with this commandment.'

(*a*) There seems no doubt that the expression 'thou shalt not kill' refers explicitly to individual murder. The Hebrew word is used exclusively for this, I am informed, and is not a general condemnation of all taking of life, for the death penalty certainly existed in the Old Testament: see Exodus 32:27, where immediately after promulgation of the Ten Commandments Moses commands every man to 'slay his brother . . . his companion . . . his neighbour,' and where a different Hebrew word is used for 'slay.' It is indisputable, and I do not dispute it, that the sixth commandment in its verbal expression, means 'thou shalt not commit individual murder.' But it is far less sure that its moral and religious significance does not extend beyond that: so serious a problem can scarcely be solved categorically by mere etymology.

The Old Testament, and Moses himself, may have intended no more than this, but once more we must qualify such an intention both because of the various texts I have already quoted which seem to imply a condemnation of war itself, and also because in anything to do with murder the men of the Old Testament went by the *lex talionis*, 'an eye for an eye,' as expressed in Genesis 9:6 and in the Pentateuch generally, more than by the sixth commandment. They apparently failed to realise that this commandment does not include the *lex talionis*.

Moreover, they may well have carried out many of their bloodthirsty punishments and waged their religious wars from a *sacrificial* concept of murder, a concept which at that time overcame the requirement of the sixth commandment, but which lost its meaning with the New Covenant, since Christ offered Himself in sacrifice for sin once and for all.

Anyhow, the Old Testament can never be normative in the sphere of ethics. We are only interested here in the Christian morality, and that is true for the sixth commandment as for the others. If we tried, for instance, to understand the seventh commandment exclusively in the light of the Old Testament, we should arrive at some very strange conclusions. The men of the Old Testament no more saw that commandment as condemning polygamy than they saw the sixth as condemning the death penalty. Yet Jesus said, 'Ye have heard that it was said by them of old time. . . . But I say unto you . . .' Certainly He did not abolish the law; it is just that He alone fulfilled it; and *His* interpretation must surely be decisive.

(*b*) It is clear that most of the Ten Commandments condemn acts and attitudes with a far wider range than the particular and characteristic act which they explicitly mention. Who would claim, for instance, that the second allows the worship of *painted* images, the fifth allows a lack of respect towards a grandfather or the king, the seventh allows incest or homosexuality, the ninth slander and lying? The Decalogue is obviously aimed at fundamental faults, which it evokes by citing a particularly striking and odious form of each. To cling to the letter of the commandment without appreciating its spirit or deeper significance, is surely the typical error of the Pharasaical Rabbinism which Jesus denounced (Matt. 15:4-5; 23:16-24; Mark 3:4; II Cor. 3:6). Anyone who argues that war is sanctioned because the commandment says only 'Thou shalt not kill,' ought in good logic to argue equally that rape, polygamy, and prostitution are sanctioned because the commandment says only, 'Thou shalt not commit adultery.'

Moreover, if the sixth commandment is concerned strictly with individual murders, it has nothing to say to ninety-nine per cent of mankind; whereas if it also condemns 'moral murders,' like anger and hatred (as is usually admitted), then we are no longer in the sphere of a strictly literal interpretation, and must also admit that there is *more* to it than ordinary 'murder.' It is doubtless not mere chance that makes the Church go on translating the commandment as 'Thou shalt not kill,' *not* 'Thou shalt not murder.' And if the airman releasing his bombs on a town is not 'murdering' people, one wonders what he *is* doing. There are quibbles on words which can only provoke disgust, like the Pharisaical discussions on ritual observances which Jesus condemned in Mark (7:11); nor should we be like the man who 'avoided' eating meat in Lent by calling his roast beef carp.

All this still does not prove that the sixth commandment condemns participation in war; but it does prove that the argument from the word used for 'kill' is invalid for our basic problem. The commandment is not concerned only with individual murders.

(*c*) It is profoundly disturbing to find that while the Christian Church for centuries (since Constantine) has given an *extensive* interpretation of the other commandments in its theology and its catechistic teaching, it has always interpreted *the sixth only* in a *restrictive* way. Christian tradition is unanimous in seeing the seventh as a condemnation of any sexual act out of wedlock, the eighth as a condemnation of all stealing, even indirect, the ninth as a condemnation of any kind of deceit in a court of law. It never makes restrictions for these commandments, and only for the sixth says categorically: 'Nevertheless, there are cases where it is a Christian duty to kill; there are cases where the Christian must commit an act which at the very least looks strangely like a murder.'

The embarrassment of the wise men of the Church is very striking when you go through the catechisms on this point. Some delicately pass over the question of war in silence, no doubt because it is a thing which would be beyond children's minds.[240] But others, foreseeing the objection which even a child will scarcely fail to make, try to justify defensive war,[241] using most high-minded euphemisms for it. Here, for instance, is Lehr: 'The Christian should also hate war. . . . But let him not think himself exempt from the duty of defending his country in its hour of danger: in any case, to take up arms is *often* a contribution to the maintenance of peace.'[242]   Charles Babut also raises the problem of war in connection with defending one's country: 'The Christian will be ready, if called, to sacrifice his life to defend it. But his patriotism will have no hate or savagery to it.'[243] Wilfred Monod is both more honest and more embarrassed: 'War started by an invader is only murder committed wholesale; and what makes so tragic the task of those who defend their homes is the fact that they cannot resist the aggression without themselves inflicting death.'[244] De Pury at one stage expressed the surprising sentiment that 'if the State is led to kill (death penalty, the just war), it is obeying, not disobeying, this commandment, and is protecting human life';[245] but in his eighth edition (p. 75) he admittedly has more qualifications: 'A war which is intended to defend a people's law or life is no longer a disobedience of the sixth commandment. Modern war, however, by its universal character and the means it uses, involves so much disorder and oppression that it brings no solution and only increases injustice.' All these catechisms admit, by their silence or their 'justifications,' that there are cases where the Christian has a duty to kill his brother. None of them admits that there are cases where the Christian has a duty to disobey any of the other nine commandments: no dispensations for adultery; no exceptions for stealing; no conditions made concerning false witness, or the respect due to parents. But there it is: with the sixth commandment alone the Church for centuries has given a restrictive interpretation.

Yet Jesus expressly gave an almost absolute extension to this commandment (Matt. 5:21-22), exactly as he did for the seventh (Matt. 5:27-28), and for the other precepts of the law in the next verses.[246] If anger and insult can be considered as murders (and this is what Jesus said), how can murder in the service of one's country be radically different from individual murder? Indeed St. Cyprian, who died in A.D. 258 (before the Constantinian heresy), was already writing: 'If a murder is committed by an individual, it is called crime; but if it is committed on the State's order, it is called courage' (Epistles 1:6). Jesus said: Not only must you not kill, but you must not even be angry with your neighbour. All the New Testament says the same. But the Church, by contrast, declares: 'You must not kill in your own interests, nor even be angry with your brother; but if the State calls you to fight your country's enemies, then it is a different matter: do your duty, that is to say—kill as many of them as you can. You are not disobeying God's Law.'

(d) Some may say that of course the sixth commandment is the only one which implies important exceptions, because it is the only one directly concerned with the sphere of the State; and that as usual I am not giving the State the place which is due to it. But what makes them think that only the sixth commandment is directly concerned with the State? In the days when the Soviet State authorised children to deny their parents, increased the number of abortions, encouraged divorces, confiscated the *kulaks'* estates, extorted 'confessions' from 'traitors,' and got the peasants' support by promising them land; in the day when the Nazi State urged children to denounce their parents, piled up its victims in camps of slow death, organised human stud-farms, encouraged the looting of non-Aryan houses, gave a free hand to its political police, and made *Lebensraum* a motive and a justification for its policies—was all that outside the scope of the last six commandments?

If this point is conceded, we are back at the same inexplicable inconsistency as before. If stealing is still stealing and lying is still lying when the State is involved, why are the murders it commits not murders? Is the State's morality so fundamentally different from the individual's that it has the right to do what it condemns in the individual citizens? This would be to put it in the terrain of nineteenth-century German philosophy, which we have seen to be incompatible with the Gospel. Why, anyhow, should an act change its nature merely by ceasing to be individual and becoming collective? We are back at the traditional State-idolatry, which I have already exposed sufficiently. You cannot maintain that murder carried out by the State is not murder without falling into such idolatry; for such a proposition assumes that the State is not subject to God's Law.

Again, where exactly would you draw the line between cases where the State 'is not killing' when it kills and those where it *is* killing? When the Soviets 'liquidated' enemies of the people, when the Nazis sent Jews to gas chambers, were they killing or just defending their State against its enemies? When the Nazis massacred the inhabitants of Oradour, was it murder—or a 'law of war', a crime—or a necessity from 'the order of conservation'? And which was it when they shot hostages, tortured, sterilised, carried out medical experiments on their prisoners? Even where the State is concerned, the boundary between murder-crime and murder-duty is very hard to trace. I know an American Christian who in 1944, at the time of the break-through at Coutances, was in command of an armoured detachment which had penetrated deep into the German lines; he told me that on that day he ordered the shooting of the German soldiers his detachment had captured, because he had to continue his advance at all costs and could not possibly deal with prisoners. It is obvious that any judgment on border-line cases will depend wholly on ideological or juridical ideas which have nothing to do with the Christian Revelation. We are in the realm of the relative, the arbitrary, where anybody at all may be a 'war criminal'.

But some think that killing in war is disobeying the sixth commandment only for the soldiers of an aggressor; while citizens 'defending' their country are not guilty of murder. Even if this were a sound principle, and you could decide quite certainly who was the aggressor, it would still lead to absurdly relative judgments. For instance, let us imagine the trenches 'somewhere in France' in 1917: French and German soldiers are facing each other, carrying out exactly the same work of death; and this has been going on for three years: we are asked to believe that on one side they are criminals and on the other they are faithfully carrying out a sacred duty. And the air raids on Warsaw and London were crimes, while those on Dresden and Hiroshima were imperious duties of conscience? No, the tragic reality goes far outside the best juridical formulas. Can the Church really do nothing else, when faced with war, but to deliver such hollow formulas, which have little apparent connection with reality and none at all with the Revelation?

To sum up: although the word used in the sixth commandment means 'murder,' the commandment in itself still implies a general condemnation of *all* attacks on human life. No human creature is exempt from obedience to this commandment, the State no more than any other;[247] the Son of God scrupulously submitted to it Himself. War cannot be put outside its competence, for to make war a separate case you have to introduce excessively subtle and far-fetched distinctions: there is *no clear line* between an individual and a collective murder, a criminal and a lawful murder. The Gospel knows nothing of such discrimination.

3. Political Significance of the Sixth Commandment

This is the sole aspect which is controversial, and it is also at the heart of our present problem; so I shall enlarge only on that, not on the commandment's spiritual and moral significance, about which theologians are generally agreed.

I would merely say that from a spiritual viewpoint it warns me that 'God wishes me to honour Him as Master of life and death, by not attacking my neighbour's life, but rather by respecting and protecting it: killing is an attack on the work of His grace.'[248] For not only am I defying God by destroying the man He created in His image, who despite His sin is the masterpiece of God's creation, but I am flouting Jesus Christ who died for every human being. By killing a man, I make it impossible for him to recognise his Saviour, to answer His call, to live for Him and glorify Him. I deny the Good News, I challenge the God of Jesus Christ.

From a moral viewpoint in the sixth commandment, as in the four after it, God is defining more exactly what is meant by loving my neighbour: first of all, and in any case, to respect his life. He warns me that I kill my brother not only when I physically cause his death, but also when I attack his life by indirect means, by hating him or being angry with him (Matt. 5:22) or even contemptuous of him. Thus, 'the true way of observing the sixth commandment is to do all we can to preserve, support and promote our neighbour's life.'[249]

Coming now to the commandment's political significance, I must first repeat that according to Romans 13:4 the State was made for man, not man for the State. The political authorities have been 'established' by God to *protect* man, taking this expression in its full and general sense. The State must not forget that it is a 'creature' in the service of men, and therefore of human *life*. Killing is the exact opposite of its mission.[250]

The State's situation can be compared here with a doctor's. A doctor too is at the service of life, though he may sometimes be terribly tempted to exploit life, notably to do experiments allegedly useful for the progress of medical science. The doctor who deliberately sacrifices the lives of human beings to abstract scientific research is violating God's Law. So is the State which deliberately sacrifices human lives to maintain an economic or political régime.

Humanity's unhappiness comes from this age-old frenzy to destroy men on the pretext of saving Man. Since the beginning of time God's creatures have been immolated in the service of false gods: political idols or delusive abstractions. It is the characteristic of paganism to glorify, at the expense of an actual neighbour, the abstract values and causes for which men are urged to slaughter other men. But the Decalogue with its sturdy good sense, dissipates these murderous chimeras; it recalls to the State that the destruction of human life is a *means* which cannot be justified by any end. God's Law strips the State of its claim to be a high priest presiding over human holocausts, forbids it to adorn itself with the sanguinary embellishments of Moloch.

It is also remarkable and significant that Jesus Himself was sacrificed because of the State, seeing that Caiaphas told the Sanhedrin, the Jewish political authority of its time, 'Ye know nothing at all, nor consider that it is expedient for us that one man should die for the people, and that the whole nation perish not' (John 11:50). So, to be rid of the Son of God, the Sanhedrin sacrifices Jesus' life to the doubtful interest of the people; it violates the sixth commandment on the false pretext that this is the only means of saving Israel from a brutal repression by the Romans (John 11:48). Jesus was willing to *identify Himself* with the countless victims of wars, with all those who have been deliberately sacrificed to the Political Necessities and Social Duty, to the millions of human beings who have been slaughtered and constrained to slaughter each other by being more or less persuaded that their deaths would be serving Justice and Law. By His readiness to become the victim of such a belief, Jesus unmasked its monstrous falsity, and showed His disciples in advance that they could never adopt it themselves.

'To such depths of wickedness are men led,' writes Calvin, commenting on the words of Caiaphas, 'who without fear of God take their counsel more from their carnal sense than from the Word of

God, and believe it will be useful for them when they do something which is not permitted by the author of all good things, the killing of an innocent man. . . . Let us learn therefrom never to separate what is useful from what is lawful, seeing that nothing good or happy can be hoped for except by the blessing of God . . . which is promised not to the wicked and rebellious, who ask help from the devil, but to the faithful who walk simply in their ways. . . . A people is no better preserved by the unjust and wicked death of an innocent man, than a man's whole body is preserved when only his throat is cut or his stomach has been run through.'[251] Of course, Calvin is here referring only to an *innocent* man's death, and this is why he had Michel Servet burnt. But in modern war the vast majority of those you kill are innocent; so that the quotation from Calvin fits in very well with my purpose. The State cannot be at man's service without being at the service of human life.

According to the Scriptures, a political order conforming to the will of God is one where, among other things, human life is respected and protected. 'God alone has the right to dispose of a man's whole life and existence,' the Synod of the Berlin Evangelical Church proclaimed in April 1950. 'A State is defending man's dignity and liberty only when it respects this sacred right belonging to God.'[252] Murder is always a major disorder, because it is a violation of God's Law. We know today, as Calvin did not, that the burning of Servet was a disorder; what would Calvinists give that this fire had never been lit! When the State kills, it is contributing to disorder, even if apparently, according to human wisdom, it is limiting disorder. By killing, it adds an extra disorder to those it claims to be putting down.

The sixth commandment has another relevance to politics which will lead us to the same conclusion. We have seen that if constraint is indispensable to the State for carrying out its function, the degree of violence or cruelty implied in the use of this constraint is by no means a matter of indifference. There is a certain limit beyond which that constraint ceases to contribute to order in society. When the State is too brutal, it becomes itself a factor of disorder. The spectacle of what goes on in totalitarian countries is an obvious demonstration of this. Our government perhaps has the right to order that a factory occupied by strikers be forcibly cleared, but when people are killed in this police operation, everyone feels that the State has failed and that the disorder is aggravated, not diminished. For in the sight of God a human life has more value than a factory or a juridical principle. It is the same with the State's constraint as with certain toxic drugs, which are useful in small doses but lethal in strong doses.

But where do you find this line the State must not pass? Without going into the problem of torture, I believe the line is given us by the sixth commandment, which properly signifies this: when the State reaches the point of killing, it has already passed the degree of violence allowed it for maintaining order in the society it has charge over. By killing, it increases disorder and injustice, whatever its declared or secret intention. Whether it lets itself be maddened by fear, or is clever enough to adopt Caiaphas' aphorism (e.g. when making war), the State betrays its true mission by shedding blood. It abuses its power, imagines that it is protecting, but is really destroying.

(c) The moment has come to consider an important and delicate aspect of our problem: are you not also an accomplice to killing when you see someone threatened with death and do not come to his rescue? If you stand by and watch someone have his throat cut you are surely participating to some extent in the murder of which he is the victim? And is not such complicity by abstention a disobedience of the sixth commandment almost as serious as the murder itself? Yes, I will say straight out, all that is perfectly true. Non-intervention by an individual or the State when faced with a murder is cowardice, surrender, participation in the murder. It is also a way of killing.

But this instinct to try to stop a person being killed, an instinct felt so deeply by any normal man, is more evidence of the sacredness of human life. You see a man who has got his enemy on the ground and is lifting a knife to finish him off; without hesitating for a second you dash in to stop that armed hand. It may be a criminal trying to murder an innocent man; but it may equally well be the aggressor who is about to receive the blow, the criminal to whose aid you are flying; and still you are glad to have intervened in time. Even if you see a wretched woman preparing to kill her drunken and brutal husband, who has long been subjecting her to the worst outrages and sufferings, you will still intervene, I fancy, even if you say to yourself deep down: 'Though he'd only have got what he deserved.' Yes, human life is sacred, one cannot allow it to be destroyed: God has said so.

But admitting this, let us take good care about *how* we intervene to protect a threatened human life. If we take concrete examples, we must not leave them in the air, and there are two possibilities in the case of the man with the knife. Either you won't have a weapon on

M

you when you suddenly see an attempt at murder—which is clearly
far more probable—and then you intervene with your hands, and
perhaps your feet, trying to separate the man on top from his victim,
to get the knife out of his hand, or at least stop him bringing it down.
Either you succeed, or you do not; perhaps the man will turn on you,
will wound you with his knife. Even if he kills you, you will have
done your duty, and have saved the victim if he has had the time to
run away while the other man was dealing with you. If not, your
sacrifice will look as if it served no purpose. But in all that there is no
moral problem.

The difficulty begins if you do have a weapon on you. If you kill
the aggressor (assuming now that he was in fact the aggressor), are
you sure you will have done right? The court will acquit you, honourably even; but before God will you not feel a murderer nevertheless? You have tried to stop a man killing another man, but if you
yourself have killed one, where is the advantage? You have committed the very crime you wished to prevent. Better that the criminal
should die rather than his innocent victim, you may protest; but
surely such a judgment is very hasty and relative. What you ought to
have done was to save the victim without killing the criminal.
'Should you kill,' Pascal asked, 'to stop there being wicked men?
That is to make two instead of one; *vince in bono malum*.'[253] You may
say you could not have done otherwise, but that is just the question
which is likely to haunt you for the rest of your life: was killing him
really something you couldn't have avoided?

Note, too, that this is a particularly simple case, in that we have
supposed a man who is plainly the aggressor attacking a man who is
innocent and passive. But as soon as you consider cases more realistic,
because they are more like war, where you try to intervene between
people fighting already, it becomes still harder to justify the death
you may cause to one of the contestants. Here are two men quarrel-
ing at a bar; after abuse they come to blows; suddenly they draw
their knives, threaten each other, and inflict injuries. If you intervene with your weapon to defend the one you think has been
attacked, are you defending a victim, or merely making a fight for
two into a fight for three? And if you deal a mortal blow to the one
you presume to be the aggressor, will you claim to have defended an
innocent who was going to have had his throat cut? You should have
intervened, but without killing, and the murder is still a murder;
you are likely to come out of the court less honourably than in the
previous case.

It is certainly a duty to defend someone whose life is threatened; otherwise you are an accomplice to his death; but that is by no means a good enough reason to believe yourself exempt from the duty of respecting the sixth commandment. The real problem consists in defending your neighbour without killing your other neighbour. Self-defence is only legitimate in the sight of God when it is not murderous; and this applies to peoples as well as to individuals. The sixth commandment shows us the 'strait and narrow way' between two crimes: it forbids us to kill a man or to let him be killed.

To conclude on this point, I absolutely agree with the commentary on the sixth commandment given by the Scottish Confession of 1560, quoted by Karl Barth: God orders us to 'protect the life of the innocents, resist tyranny, help the oppressed,' and forbids us to 'tolerate the shedding of innocent blood when we could stop it.'[254] Probably the authors of this text saw it as an *implicit* justification of defensive wars, but I gladly accept it in its explicit formulation, even seeing it as a formal condemnation of war: for how can a Christian claim to be protecting the lives of the innocent if he begins destroying the lives of other innocent people? How can he claim to be resisting tyranny if he begins exercising a tyranny as brutal and odious as the other? How can he help the oppressed if he becomes an oppressor himself, helping the oppressors on *his* side? How can he stop the shedding of innocent blood if he *contributes* to the shedding of innocent blood? Common sense agrees with God's law in crying out: do not use high-sounding hypocritical euphemisms to gloss over a mutual slaughter which is nothing but a collective criminal madness. Murder does not protect anything, it destroys.

Chapter 2

THE DEATH PENALTY AND THE POLICE

'BUT the State is obliged on occasions to apply the death
penalty, and consequently it has also the right to kill the
soldiers of an enemy State which threatens it in criminal
fashion.' This objection, intended to legitimise war, rests on a
syllogism the premises of which are disputable: war is like the death
penalty, the death penalty is legitimate, therefore war is legitimate.
What is such reasoning worth?

(*a*) First, is it sound to compare war to the death penalty? After
all, in civilised countries where it still exists,[255] the latter is reserved
in principle for criminals whose crime is defined by law. Impartial
judges, having, that is, no personal interest in the matter under
judgment, deliver a verdict only on the guilt of the accused according
to the directions of the law. If the court's sentence implies the death
penalty, the executioner, who is also completely uninvolved till
then, will carry out the execution impersonally. The guilty person
alone is put to death; his wife, children, and friends are not hanged
or guillotined with him.

But in the case of war there is no international law to guide men,
although treaties and great legal principles are invoked on both sides.
There is no definition possible of the criminal, or even of the aggressor, when each side, like quarrelling schoolboys, shouts at the other:
'You began it!' Each side is convinced of its own rightness and that
it is the other side who are criminals, because their governments have
subjected them to intensive propaganda, biased and often deliberately dishonest. They slaughter each other on a vast scale, without
regard for any moral law, limited only by the fear of reprisals. It is
not criminals who are killed, but women, children, old men, and
soldiers whose sole reason for marching is that they are threatened
with death if they refuse, exactly like those on our own side—and who
would declare that *they* are criminals? In war every nation in its
madness tries to administer justice itself by any and every means.
Every government is at once judge, party to the dispute, and executioner (what an executioner!). They do not seek the triumph of

Right, but *their right*. And when the carnage is over, despite the hypocritical proclamations of the conquerors, it is not law which has triumphed, but brute force.

The death penalty is intended to inspire a salutary fear in those who might be tempted to commit a crime; but war has no educative aim: it is a senseless disaster which leaves the survivors panting with hatred and fear. Neither morality nor justice nor right nor civilisation has gained anything by these monstrous orgies of destruction. No real value has been protected. War cannot be compared to the death penalty, and even if the latter should be legitimate, it would be absolutely no reason for considering the former so. War is far more like a pitched battle between rival gangs than it is like the death penalty.

(*b*) 'But if the State has the right to put a criminal to death, then the sixth commandment does not apply to it so rigorously; and once you make an exception for the State in this, may it not have the right also to kill in war (defensive war, of course)?' Well, let us make sure that even the death penalty is legitimate from a Scriptural point of view.

Calvin, who sees the magistrate as charged by God with the mission of making the world obedient to the rule of the Decalogue, falls into a serious inconsistency on this. After writing: 'Here arises an important and difficult question, whether it is not forbidden by God's law for any Christian to kill,' he still concludes by asserting the legitimacy of the death penalty. Chenevière tries to explain Calvin's position thus: 'In other words, the commandment applies only to ordinary citizens, and by no means to the magistrate, who is subject to a different rule.'[256] Calvin claims, in effect, that because they are entrusted with instruments of divine justice, magistrates 'are not at all subject to common law in this respect.'[257] But this only pushes the difficulty further back, for are there then two moralities? And to what other rule is the magistrate subject? Where does Calvin find the strange dispensation he grants the magistrate, and what is its scriptural basis?

Of course the magistrate does not behave exactly like ordinary citizens, of course it is his business to *punish* criminals. But has he the right openly to violate God's law, of which he is supposed to be the guarantor? But the individual murders from self-interest, it may be objected, whereas the magistrate puts to death to safeguard justice. Yes, that is very often true, but unfortunately not always. In fact, it is seldom completely true, for 'justice' is always defending, more or less, certain privileges, and if killing is a violation of God's law, it will remain so, however disinterested. In any case, to reject such a conclusion, arguments with more weight than Calvin's would be needed. Moreover, how can the State hope to ensure respect for the Decalogue if it is itself ready to violate that rule? The authority of those who say, 'Do as I tell you, but don't do as I do,' has never been very great.[258] The least one can say is that the State is faced here by a terrible dilemma.

Barth would make a clear distinction between *homicide* as a just punishment and murder as criminal killing.[259] But was the killing of Jesus murder or homicide? From one point of view Pilate had the right to ensure the maintenance of the *pax Romana* by suppressing Jesus, a trouble-maker. This is only one example showing the inadequacy of this 'scholastic' distinction, for in the most 'justifiable' homicide there is always an element of murder. Despite Barth, I don't think there are cases, however rare, where the Church can tell men that 'if they must kill then, they are *not* murderers.'[260] The whole of Barth's theology seems in contradiction with such words, and whatever you call killing, it does not alter the facts. Let us now seek instruction from the Scriptures.[261]

We have seen that the Old Testament uses and even abuses the death penalty, notably as a sanction against many crimes which today we should find it barbarous to punish in such a way. It seems, however, that these penalties were not put into practice as strictly as one might think from reading Leviticus and Deuteronomy. Not all children rebelling against their parents were stoned to death (Deut. 21:21), nor everyone guilty of adultery (Deut. 22:22): far from it. All these terrifying threats of capital punishment scattered through the Pentateuch must doubtless be treated with circumspection. Moreover, according to Genesis, God Himself was opposed to Cain, the murder of his brother, undergoing the death penalty according to the *lex talionis*: 'And the Lord set a mark upon Cain, lest any finding him should kill him' (Gen. 4:15). There is surely a serious breach here in the theory of the death penalty; but in any case the Old Testament can only be normative for us by reference to the New Testament.

What do we learn from the New Testament on the death penalty? We have already seen that the only two texts which might possibly be invoked in its favour, the episode of Ananias and Sapphira (Acts 5:1) and the punishment of the incestuous man (I Cor. 5:5), cannot in fact justify it from a Christian point of view. Nor without sophistry can Jesus' words to Peter after his arrest: 'Put up thy sword again into his place: for all they that take the sword shall perish by the sword' (Matt. 26:52). For Jesus did not say, 'They ought to be put to death,' and still less, 'You, my disciples, ought to take it upon you to carry out such an execution.' He did not give His authority to a juridical principle,[262] and He certainly did not charge His Church with the duty of seeing it was respected. He stated a fact, 'they *will* perish by the sword,' and rightly warned Peter that violence always breeds violence and therefore never 'leads anywhere.' Tertullian has more of the truth when he says that Jesus 'by disarming Peter, disarmed all soldiers.'[263] Let us at any rate say, 'all Christians.'

There remains Romans 13:4: 'For he (the magistrate) is the minister of God to thee for good. But if thou do that which is evil, be afraid; for he beareth not the sword in vain; for he is the minister of God, a revenger to execute wrath upon him that doeth evil.' Calvin naturally sees this verse as justifying the death penalty: 'The magistrates must with force and violence put down the presumption of the wicked, who refuse to be governed by the laws, and must inflict punishments for their offences, such as the judgment of God requires. For He says notably that they are armed with the sword, not only for dignity or display, but to strike the evil-doers. . . . And here is a notable passage to prove the power of the sword. For if the Lord, by arming the magistrate, also committed to him, and ordered, the use of the sword; then whenever he punishes evil-doers with death, thereby executing God's vengeance, he is obeying God's commandments. Let those who say it is bad to shed the blood of evil-doers go and plead against God.'[264]

Very well, we will plead against God—in the name of Jesus Christ. This one verse from Paul's epistle cannot stand against the whole of the New Testament. What exactly does it say? We are all so much influenced unwittingly by the Constantinian heresy, that it needs a big effort to free ourselves from time-honoured habits of thinking.[265] So we must look at things very closely.

'It is not in vain that he beareth the sword'—who is the 'he'? From the grammar it is evidently one of the ἄρχοντες referred to in the previous verse, a word generally translated by 'magistrate,' and doubtless to be taken here in its restricted sense: the judges in the court.[266] This translation is confirmed both by the context, which deals with punishments inflicted on criminals for their offences, and also by the fact that at this time court trials were still one of the State's essential activities, perhaps the most important of all. The expression 'who beareth the sword' may even have designated the judges or praetors during the exercise of their functions! In any case they are magistrates and not soldiers, as has been believed too often and too lightly; the army is not alluded to here! The problem discussed in these verses is of the penalties inflicted by the courts on criminals against common law.

Among these penalties does Paul refer expressly to the death penalty? Calvin answers with a categorical affirmative: according to him, this sword should serve not only to frighten and threaten evildoers, but definitely to 'strike' them. This does not seem so obvious, and Calvin is putting more into Paul's mouth than the words warrant. The word 'sword' may quite well be used here in a symbolic sense, to designate the physical constraint available to the judicial system for dealing with criminals. Perhaps Paul merely meant: Look out if you 'go off the rails,' for the judge has power enough to make you appear before him, to punish you and have you chastised (by whipping, for instance) or keep you in prison. 'He beareth not the sword in vain' would then mean: the sword he bears on him, as a sign of his dignity and his Judge's authority, should remind you that he has the power to deal with your person and have punishments inflicted on you.' The sword is known to have been the symbol of justice at Rome, and I do not think it can be seriously maintained that this latter interpretation is *a priori* less legitimate than the former; I have serious reasons for thinking it preferable.

First, it is doubtful whether the Christians of Rome whom Paul is addressing here were tempted to commit crimes grave enough to be subject to the death penalty. They were probably tempted, like anarchists of all ages, and as the context clearly indicates (verses 6 and 8), either to commit ordinary offences against the law, such as slanders, perjuries, violations of local laws, refusals to pay tribute, insubordination by slaves, etc., or else to be disrespectful to the Roman political authority, discreetly to make light of the laws and have a generally scurrilous attitude. But Paul can scarcely have thought they would go so far as to commit murders, robbery with violence, or take part in 'plots against the security of the State'. The whole text agrees with common sense in suggesting that he is simply afraid of licentious behaviour on the part of his future parishioners and not of sanguinary or revolutionary crimes liable to incur the death penalty for them. He cannot have been referring here to the capital punishment inflicted on Christians because of their faith; for he speaks expressly of the punishment due to those who do what is *evil*, and besides, he wrote this Epistle seven years before the first great persecution. Besides capital punishment the Roman courts obviously had a whole range of less serious punishments and Paul was undoubtedly thinking of these; it is improbable that he had capital punishment in mind at all, as is also suggested by his calm, almost light-hearted tone, in contrast with his fierce indignation against the incestuous man in I Corinthians 5.

The other considerations lead us to the same conclusion. One is that the magistrate (*princeps* in Latin, ἄρχων in Greek) never himself executed those he had judged. The execution of those condemned to death, as also various forms of corporal punishment, were always entrusted to lictors or executioners, never to the judge;[267] so if the text is taken literally, the sword which the judge carries cannot evoke the death penalty, without forcing the words, but only the judge's authority. This seems confirmed also by the use of the definite article before the word 'sword'; the expression 'bears the sword' suggests the dignity of a free citizen and the magistrate's power; whereas had Paul been referring to beheading, he would have been more likely to say 'bears *a* sword.'

The second point is that execution by the sword was reserved for citizens alone, while slaves and aliens were executed with an axe. Now, free citizens must have been a minority within the Church of Rome, so if Paul had been referring to the death penalty, he would have said 'axe' rather than 'sword'.

Next, we must ask what exactly Paul is approving in the magistrate's 'ministry'. Is this the whole judicial and penal system of Rome, including the death penalty, or simply the fact that the magistrate, whether Roman or otherwise, punishes evil-doers and honours good people (I Peter 2:14), to the exclusion of any value judgment on the Roman legal system? The second interpretation is obviously right. The magistrate is servant of God 'for good': that is, to see that good is respected in society, and to punish 'him that doeth evil'. Paul is only approving here the fundamental *function* of the magistrate in general, not the particular way in which Roman magistrates carry out that function.

This different shade of meaning, which is vital for our subject, will appear obvious if it is first remembered that all magistrates, in Greece as well as in Rome, had an essentially religious, and therefore pagan, function: from the day of their entry into office they carried out sacrifices in honour of the city's deities, and it was the same throughout their term of office. Paul cannot possibly have been approving this pagan aspect of their functions, so the text cannot possibly be considered an unqualified approval of the Roman legal system. The magistrates, too, were in the service of the Emperor, and he was already deified in Paul's time; they took an oath of absolute obedience to him: Paul cannot have given his approval to this either.

It is equally implausible to interpret our verse as if Paul were expressly approving the punishments practised by the Romans, giving them the preference, for instance, over those known in Israel: crucifixion rather than stoning, Roman whippings rather than the thirty-nine strokes of the Jews. Quite obviously he has no intention here of going into such details, and is not making any value judgment on the methods by which Roman justice is applied, let alone on the death penalty. The magistrate is a servant of God only in punishing the evil-doer, not because he inflicts any particular punishment: Paul approves the principle of punishment, not its forms. So even if it were shown that he is referring to the death penalty here, it could not be stated that he approved of it from a Christian point of view.

As we have seen in connection with the definition of good, Paul clearly implied that the judgment pronounced by the magistrate is only legitimate, approved by God, if it strikes at an action which is genuinely bad by God's norm, not a mistake defined by reference to some arbitrary system. So if the magistrate is only effectively in God's service *in his judgment* if he is condemning a real evil-doer, it is tempting to think Paul may have made a similar implicit qualification on the *penalty* pronounced. At any rate he does not raise here the problem of the degree and nature of the punishment; he merely says that the magistrate is a minister of God when he *punishes* the evil-doer. He does *not* say that the penalty inflicted by the magistrate is necessarily legitimate, that is, consonant with God's will.

Finally, it would be foolish to draw conclusions in favour of Roman justice from this text without comparing it with the other New Testament texts where Roman courts are referred to. The three texts from the Epistles are scarcely eulogistic; not much can be deduced from I Corinthians 4:3 and James 2:6; but I Corinthians 6:1-9 is frankly pejorative: 'Dare any of you, having a matter against another, go to law before the unjust ($\dot{a}\delta\acute{\iota}\kappa\omega\nu$)[268] and not before the saints? . . . Ye set them to judge who are least esteemed in the church. I speak to your shame. . . . Brother goes to law with brother, and that before the unbelievers . . .' This seems rather different from the praises of the magistrates which theologians have thought they could see in

Romans 13! Is it not strange that Paul disapproves of resort being made to the services of judges whom he had elsewhere called ministers of God? Why does he blame the Corinthians for applying to these pagan magistrates?

We must confront the two texts, and seriously modify the apparent serenity of Romans 13 by reference to the severity of I Corinthians 6.[269] Supposing again that in the former Paul was thinking of the death penalty, the fact that in the latter he calls the Roman judges 'unjust' forbids the conclusion that he considered this penalty legitimate. He certainly had no complacent admiration for Roman justice—not after the Cross.

One important thing remains to be said: in Romans 13 Paul is not thinking of a *Christian* magistrate: he speaks only of the Roman judges as they existed in his time; the whole development of his argument is from the point of view of Christians, not of the magistrate. The idea of a Christian magistrate was doubtless unthinkable in those days,[270] notably because of all the pagan sacrifices the magistrate had to preside over in exercising his functions; also, the Empire did not confide these important posts (praetors, etc.) to any but reliable citizens, who had no other king than Caesar.[271] So it is a childish anachronism to interpret this text as if Paul had been in a 'Christian country', so that what he said of the pagan courts of his time would be directly valid for the 'Christian' courts of our time. The agonising problem of the death penalty comes up as soon as it is a Christian who is called on to pronounce or execute it. Paul does not touch on this problem, and probably never even thought of it.

No Christian justification of the death penalty can be deduced from Romans 13, so there is no single text in the New Testament which approves it.[272] There is, however, one which condemns it, and it is surprising to see how little attention those who deal with this question accord to it: I refer to the episode of the adulterous woman (John 8:3-11).

(c) Unlike so many of the texts usually invoked in favour of Christians' participating in war, this episode clearly comes in the framework of the order of conservation, not that of redemption: it is undeniably concerned with protecting human society, notably the family; the State's role is brought up, and we are shown a real trial sequence. This text is rarely brought up, however, no doubt because it contradicts certain Constantinian propositions.

It is clearly no concern with public morality which makes the Scribes and Pharisees bring Jesus the woman 'taken in adultery'. If they come right into the Temple to disturb His teaching, it is because they are in haste to use her to set a terrible trap whereby they hope to get rid of Him. If Jesus confirms the ruthless verdict of the Law of Moses (Lev. 20:10), they will quickly stone her to death, pleased to tarnish His reputation by making Him shoulder the responsibility for this execution; He will be seriously discredited after this if it can be said: 'It's he who had that poor woman put to death, the man who claims to have come to save sinners. He shouldn't have done it.' He will have blood on *His* hands too, people will be frightened of Him, they will stop following Him; and besides, by taking responsibility for this execution, He will be boldly challenging the Roman law, which gave nobody but the Roman governor the right to pronounce a death penalty (John 18:31). This might cost Jesus dear, for Pilate did not take his prerogatives lightly.

If, on the other hand, Jesus tries to save the woman's life, if He decides for their own custom whereby this kind of punishment for adultery is carried out very seldom, then the Pharisees will be able to accuse Him of openly contradicting the Law of Moses, which is the surest way of destroying His authority among the inhabitants of Jerusalem; they will have a very strong argument against Him in the eyes of the people, and perhaps even a pretext for having Him condemned to death, since contradicting the Law was a real blasphemy in Israel (Deut. 4:2; 12:32; 27:26). So it is indeed a clever and dangerous trap: He can only condemn the woman or condemn the Law, and doing either will irremediably condemn His own ministry.

It is Jesus' own person the Scribes and Pharisees are attacking, it is Him they wish to destroy, His claim to be the Messiah they want to eliminate for good. In this sense the episode is also a Messianic text; but it is equally one where the death penalty is frankly tackled. The question of that penalty's legitimacy is explicitly involved here (which was not the case in Romans 13). Jesus is consulted not only as a religious chief, but as citizen; and all these men gathered round the guilty woman are perfectly qualified by the Law to judge her, condemn her and even execute her forthwith: the irregularities of detail in procedure matter little (they have not brought the *man*, despite Leviticus 20:10). Jesus, in fact, is abruptly involved, despite Himself, in the jury of a sort of civil court; and the scene develops, in the most highly dramatic manner, on the level of the State, its mission and its rights. Jesus' enemies have succeeded in putting Him on a ground which is not His usual one; they will learn to their cost that He is perfectly at ease in His role of King.

When He finally straightens up to answer the questions they are harassing Him with, doubtless believing they have 'got him', He confirms the condemnation of the woman to death: 'He that is without sin among you, let him cast the first stone at her.' He definitely cannot be made to say the opposite of the Law, He confirms the death penalty and apparently its legitimacy. He quietly submits to the ordinances of Leviticus, and sanctions with His authority the sentence against the woman: she does deserve *death*; and He quite agrees that the men present should execute her at once. But He discreetly introduces a new clause, in the name of common sense and equity, for it would indeed be inequitable that a man worthy of death should condemn anyone else to death. Only a judge can condemn, an accused person cannot condemn another accused person.

In a second the situation is reversed: the accusers feel themselves exposed and accused, and Jesus instantly resumes His true place, that of judge who alone may speak, since He alone is without sin (John 8:46). He has formally confirmed the legitimacy of the death penalty, but has yet prohibited it in fact—and not only to His disciples, to the Church, but also to the State. He does not contradict the Law, He even admits the principle of the death penalty; but by His words He makes its execution impossible, not in the name of any indulgent tolerance, but along the lines of national custom, for which the rigour of this law had fallen into disuse. Yes, He says, she deserves death, but you have not the right to put her to death. Thus magnificently does He break out of the trap in which His enemies think they have already caught Him.

He does more than escape Himself from the danger: He reveals to us the real meaning of the Old Covenant's condemnations to death. All these capital punishments provided for by the Law were not so much intended to be carried out, for then almost everybody would have had to be killed, as to warn the Jews of the punishment awaiting them at the day of the Last Judgment if they infringed the commandments of the Divine Law. Each of these terrifying texts tells us: here is what you deserve if you flout God—death! For the wages of sin are death. And he who commits sin must expect nothing else but death when he appears before the supreme Judge.

Death, whether inflicted by men in the name of civil justice or reserved for the guilty man at Judgment Day, will be his only way of expiating his fault. We can see here the religious character of the death penalty, which is a sort of expiatory sacrifice (and only those who have watched an execution from very close quarters know the extent of pagan sadism involved in such human sacrifices). See how hard it is to draw a distinct demarcation line between the orders of redemption and of conservation! These cruel expiations could only have a provisional value, an eschatological meaning; and if such is indeed the theological significance of all the threats of death scattered through the New Testament, we can appreciate at once why Jesus confirms the death penalty while making sure it is not put into practice: He is not playing with the letter of the Law but restoring its true eschatological meaning. In the Old Covenant executions and threats of execution are both *signs* of the Last Judgment.

But now comes a new dramatic stroke: Jesus, who alone would have the right to condemn this woman, does not condemn her either; instead, He forgives her fault, or crime, and heals her—'go, and sin no more.' Some are scandalised: He tolerates people's vices, even encourages them, acquitting this woman without imposing any punishment on her for her offence. Is not this a reversal of morality? His attitude would indeed be inexplicable and unjustifiable if we did not know that He is Himself soon to undergo in her place the sanction of death which she has justly earned by her crime. The sanctity of God and the Law's requirements are thus respected: the wages of sin are still death; but it is He, the Righteous one, who is struck down with death in the place of the sinner, to deliver her and obtain for her the forgiveness of God. There will still be the cruel, expiatory sacrifice, but it is the Son of God who will offer it with His own blood. In this sense the Old Testament's condemnations to death are also *prophetic* texts announcing in their own way the redeeming death of Christ, exactly like the sacrifices in the Temple services.

Thus, while capital punishment in the Old Testament is both a sign of the Last Judgment and a prophecy of the tragedy of Golgotha, in the New Testament we watch the idea of judgment splitting into two different concepts: on the one hand the Gospel proclaims that everyone will have to render account of his acts 'in the day of Christ', after His 'advent' (Matt. 25:19; II Cor. 5:10), but on the other hand it proclaims that the divine judgment has already been fulfilled in Christ when He underwent once for all time, and for all men, the death penalty which all of them have deserved by their sin. The Gospel affirms simultaneously that judgment *will* take place on the last day (John 5:29; 12:48), and that nevertheless it has *already* taken place (John 3:18-19; 12:31; 16:11).

In the New Covenant human courts remain legitimate and necessary, but they are simply stripped of their right to inflict the death penalty; and this can no longer be an expiation nor a prophecy of Christ's expiation; it can only be a denial of the cruel sacrifice He underwent, an insult to the Crucified.

I hope I shall not be misunderstood: I am not denying the State's right and obligation to punish criminals. I believe with Calvin that in some cases the magistrates 'will defile their hands by pardoning.'[273] I only deny (precisely because Jesus was put to death) that the State, any more than an individual, has the right to put criminals to death. I am not discussing whether from the point of view of expediency a country is more prosperous when it has abolished the death penalty or has reintroduced it. I simply believe that the sixth commandment is addressed also to the State, telling it: you are putting yourself in God's place when you arrogate the right to cause a man's death; for since Jesus Christ died for all men, no other death is now necessary.

If I am accused of again confusing the orders of redemption and of conservation, I would reply: Jesus was very much within the order of conservation when, not content with stopping the Pharisees from stoning this woman, which would have been regular according to the *civil* law, He went on to take the daring, revolutionary initiative of not stoning her Himself. In relation to her He accomplished two acts: as citizen He refused to inflict the death penalty on her, while as Son of God He gave her forgiveness for her sin. But as regards the first of these two acts, we must choose between two contrasting appreciations: by not condemning her, Jesus either took a scandalous liberty with the Law, definitely flouting the State's requirements and the laws established by God to preserve human society, laws He had just sanctioned by His personal authority; or else He was truly fulfilling the Law, because He knew that His own death, imminent and already present, would inaugurate a new system in which the execution of criminals lost all meaning and all theological justification. Surely we must adopt the second alternative!

In short, from the point of view of the Gospel, to execute a man (I am deliberately not saying 'a criminal', for in face of the Cross that word becomes singularly relative, even on the level of the State[274]), is to deny that Jesus Christ was executed once for all time and for all the sins of all men; to deny that the Cross of Golgotha is the only sanction valid for men's sin, the only one which satisfied God's justice. On the one hand, to execute a man is to anticipate the Last Judgment, God's judgment on the Last Day, instead of leaving it to the only just judge to whom God has committed all judgment (John 5:22). For the death penalty, let us remember, expresses an absolute judgment, whereas all the other punishments, even life imprisonment, express relative and provisional judgments. To execute a man is somehow to reject the return of Jesus Christ, to refuse to live in an eschatological perspective, awaiting His advent. To kill a man is always to forget that Jesus came to die for us, and will return to *judge* the quick and the dead.

This is as true for the State as for Christians; and if the State ignores Jesus Christ and the Christian significance of the sixth commandment, if it flouts that commandment, Christians cannot but refuse to obey it when it wishes to constrain them to execute a man, that is, to make them deny Jesus Christ. This raises formidable problems of conscience, I know: what should a Christian judge do, or a Christian called to serve on a jury in a court of assizes? But I cannot here go into these problems in detail.

In the whole episode of the adulterous woman, the trap laid down for Jesus turns on the right not of judging the guilty but of inflicting the death penalty. Failing to realise this and obviously embarrassed by the episode, Calvin merely asserts, against the evidence of the text, that our own offences should not stop us 'correcting the vices of others', and sets his mind rather easily at rest by saying that Jesus 'by no means reverses the law and by no means abolishes the judgments and punishments ordained by the law.'[275] Certainly Jesus does not reverse the political order, nor does He make impossible the work of human courts. He does not abolish all punishments, but He does abolish one of them, which is blasphemous: the death penalty. For He makes it impossible in practice, illegitimate; He declares it superseded, with the other cruel sacrifices of the Old Covenant. If Calvin had understood that, Calvinism would have had a different history.

For the Gospel the death penalty is an anachronism. But Christians never succeed in believing the Good News: they have re-established what the New Covenant had rendered null, notably, among many other practices of the Old Covenant, the practice of blood sacrifices, whether religious, juridical or military (Heb. 9:22 and 26; 10:12).

2. The Problem of the Police

Many readers will doubtless concede that the death penalty is at the very least disputable from the Christian point of view, but even so, they will say, a State without police is unthinkable and since the police are indispensable for preserving the country from criminals inside it, why should the army not be just as indispensable to pre-serve it from enemies outside? Again we have a syllogism: the police are legitimate, and the army is a sort of police, so the army is legitimate.

I will ask two questions analogous to those I asked in the previous section. First, can the army be compared to the police? There are certainly resemblances between them, such as uniform, passive obedience to the State, and in most countries the use of certain arms —but there are also substantial differences: the police are at the service of the law, which is the same for all the country's citizens, and which transcends both the police and the people they have dealings with; whereas the army is at the service of the nation, or rather of the State, which arrogates the right to be supreme judge of the nation's interest; and the army makes its own law. The police try to deter criminals, whose offences are defined by law, and not to kill them; whereas the army tries to kill the soldiers of the enemy army without worrying unduly about any civilians present among the soldiers.

In principle the police make a *minimum* use of force; this is even its real art and its strength; whereas the army always makes a chal-lenging display of its power; and when the moment comes to act, it gives itself up to a veritable orgy of blind destruction and slaughter. The police works for the triumph of right, as defined by the country's official laws; a citizen suffering injury can lay a complaint against it in the name of the law; whereas the army works for the triumph of force; its law is that of the wolf—might is right. A genuine police inspires in citizens (the vast majority anyhow!) a comforting feeling of security, whereas the army inspires feelings of fear and insecurity in neighbouring peoples, who believe themselves threatened, and by an inevitable reaction, in their own country: a military parade may be partly reassuring to the citizens themselves, but it is also alarming.

Then there is a point which concerns our problem still more directly: there are countries, such as England, where the police are unarmed; and in most countries the police are seriously limited in their right to use arms, which are theoretically intended only for their personal security, and which they can only use in cases of self-defence. If in the course of his duties a policeman kills a man, he is charged with murder, and must prove that it was genuine self-defence, or that he could not do otherwise if he was to carry out the express orders he had received—or else he is punished like anyone else. It is quite exceptional for a policeman to kill anyone; many complete their career without ever having killed (except in wartime). Whereas for the army the thing is to kill the maximum number of enemies with the minimum of effort. If the police kills, it is a regrettable accident, or an offence; but if the army kills people, a lot of people, it is a glorious success, something to be proud of.

These differences rapidly sketched, are enough, I think, to invalidate the comparison of army with police, and thus to ruin the syllogism whereby the former is whitewashed by reference to the latter. But the second question I would ask is no less serious: is it legitimate for the police to do absolutely *anything*? I am far from minimising the devotion of those who carry out, often both inconspicuously and heroically, an essential task for which we can never be grateful enough: that of ensuring people's safety, public order, and a minimum of justice among citizens. One must add, however, that not everything in the police is to be admired. Doubtless it is impossible to imagine a nation which could do without the police, but this does not mean we must find everything they do legitimate.

A Biblical study of the police would be as painful as it was dramatic. Let us merely say that the New Testament (notably Romans 13) does seem to admit implicitly the legitimacy of the existence of the *principle* of the police, as an indispensable instrument to ensure respect for laws and public order by the constraint it exercises over its citizens. But admitting this—what crimes are not committed by the police operating in the New Testament, to speak only of *them*! The massacre of the innocents (Matt. 2:16), the execution of John the Baptist (Matt. 14:10), the slaughter of the Galileans (Luke 13:1), the bribery for a denunciation of Jesus (Matt. 26:15), the arrest of Jesus (Matt. 26:50), the scourging and crucifixion of the Saviour (Matt. 27:26 and 31): these are some examples from the Gospels. In the Acts we have the double imprisonment of the apostles (4:3; 5:26), their scourging without definite offence being charged against them (Acts 5:40), the beheading of James and arbitrary arrest of Peter (Acts 12:2-3), the scourging (without judgment) of Paul and Silas (Acts 16:22), the 'examination' by scourging which Paul had to undergo (Acts 22:24)—there would be plenty to say, incidentally, on the subject of tortures and third-degree methods used by the police both then and now.

Admittedly most of these crimes were committed by the police on the orders of the king, the governor or the Sanhedrin, but the fact remains: the police referred to in the New Testament are often involved in very dirty work; the police of the temple and Pilate's police play an important part in the crucifixion of our Saviour. In the New Testament the police contribute more often to disorder than to order, and above all to the major disorder of executing the Son of God: again we are brought back to the Cross. After this we should be very much on our guard against the optimistic benevolence with which so many theologians talk of the police, one of the characteristics of the Constantinian heresy. For that heresy is perhaps essentially a refusal to accept all the implications of the Cross.

No, I am not trying to make the modern 'Christian' police responsible for the crimes committed by the police of Jesus' time! But even if God wills the existence of police, it certainly does not mean that we can automatically declare the modern police 'legitimate' without first carefully considering their ends and their means. Once again God has created a ministry outside the Church, that of the police; but it remains to see how the police fulfil their ministry. Not everything is legitimate in the police of our time, any more than it was in the police of the first century. In a sense, and to a greater or smaller degree, the police in every country continue to crucify Jesus Christ.

In effect, from the Christian point of view, we can only approve the police who are in the service of right, of justice, of law, in a word of 'good', on the understanding that the Scriptures, and notably the Decalogue, constitute the criterion of good. But in fact the modern police are often government police, whose essential function is to help the government to keep in power; while some para-military police formations are veritable civil-war armies intended to protect private interests rather than the law. Then there are the 'security' police so characteristic, alas, of modern totalitarian States; but the Gestapo, etc., have provoked such disgust that it is unnecessary to stress their function, which is to ensure the tyranny of a ruthless dictatorship by every means, regardless of moral principle. The defenders of 'militarism' will hardly try to justify the army by reference to the Gestapo-type police; so there are obviously indispensable distinctions, and one cannot say without qualification that 'the police' is legitimate.

The same applies as to the magistrate in Romans 13: the police is only legitimate in the view of the New Testament if two important conditions are fulfilled: first, in relation to the end it is pursuing, it must be in the service not of an arbitrary and more or less pagan ideology, or a State which takes itself for a god and is its own norm;

but of good as defined in the Decalogue. Second, in relation to the means it puts into operation, these must be appropriate to the end aimed at and must be acceptable to God, that is, in the last resort, submitted to the criterion of the Decalogue. We are brought back again to the sixth commandment, from which it is decidedly hard to escape in these matters.

It is by reference to this that the police must be judged, for the Revelation should not be amended in the light of empirical 'realism', however reasonable, and actual practice—but the other way round. Taking the line of the Constantinian heresy, our theologians decide too easily that the Scriptures have no authority in relation to certain problems raised by human society. They are very ready to accuse the non-violent of resigning from the struggle; but that is just what they are doing themselves.

Chapter 3

THE ARMY*

IT can scarcely be attributable to mere chance that Jesus was crucified by soldiers, properly commanded by their *officers*. Here again it is strange that this tragic confrontation between the world of the *army* and that of the Gospel should be passed over so easily, as if it were without significance.

1. The Country's Defence

If the sixth commandment, in its Christian political significance, condemns the institution of the death penalty and also murders committed even accidentally by the police, what is the position with war? Are we faced after all by a situation where we must admit a reversal of principle to what is required by this commandment? Can one speak of a case of *force majeure* where God Himself would consent to His children violating His law of love, although, as we have seen, this is the minimum guarantee and the *sine qua non* for true humanity in the life of society? But perhaps any State has the right, and even a duty, to organise the defence of the country it has jurisdiction over?

We have already noted that neither the term nor the idea of national 'defence' is to be found in the New Testament, which seems completely indifferent to this problem. The main reason for its silence may well be the exceptional historical situation in the age when it was written: for a century the Pax Romana had not been menaced by external wars of aggression, though it had been by internal revolts. So the New Testament never speaks of contemporary 'wars'; this word is used only to designate either the wars of the past (Heb. 11:34) or the apocalyptic wars of the end of the world (Matt. 24:6 *et passim*); apart from three occasions when it is used to serve as an image (Luke 14:31; I Cor. 9:7; I Peter 2:11). The agonising problem of 'going to war' does not seem to have arisen for the men of the New Testament.

* Translator's note: For the sake of convenience I have retained the use of 'army' in its wider sense, common in France and other European countries, of 'all the armed forces', naturally including navy and air force as well.

On the other hand, the attitude and message of the Jewish prophets do not seem to give a firm scriptural basis to the concept of
national defence: for them the Lord is the only true defender of
Israel; the people's only true protection lies in repentance and in
obedience to Him who is its fortress and shield; the chariots and
horsemen attract sarcasm from the prophets more often than
anything else (see II Kings 6 and Isaiah 30 and 31).[276] 'Oh, but of
course the case of Israel is exceptional, given the essentially religious
foundations of its mere physical existence, which doesn't apply to
modern nations.' But then why give Israel as an example on some
occasions, and reject it on others?

We are obliged to return to the sixth commandment, and look
honestly, in the light of the Gospel, for its relevance to national
defence. Two separate questions arise here.

First there is the problem of the *end*: can one dispute the right and
duty of any government to protect materially the physical existence
of the people it has in its charge, the right to maintain and defend its
frontiers and its independence? To these questions the only possible
answer is an unequivocal 'no'. On occasions the State will unfortunately show wisdom in preferring to accept a momentary impairment
of its territorial integrity or national independence rather than run
the risk of causing the destruction of its people by a vain and desperate military defence—see Luke 14:31-32 and many passages in
Jeremiah.[277] The Vichy government certainly surrendered too readily
to the occupying power, but the Nazi government was also mad and
criminal in the spring of 1944 to continue a war that was plainly lost.
Still, the State is *responsible* for the country, so one can scarcely dispute its right to provide for and organise the country's defence as
best it can.

But there is also the problem of *means*, and here is the only real
difficulty; it is amazing that the defenders of 'militarism' keep silent
on this, while spending so much effort proving the legitimacy of the
end—do they think any means is justified when the Nation is in
danger? Is God's law, and above all the Decalogue, suspended as
criterion for the Christian's obedience the moment his country is in
a state of war?

Here again there are two different questions: are military means
of defending the country permitted by God; and are they effective?
Generally the order of these questions is reversed: it is asserted,
though without any proof, that recourse to arms is the *only* effective
means of defending the country; and therefore that it must certainly

be authorised by God. But we should be crystal clear about priorities on this essential point, and in Calvin's words must ask first what is 'lawful' and only after that what is 'possible': as I said at the beginning of this book, the problem of effectiveness arises only after that of legitimacy and is dependent on it. But the only clear criterion of the legitimacy of an enterprise or an order from the State is the Decalogue; so I do not see how a Christian, respecting the authority of the Scriptures, can avoid the challenge of the sixth commandment to the legitimacy of the army. The real problem is surely put plainly enough by the very terms of the commandment: one must prevent killing, without oneself killing. Is it not true here again that when the State reaches the point of killing, it has ceased to be a factor of order or *protection*?

Let us note in this connection that any theory claiming to justify the army necessarily implies the idea that the moment hostilities are started the State ceases to be responsible for the nationals of the enemy country—or even for those who merely happen to be in the army's path. This is the basic weakness of any such theory, the point which makes it incompatible with Christian thinking. For the Scriptures are categorical: the State is in the service not of certain men but of man, for his good, notably in protecting his life. The army believes itself exempt from the obligation of protecting enemy citizens, on the pretext that they have undertaken a criminal action, the invasion by force of national territory. The State must certainly resist illegal invasion, but without ceasing to consider the invaders for what they are: men. This is the real problem, and it is here Gandhi has much to teach us. That the State should be more responsible for its own citizens than for foreigners is understandable; but that it should be the protector of the former and murderer of the latter is something which cannot be maintained without giving an absolute and idolatrous value to nationality. When by this distinction the State awards itself the right to slaughter 'foreigners', it is betraying its vocation. 'Reasons of State' have supplanted God. As Pascal put it, ' "Why do you kill me?" "Why? Don't you live on the other side of the water? My friend, if you lived this side, I should be a murderer, and it would be unjust to kill you in this way; but since you live the other side, I am a brave man and this is just." '[278]

The International Red Cross, showing here its genuinely Christian inspiration, has made great efforts to modify this *irresponsibility* towards enemies by the agreements it has proposed to governments.

But in trying to humanise war, it has emphasised war's intolerable absurdity: after each battle you treat with all conscientiousness, in prisoner-of-war camps and hospitals, the men you have been trying to slaughter a few hours before. At the heart of the 'militarist' philosophy lies the irresponsibility of the State, which thinks itself exempt from the duty of protecting certain categories of human beings, as soon as the colour of their skins, their political opinions or their uniform is different. People are no longer responsible for those they kill.

But God asks both the statesman and the State's man—the soldier—the same question as He asked Cain: 'Where is thy brother? . . . The voice of thy brother's blood crieth unto me from the ground' (Gen. 4:9 and 10). To escape this terrible question, men have deadened their hearts and minds by letting themselves slip into the twilight where the pagan deities of the City and Mars and Fate are thronging. In the heady darkness where all divine objurgations and moral standards are shaken,[279] these cozening deities persuade the soldier that he is no longer an ordinary man subject to common law. This is the dreadful imposture of militarism: Mars literally dehumanises the warrior by reassuring him, distressed despite himself at having blood on his hands, by giving him the magnificent feeling that he is a superman who holds in his power the destiny of nations and who therefore has all rights over other men, including that of exterminating them like flies. By intoxicating him with grandiloquent abstractions, old as the hills, and false, Mars convinces him that he is no longer responsible for his brother. Recourse to war, even defensive war, is a surrender. For the magistrate is in God's service to protect, not to destroy.

I believe firmly and serenely, in fact, that the Christian will put himself at the State's disposition to take part in its legitimate defence, that is, defence in accordance with God's law; but must refuse, because of the sixth commandment, to use murderous or military means for such defence, or to obey orders which would force him openly to violate the Decalogue. I believe that the arguments generally used to justify the 'suspension' of the sixth commandment, declared incompetent before the reality of war, are arguments from human wisdom, which cannot take precedence over the Revelation. I even find them highly debatable on their own ground, that of common sense; and I am amazed that so many writers can talk lightheartedly of the need and obligation to 'defend' their country by military means, without bothering to justify their confidence in this concept. Is it really so obvious that when the nation is in danger it can be defended by the army? Let us now examine the consistency of the argument that a general resort to arms is the only means of ensuring national defence *effectively*.

2. Does the Army Spare the Nation the Horrors of War

'You are playing the enemy's game,' pacifists are told. 'By refusing to carry out your military duty, and through your example encouraging others to do the same, you are weakening your own nation and making it an easier prey for the aggressor who covets its land and its wealth. Every conscientious objector is an invitation to aggression.'

First of all, it is not all that easy to define the aggressor, to decide between two nations at war which has borne the heaviest responsibility, which has done the most to cause the conflict. In all wars all armies believe they are to some extent *defending* their country. Even if we had a universally adopted definition of the aggressor, which we do not, we shall still need to be suspicious of it, for a legal formula can never correspond exactly to the complex realities of life. There are always wrongs on both sides, and only God can assess the respective proportions. This is not to say, of course, that at the actual moment when hostilities start some nations are not far more guilty and responsible than others; but the discussions round Article 231 of the Treaty of Versailles showed the hypocrisy of statesmen who attach immense importance to the incident, however monstrous, which forms a transition between 'cold' and 'hot' war.

In any case, how can I be sure that the aggressor, the government which wants to provoke war, is necessarily the other government, not my own? Only those saturated in a nationalist ideology are convinced that their country is always right, always an innocent victim, that the wicked are bound to be discovered only outside its frontiers; whereas anyone looking at history and human experience objectively must admit that his country is just as likely to be guilty as to be the victim of aggression. So by accepting military service, I am just as likely to be contributing to the crime as working to prevent it. This, of course, does not apply to nations which are genuinely neutral; but then *they* are carrying out an act of conscientious objection, so to speak, in the community of nations?

Today, indeed, most nations belong to one or other of two immense power *blocs*, and in this respect they do not enjoy any real independence. Each nation is usually concerned to achieve solidarity with the rest of the *bloc*, to resist aggression, or as the other side may see it, to encourage aggression. All I have just said about the chances of a nation being innocent apply even more strongly with the *bloc* system; and by submitting to my country's military laws, I am probably reinforcing the *bloc* defending capitalism or communism, as the case may be; and both seem quite capable of being aggressors!

Nor is it so obvious that the pacifist weakens the camp of his country and its allies to the point of encouraging enemy powers to attack them. It might equally well be said that by contributing to the increase of war potential through my presence in the army, I am increasing fear and suspicion among neighbouring countries presumed to be hostile—who might therefore be more inclined to forestall attack by themselves attacking. In the armaments race, which forms the real background against which we are living, every increase in military power by one of the rival *blocs* leads the other *bloc* to increase its own military power from prudence and fear. This is the devilish vicious circle, often with additional 'promotion' from armaments manufacturers, which always leads to war: 'He who prepares for war inevitably creates the spirit of war, whether he intends it or not, and thus precipitates the war he fears.'[280]

Any programme for the strengthening of national 'defence' must inevitably help bring war nearer for other reasons too: for one thing it delivers up the nation as a helpless prey to the terrible parasites I have already referred to who grow rich by preparations for war. Their appetite is insatiable, they quickly become the masters of governments, even socialist governments; they paralyse the effort made to settle international conflicts peacefully; they assassinate men like Jean Jaurès; they sabotage international organisations and interviews between heads of State; they discredit peace movements and stifle the voice of the people, who long for peace. Slaves to Mammon and caught in their own grisly network, they work towards getting more and more commissions: this alone counts in their eyes. If possible, they sell their arms and products to both sides at once, and anyhow they close their eyes to the real destination of the arms they sell. The world can be destroyed so long as their profits continue and preferably increase: at the beginning of April 1953, for instance, the announcement of an imminent resumption of armistice talks in Korea immediately produced a slump in stock markets.

All this can only lead to war; and I, a Christian, am supposed to go on being an accomplice to it, to offer my submission as an edifying example to the wretched thousands destined as cannon fodder!

Again, it is clear that wars could at least be reduced in number and importance if there were an international organisation capable of judging equitably the conflicts between nations, and of imposing its judgments by its moral authority, whether or not supported by an international police force. For centuries this has been the longing of humanity. But if you look for the causes of the impotence of the International Court at the Hague and the failure of such bodies as the League of Nations, you find first and foremost the principle of national sovereignty. But this principle, so destructive of peace, is only a real 'power for evil' in so far as it rests on powerful armed forces. Again and again we come across the same vicious circle: the only way of lessening the danger of war is by strengthening international organisations; but the only way of strengthening these is by reducing national armed forces to the point where they cease to be dangerous for neighbouring nations. How do we escape from this circle? Shall I be told that until the international police force is capable of ensuring our safety, we must certainly ensure it ourselves with our own armed forces?

But suppose by their very existence these forces help to stifle at birth any attempt to bring about international law? Once more, it is by no means certain that my acceptance of military service is more effective than my conscientious objection for saving my country from war. At any rate it is hard to say on which side the balance comes down.

It may be remarked that I am leaving out of account imperialism, which is also a cause of wars. But if the lust for empire helps to produce aggressive armies, it is the other way round as well, as can be seen from the history of the last century and a half. Often a 'secondary power' gradually becomes involved by circumstances in the maelstrom of international diplomacy, and when threatened by other powers, sets about increasing its 'war potential' though at first chiefly for its own defence. Then, sooner or later, its army comes under the domination of some politician or political general imbued with militarist ideas and capable of putting them into practice. One day this army is revealed to be among the most powerful in the world. Henceforward the country is intoxicated by its own power, and launches into imperialist activities, because it cannot resist the temptation of using its forces to put pressure on its neighbours so as to obtain what it covets. Its government is the slave of the national hysteria which it has itself provoked so as to justify the crushing military expenditure imposed at home—to the profit of those mentioned above. After this, imperialism will know no bounds till the final catastrophe: has there been a single case of imperialism in the last 150 years which has escaped such a cycle? Imperialism is really much more the product than the cause of militarism, and far from fighting against it by 'joining up', I shall only be increasing its strength—in my own country.

The formula 'Si vis pacem, para bellum', may have had an element of truth when the Roman Empire was the only great power in the world, with a military superiority so overwhelming that the barbarian peoples hardly dared to move; but it is thoroughly fallacious since the world has been divided between rival powers capable of challenging each other. As far back as 1927 Field-Marshal Robertson said: 'We no longer agree without qualifications that the best way of preventing a war is to prepare for it. The preparations for war only hasten the war.'[281] In theory it is no doubt undeniable that every conscientious objector lessens his country's military power and so risks encouraging enemy nations to attack it. But it can equally well be said that every soldier, by his mere presence in the army, increases the distrust and fear-reflexes of these enemy nations, brings into play secret or overt forces which work towards war, and so also helps to make war more likely. If, for instance, in civilised countries civilians are forbidden to bear arms, this is doubtless because their doing so is considered a factor increasing the chances of disorder and injuries. So both these positions can be maintained; but if armaments and armies destroy instead of ensuring a country's security, if it is not *obvious* that my submission to military laws will allow me to work effectively to spare my country the horrors of war—then the objection I have imagined at the beginning of this section loses all its force.

Jesus denounced the vicious circle, and the false philosophy of 'militarism', in that one terse sentence: 'All they that take the sword shall perish by the sword.'

3. What is the Nation's Military Defence Worth?

'Perhaps you are right, but even so, once war has begun, it is better for our country to be as strong as possible, so as to have the maximum chance of coming out of the war victorious.'

This objection raises two questions: is the military method an *effective* method of defending the country, and is it the *only* method?

(*a*) Since the beginning of time, for generation after generation,

half the combatants inevitably—since there are always victors and
vanquished—have made the bitter discovery that it is not enough to
have an army and fight to be able to defend themselves *effectively*:
the invaders are not always beaten back—far from it—and those
who take up arms to resist the aggressor should realise that in general
their chances of being victorious are only fifty per cent; so are their
chances, whatever the respective alliances on both sides, of having
fought for nothing and of suffering at the hands of their conquerors
a fate worse than if they had not fought. Jesus Himself, with His
sturdy common sense, asked: 'Or what king, going to make war
against another king, sitteth not down first, and consulteth whether
he be able with ten thousand to meet him that cometh against him
with twenty thousand? Or else, while the other is yet a great way off,
he sendeth an ambassage, and desireth conditions of peace' (Luke
14:31-32). Let us forget here the spiritual significance of this parable,
and merely see in it one condition for the answering of our first
question: military defence can be effective only with a clear military
superiority, in the widest sense, over the enemy. I do not see how
this proposition can be disputed.

But superiority is very hard to assess, especially today with all the
secret weapons at various countries' disposal and with the fantastic
complexity of the technical, industrial, and diplomatic elements
which make up such superiority. Twice in thirty years the German
government has made a disastrous mistake in its assessment; and no
government today can assert that it has enough superiority over a
potential enemy to make military defence of the country *effective* for
sure; there is always a doubt, and accordingly the risk of failure is
always there.

The modern army is surrounded by so many technicians that
you might think the scientific method would be applied also in the
conduct of a war; but not at all. The government declaring war is
rather like an industrial chemist who undertakes a series of very
dangerous experiments in his laboratory, having no idea whether
he is likely to blow up the whole laboratory, killing all the staff and
even the inhabitants of the whole area around.

That is why I doubt whether the word 'effective', 'producing its
effect', is adequate for the conduct of a defensive war: it assumes a
certain constant and rational relationship between the means used
and the effect obtained; but there is nothing like that in the military
defence of a country. Firemen have an effective means of fighting a
fire, because experience proves that they almost always succeed in

limiting and stopping the fire; but would they be considered effective if on every other occasion that a fire broke out, it burned still more violently after their efforts, setting the whole town ablaze, not to mention killing the firemen themselves? The army is an effective means of *destroying*, it produces its effect there all right; but not for *defending* the country.

War is a kind of collective frenzy, which sweeps and rages through whole continents, till it suddenly and mysteriously stops—as a forest fire might stop, finding nothing left in its path to burn or because the wind has dropped. There are wars which have ended just because one of the combatants ran out of petrol or oil, or because certain secret weapons could not be perfected in time. There have been 'reversals of fortune' (the phrase is significant) which have occurred by the very narrowest of margins.

This is the terrible thing: today when a country is attacked, its government can never assert with certainty, leaving aside all question of 'honour', that it is worth defending the country by arms; can never prove that there are reasonable chances of repulsing the enemy nation and conquering it before it has inflicted too much damage; can never declare that the country has enough effective means to deal with the threat hanging over it. Everyone goes off to the war, but not in a reasoned manner, from the conviction, carefully considered, that here is the only useful and effective thing to do. No, they go under the impulse of a secular atavism, that is irresistible and somehow religious (though pagan), because they have been psychologically prepared for it by a skilful propaganda of fear and hatred, and because (I must repeat) there are some who satisfy their ambitions and others who become rich through war and its preparations.

'Still, we were delivered from the German occupation thanks to the allied arms.' True; but would you reason like this if you were German, Polish or Czech? Of course in any war there are victors and vanquished, but they have both used the same methods; so the success of the former does not derive from the so-called effectiveness of armed defence, since they all resort to that, but from a whole complex of circumstances of all kinds, many of which, strictly speaking, are unconnected with the country's armed forces, but which have finally worked in favour of the victorious side.

'But we cannot just stand and watch our country being invaded, our families being killed, our towns burned.' True; though the invader will kill our families and burn our towns much less if we do not defend ourselves with arms and kill the invading soldiers. In a sense, our families will be slaughtered, our towns destroyed, our villages plundered, chiefly because we have taken up arms on the pretext of protecting them.

Luther, following Thomist scholasticism in this, was aware of the problem: 'One must act with the greatest prudence in proceeding against malefactors, so as not to put the innocent in peril. . . . The prince should not destroy a bowl to recover a spoon, nor put the country to fire and the sword for the sake of one guilty man. . . . For it is not lawful to fight evil by a means that is still worse. . . . In cases where a prince cannot punish an injustice without causing worse misfortunes, he should renounce his right, however solidly established it may be.'[282]

In recent times E. Gounelle, in agreement with the unthinking opinion of thousands of people in all countries, has written: 'I have not got the choice between a good and an evil, but between two evils: to kill and to let kill.'[283] This may have been partly true in the days of halberds, but it has long ceased to have any truth. When you kill, you are also 'letting kill', if only through the working of reprisals. In September 1944 during the German collapse a French 'resister' in one village fired at a retreating German column; the German stopped a dozen civilians at random and shot them on the spot. Thousands of similar examples could be quoted, and the real dilemma is between 'letting kill' by killing or by not killing. It could even be maintained that the more enemy you kill (soldiers and civilians), the more of your own nationals and your allies (civilians and soldiers) you cause to be killed. Gounelle's false dilemma hides the truth: war is a terrible and blind industrial machine, and anyone who takes part in it can only achieve self-justification by duping himself with words.

Of course you cannot stand by and watch the invasion of your country; but you must also be sure your intervention will not increase the evil instead of diminishing it. The experience of recent wars is scarcely conclusive on this point: there have been many countries ravaged in the attempt to 'defend' them; the example of Korea, where there were ten times more civilians killed than soldiers, is so painful that Europeans can hardly like the prospect of being defended against a potential enemy in such a way. It would be very interesting to have exact statistics of the Frenchmen killed in the last war by the Germans and Italians on the one side and by the allies on the other; and you would have to transfer from the former class to the latter all the hostages shot, all the Frenchmen massacred by the Germans in reprisal for acts of war carried out against their armies. How many houses in France were destroyed by enemy bombs and how many by allied bombs? We have seen that the 'final result' argument, which some may have felt like bringing up, is not valid here; so what exactly do people mean when they claim to be 'defending' their country by arms?

Let us look squarely at the facts: when the invading armies have entered your country, you are bound, in trying to hit them, to hit your fellow-countrymen as well: like the gunners or bombers who are obliged to destroy whole villages and towns where there are as many civilians as military. Is it so sure that you will defend France by killing Frenchmen and destroying their homes? To the time-honoured question: 'If a criminal attacked your wife, would you not defend her?'—I would answer: Of course I should; and if I only needed to knock him out, I shouldn't hesitate. But there are two things I should certainly not do: throw a grenade at him and risk killing my wife as well as him; or run off to his house (while he carries out his crime) to throw a grenade at the window and try to kill *his* wife and children.'

When you try to defend a country by arms, you not only turn it into a battlefield; by terrific air-raids on enemy towns, you make the enemy more savage and ruthless, and so indirectly increase the amount of destruction and slaughter in the very country you were trying to defend. Who can deny this vicious circle of war? How many farms, villages, towns, have been destroyed because the inhabitants resisted?—while Paris remained intact because twice in five years it was not defended. How many men and women have been shot because the invading army accused them of having fired at its men![284] A soldier notoriously becomes more cruel when his comrades have been shot down at his side: that is a law of the human heart, which has sometimes been cynically exploited by selfish interests. And when the invader's soldiers hear that the towns where their families live have been bombed, instead of demoralising them, it galvanises them and makes them all the more barbarous in the general slaughter.

Is throwing oil on the fire the way to put it out? Is fighting the invader the way to defend your country—or to destroy it—or both at once? This is the question, agonising and terrible, and I doubt whether an intelligent and honest person can evade it or resolve it in a way that excludes all doubt. The great military chiefs have always understood this; which is why they have always been at pains to

carry the war to enemy countries. But in that case it is not a defensive war, so one way or the other the arguments put forward by
theorists of military 'defence' still fall to the ground.

'But that's the *only* way of defending yourself against an invader.'
Even if this were proved, it would be no proof that military defence
was an effective and adequate defence, to which I must therefore
resign myself. And if you cannot prove, in a clear and pertinent
manner, that by 'joining up' I shall be doing more than just joining in
the general slaughter and destruction, then you cannot reproach me
with shirking my duty of 'defending' the country.

'No, we cannot be sure that it is sensible to try to defend our
country by arms against a "civilised" invader. But if we are invaded
by a totalitarian régime, should we not by all possible means try to
stop it destroying our liberties, deporting the fine flower of our
country and wiping out our civilisation?' I ask the reader to believe
that I realise the emotional force of this objection and that like
everyone else I shudder at the prospects it conjures up. But I am
trying to assess, as calmly and objectively as I can, whether military
defence is an *effective* method of avoiding such a disaster.

Let us first note that we have shifted the ground from nations to
ideologies; but does this make much difference to the problem? All
the doubts I have cast on the effectiveness of military methods surely
remain just as valid, whatever the invader's ideology. If we are not
sure of driving back a 'civilised' aggressor, even at the cost of destroying our own country, why should we be any more sure when the
aggressor is totalitarian? On the contrary, the chances of successful
defence will be still fewer, because an international and ideological
war will be complicated by civil wars; to the horrors of mass air-
raids (to speak only of those suffered by our own country, the
so-called victim of aggression), must be added the horrors of
mutinies, political assassinations, fratricidal 'partisan' operations
and concentration camps. Can such a prospect be envisaged other
than with grim resignation? Who will dare say it is my *duty* to take
part in all this?

Moreover, you do not kill totalitarianism by war; war is the best
method of injecting the virus everywhere. Faced by the necessities of
total war, the armed forces become totalitarian themselves, and
wherever they go, spread the germs of totalitarianism—which is
really nothing but a political régime, completely militarised. We have
already had the experience that to fight totalitarianism by arms, one
is obliged to use the same methods as it does.[285] When people claim

o

to be defending the essential values of our civilisation by arms, I would remind them that, as Visser t'Hooft has put it, 'the so-called spiritual values have an annoying tendency to evaporate as soon as you start fighting round them.'[286] Also, if there are some totalitarian régimes which collapse under the effects of war, there are others which emerge from war remarkably strengthened.

H. Bois, reverting to an image used by Luther,[287] has compared the army of defence to a surgeon who cuts up a body and makes the patient suffer but cures him.[288] But a conscientious surgeon would scarcely undertake a dangerous operation unless there were some slight chance of its being successful and in particular unless he had sterile instruments available. He would show criminal negligence if he rushed into such an operation with infected instruments, and without good reason for hoping that his intervention could save the patient. 'Unless the patient is at the point of death, and the surgeon thinks it is worth while trying an operation, although probably hopeless, rather than watch helplessly while the patient dies.' Yes indeed, so long as the surgeon is absolutely sure the patient is going to die; otherwise in the conditions imagined above, he had far better not operate, for he may very well kill the patient.

But this analogy certainly brings us to an essential aspect of the problem: if our country were occupied by a totalitarian régime, would it necessarily mean the nation's *death*? Such a judgment is plainly introducing ideas and feelings to which absolute value is given, when they are really very relative and disputable, and derive more from political ideologies than from common sense or the Christian Revelation.

'Better to die than be under Russian domination.' How can anyone be so sure, how can anyone know that the old adage, 'while there's life, there's hope', is completely false? 'There is one thing worse than death,' writes Miéville, 'and that is slavery and the degradation of a whole people by a régime which debases their minds. . . .'[289] But out of 100 men, including Miéville himself, who were given the choice of Russian rule or immediate death, how many would choose the latter? '. . . a régime which debases their minds,' the quotation goes on to say, 'by bending them to a servility and obedience which stifles them, and which if they resist sets out to break them by all the ingenious means which technical refinement puts at modern man's disposal.' Yet this description of a totalitarian régime could often apply to the army itself: in the last war, for instance, according to La Gravière, conscientious objectors in

France were kept in a bare cell for months, or paraded naked in front of the whole guard; one of them was beaten into unconsciousness, had all his lower teeth knocked out, and was left with a permanent scar below his chin.[290] The fact that in France conscientious objectors are put in prison indefinitely shows that we civilised French use the same techniques of degradation as we denounce in totalitarian countries. 'By techniques of degradation,' writes Gabriel Marcel 'I mean all the processes deliberately undertaken against individuals belonging to a particular category to attack and destroy in them the respect they can have for themselves and their convictions.'[291]

Still, 'better to die gloriously with a weapon in your hand, than a slow inglorious death'; or as Horace said equally romantically, 'dulce et decorum est pro patria mori.' But why should it be more glorious to be dismembered by a bomb or to suffocate in a collapsed trench, your fist still gripping a tommy-gun, than to die in a concentration camp where up to the last minute you can keep the inward attitude of a *man* and render a Christian witness? Which is the more glorious from the point of view of the Gospel? Christ and the apostles died as brave victims of totalitarianism, but not with weapons in their hands; and in times of suffering Christians must surely be witnesses of Jesus Christ by their *patience* (which, etymologically, *means* suffering).

Military defence of a country involves such appalling risk of destruction both material and moral, of final defeat to be followed after all this by the hated totalitarian domination, that on grounds of effectiveness—all I am concerned with at this stage—you cannot say *with certainty* that it is better to run such a risk than simply to endure occupation. All the impassioned speeches about honour and manhood and gallantry avail not at all; bombardments, alas, talk louder.

All the mystiques and ideologies, including the most brutal, including Nazism, communism, and aggressive nationalism, have in common this dogma, which Miéville, though a believer in peace by law, also considers as established: 'Above the life to be preserved, there is that which makes life worth living and preserving.'[292] Although the emotional and ideological content of this dogma varies according to the different cases, its authority has always helped to inspire men with the fear, hatred, and anger which will lead them to mutual slaughter. 'You don't convert fools and fanatics, you reduce them to impotence,' we are told—not by Hitler or Mussolini, but Miéville himself,[293] who adds elsewhere: 'We are dealing with a point where all reasoning ceases, where the attitude a man takes up will be determined by the values which he has chosen or which have been imposed on his mind as dominant and most important.' Yes, indeed, in the last resort the fundamental and decisive choice is irrational, mystical; that is just the trouble, for no romantic convictions or mystique should take the place of the one Lord. For a Christian only obedience to Christ is worth more than life itself; from the Christian point of view, to put a political régime 'above life' is to make vain and idolatrous propaganda. The first Christians were not so hard to satisfy: they died for Christ, not for a régime.

I suspect, too, that some of those who declare most bravely that arms must be taken up to defend spiritual values against 'godless communism' might soon find, if they had to face a communist occupation of their country with no help of intervention from outside, that to continue the struggle would be criminal, an incitement to civil war: where is the clear, precise line between this sort of war and that which is a sacred duty? According to Barth, the Christian should not refuse to go to war unless his own government seems to him frankly in the wrong; 'does this mean,' Rutenber asks acutely, 'that if justice is on the side of the enemy, he should take up arms against his own country?'[294] Why not indeed?

Again, are you quite sure, I would ask my imaginary critic, that your own country is not seriously infected with the appalling disease of totalitarianism? Have we no symptoms of it at home, and have police actions in Algeria had nothing in common with those of the Gestapo? So you may be making war against something which, alas, is nothing but a sinister caricature of our own degenerate and de-Christianised civilisation. Don't you see that your position is terribly arbitrary,[295] and that by sanctioning wars of defence in certain cases only, you are introducing, no doubt unwittingly, the pagan mystiques of Mars and the Nation?

Poor Church of Jesus Christ! Where is your *resistance* to these scourges? You keep nice and quiet in face of so many forms of tyranny, oppression, and social injustice, you collaborate so 'sensibly' with so many exploiters and unjust governments, that it is strange to see you standing out with such fervour against a particular form of oppression. You surrender to ten manifestations of Satan's triumph, but now and then you let yourself be mobilised against what is merely an eleventh form of that triumph. Why not against the first ten? Because such is the State's whim? And are you not afraid, by letting yourself be involved in this criminal slaughter, to surrender again to the Enemy—even this eleventh time? For are you not playing his game just as much as you did before by your silence and condonement?

The real problem, going beyond and dominating that of war, is the problem of *resistance* to evil, of non-collaboration with Satan. In face of invasion of the country by a foreign power, the real question is that of resistance to the evil represented by that invasion. It was remarkable to see how, directly after the Armistice of June 1940, all Frenchmen except for an admirable but tiny handful began collaborating with the Germans, from Marshal Pétain to the ordinary private, from the big industrialist who offered them his capital and his factories to the farmer who delivered them his butter and the munitions worker who turned out shells for them. It can hardly be denied that in their efforts to Nazify France, including the deportations, the Germans found all the collaboration and complicity they needed from the French. It seemed as if, the moment the Armistice was signed, there were no further resistance to be offered to the occupying power. The organised 'Resistance' came into being only very gradually, and in the early stages it was extremely timid.

A people's resistance consists in its capacity to say 'no', even at the cost of life itself; but military discipline teaches you to say 'yes', 'jawohl',[296] rather than 'no'. It helps to destroy individual judgment and personality after the manner of totalitarian states. Because it uses all means, even the most criminal, it may well destroy citizens' moral conscience, the very root of potential resistance to injustice and tyranny; and by training men for killing, it induces a whole series of surrenders to sin. 'The development of irresponsibility by a blind discipline,' writes Biéler, 'breeds individuals ready for any reversal of action, trained to respect only that authority which is at the moment in power.'[297] And in Van Lierde's words, military training is 'a laboratory which puts men's consciences to sleep by encouraging them to lose their sense of responsibility, thus allowing them to slaughter their fellow men in millions.'[298]

The tradition of National Defence cannot imagine any struggle being carried on except with arms, so that when the military battles are over for the time being, the soldier is a ready-made slave; now that he is a civilian and disarmed, he believes he must resign himself to anything. But this tradition teaches men to fight their fellows instead of fighting evil, an error as childish as it is tragic, for instead of limiting the evil, it increases that evil a thousand-fold: as Gandhi said, it is a barbarous illusion to think you can kill a régime by killing its officials. National Defence is also so fantastically expensive that it makes a great contribution to ruining the country, preserving poverty and thus social strife and class warfare; moreover as it gives the impression, rightly or wrongly, of being an immense waste of time, resources and money, it helps to destroy a country's civic spirit. It is more than a paradox to say that the military system does not encourage a true spirit of resistance.

Of course there are exceptions, and some great military men have been at the heart of resistance movements; but I think enough has been said to show that it is not at all obvious that the military defence of a country is an *effective* means of protecting it against foreign invasion. An army is like a sword without a hilt which hurts its user as much as it does his enemy. Militarists ask us to believe that the use of war methods will still have a favourable issue, taken by and large, and that it is therefore still worth risking all this destruction and slaughter. Exactly as in all the pagan mystiques of Force, including the Hitlerian and the Marxist, we are promised the Golden Age of Peace and Liberty *after* the catastrophic apocalypse of blood and fire—as if good should come out of a frenzied outburst of evil. Only this is something you certainly have to *believe*; but the god to be believed in is not the God of Jesus Christ, and such a faith has nothing in common with the faith of the Gospel.

(b) Is military resistance the only possible means of defending the country? For that is the second presupposition of the original objection made. It may seem strange that humanity, despite the advanced degree of civilisation it has apparently reached, should have found no other way of settling the conflicts which are bound to divide it than by such a cruel and ruinous process as that of war. No doubt the army is an institution and an industry from which so many people live and grow rich, an adventure which flatters so many heady emotions and deep instincts, that it has never been easy to talk of dethroning it.

All the same, in view of the tremendous destructive power of modern armies, and the abject immorality in which they are bound to fall, the time has perhaps come to consider another method of resistance to protect a country against the enemies who threaten it A systematic non-violent resistance, including civil disobedience, in short complete non-collaboration with the invader, seems a means more moral, more 'manly' (in its truest sense), more compatible with the Christian faith. I do not claim, of course, that this sort of resistance is less Utopian, less ineffective, less costly in lives even than military defence; but it exists and shows more humanity: for that alone it is worth considering.

I hope people better qualified than I will work out in detail this technique of non-violent resistance, in the light of Gandhi's experience, of the trade union movement,[299] and of certain non-violent struggles like the German passive resistance to the French occupation of the Ruhr. The vast literature concerned with resistance to Nazism, and the history of the beginnings of the Reformation in France, should also prove immensely instructive on this subject.

Such a resistance, like the military form, would have to be organised minutely and methodically in advance, including such problems as rations and the consequences of the general strike; the population would have to be systematically educated, non-armed 'forts' prepared, with food for the men who refused to work for the occupying power, in particular technicians and specialists, and for all who were threatened with commandeering or deportation. To apply the two principles—mutual aid and real solidarity between fellow-countrymen, on the one hand, and complete non-collaboration with the invader on the other—would certainly cost time and money; but a great deal less than the present National Defence; and the population's living standards could be tremendously improved thanks to the millions thus freed. Let us remember that a population's 'morale' is an essential element in its resistance.

No doubt it would be a very long struggle, a sort of guerilla warfare. Nevertheless, do not let us say too hastily that war is the *only* possible means of defending the country. And to finish with this charge against conscientious objectors, that they are shirking their duty by refusing to be integrated in the armed forces, I suggest that the charge cannot be upheld, since the objector will take part in the defence of his country by his non-violent resistance—until he is put in prison! He does not refuse to defend his fellow-countrymen, he only refuses to do so in a way he finds crazy, criminal, and incompatible with his Christian faith.

The Roman Church leaves 'open' the question of conscientious objection, and does not reproach those who refuse to take part in the military defence of their country: this must surely mean that it is uncertain about a Christian's obligation so to take part. The same conclusion (of uncertainty) may also be drawn from the recognition by the Oxford Oecumenical Conference that conscientious objection is *one* of the attitudes legitimate for Christians. For his part Karl Barth acknowledges 'that the rigorously negative response of the pacifist ethic contains almost an infinity of truth.'[300] One might easily conclude therefrom that the militarist response contains almost an infinity of error!

The so-called *duty* of *defending* your country *by arms* is not a rational or moral obligation well enough founded to be able to modify or overcome the obligations of the Scriptures; and if any theologians are surprised at my devoting so many pages to a discussion outside the range of Christian theology, they would do better to be surprised at the way in which Christian theology has for centuries calmly assimilated a pagan ideology.

4. Military Service

It seems to me, then, that recourse to war by the State is not an obvious aspect of the task confided to it by God; the intention may be good, but the means used are foolish and criminal, being a flagrant contradiction of the Decalogue; this is why war is in the last resort a betrayal of the State's real mission. It *must* find other methods of resolving international conflicts and obtaining respect for its legitimate independence. A nation's honour and interests cannot be defended by war any more than an individual's can by duels, nor has it any place in the Christian ethic.

Military service consists in killing our neighbour, and preparing for that. God has forbidden us to kill, in His Law as in the Gospel. And His commandment, illuminated and confirmed by the Gospel, has more weight than all the semi-reasonable arguments generally used in favour of such service.[301] The Christian must cease to be an accomplice in the State's murders as in its other crimes.

Whether we like it or not, to accept being integrated into the armed forces is to adhere to the paganism of Mars, and therefore to deny Jesus Christ. It is indeed a paganism, because the army demands a total surrender of my will and my judgment (different from my surrender to Jesus Christ), in that it 'falsifies all moral standards',[302] is founded on the anti-Christian principle that the end justifies the means, and demands a false faith, an optimistic confidence in the justice of men, as if good could come out of the evil they accomplish. If totalitarian paganism is incompatible with Christian fidelity, so is military paganism: the two are almost identical.

On the other hand, I believe that a Christian has no reason for refusing to take part in the non-violent—that is, non-murderous non-military—defence of his country.

CONCLUSION

THE Christian ethic is a morality of *gratitude*. The expression of gratitude is at once its end, its motive, its content, and its standard. For the Christian lives from the grace of Jesus Christ. For him, to live is joyfully to count God's blessings. But how can he give thanks when destroying God's creatures, when shattering the grace which is at work in his neighbour's life? He cannot thank God while at the same time despising His mercy and His patience: the two attitudes are irreconcilable. The 'Christian soldier',* once the lies of war's mystique have been strained off, can neither express nor excite praise but only bitterness and blasphemy.

The Christian ethic is a morality of victory; it is founded on the *faith* in the resurrection of Jesus Christ; it is the concrete, daily expression of that faith in the victory of God. There is no Christian obedience outside this joyful proclamation that sin has been overcome, and that through Christ there is an issue, a release, for all the fatal outbursts of evil. But military service necessarily implies a sad submission to the terrible law of sin, the pride of revenge and reprisals, which it proclaims as not to be avoided and beyond atonement. It is above all an acceptance of Mars' triumph. The 'Christian soldier' can bear witness only to the impotence of a Christ irremediably vanquished.

The Christian ethic is wholly orientated towards Jesus Christ's return; it is therefore a morality of *hope*. In his behaviour towards his neighbour, and particularly towards his enemy, the Christian knows that everything is relative and provisional, subordinated to the Master's intervention, return and judgment, and altered by this expectation to which His heart thrills; for everything is possible to him that believes. Whereas deliberately to kill a man is to consider the present as decisive, and the judgments men deliver on it as definitive: in other words, one expects nothing more for that man or from him. The 'Christian soldier' no longer has any good news to

* Translator's note: In English, of course, the two words have an even more unfortunate and tendentious association, owing to the words of the famous hymn: 'Onward Christian soldiers'.

proclaim; his witness can only be the despairing one that the Saviour will not return.

The Christian ethic is a morality of *love*. Anybody who has discovered how much the God of the Crucified has loved him cannot do otherwise than show his neighbour a mercy analagous to that which he has himself been shown. There is no true obedience for the Christian outside this concern to bring down on his brethren's head the charity of Christ and His forgiveness: for whatsoever ye do unto the least of my brethren, He said, ye do it unto me. The Christian life is wholly a ministry of reconciliation. Military service can find no place in it, for despite the 'alibi' and the fallacy of 'defending your country', there is a complete and pitiless break with your neighbour. The 'Christian soldier' can bear witness to nothing but this: that love, and therefore the Gospel, are inadequate and Utopian.

The Christian ethic therefore implies and demands conscientious objection.

Of course non-violence will appear to be folly in face of modern cruelty.[303] But the time-honoured acceptance by Christians of military cruelty is one of the decisive causes of today's barbarism. Must the Church continue to encourage and nurture that barbarism? We have the choice between folly and crime; but all hesitation disappears as soon as we sense, behind that folly, the shadow of the folly of God (I Cor. 1:25).

But the pacifist thesis may lead the Church to the Cross? It certainly will. It might also lead the Church to glory, whereas today, its Gospel falsified, the Church is without the Cross, and without glory.

So many people at present are preparing with great earnestness to 'defend' Christianity. I believe the more urgent thing is to live it.

REFERENCES

Preface

1. The Churches faced by their present Task (the record of a recent Œcumenical Conference at Oxford), p. 243.

Text

1. In Albert Camus' '*L'Homme Révolté*' there is an impressive anthology of modern glorifications of war.

2. War, of course, is only one aspect of collective murder and social sin; and certainly in peacetime also men are starved to death and left to rot in concentration camps. But any criticism that the book is silent over this would be beside the point; there is simply not the space here to go into all the problems which the Church is facing. In any case, the reader will see that I am by no means unaware of these things; I am far from thinking that it is only over war that Christians are in error.

3. *Revue de l'Evangélisation*, June 1950, p. 107.

4. *Cahiers de la Réconciliation*, September 1950.

5. Oxford, *Task*, 65.

6. 'The End and the Means', *Foi et Vie*, April 1948, pp. 218 and 221.

7. *Foi et Vie*, July 1950, p. 335.

8. Quoted by Chènevière, *Politique*, 55.

9. 'It is perhaps one of the great disgraces of our times that it should have needed the example of Gandhi to illuminate again this simple teaching of our Master, and that even this example often caused more derision among us than repentance' (Philippe Vernier, *Avec le Maître*, 1, 12).

10. Which certainly does not mean, as some would seem to think, that *in*effectiveness is the criterion of fidelity.

11. In his study on *Justice and Justification*, Karl Barth does not quote a single text from the Old Testament.

12. Paul Gliddon has justly remarked that there are extremely few people who would wish to be loved in this very special way! Hartill, *Way*, 40.

13. *Guerre*, 105.

14. *Servir*, 55-9.

15. Evidently it needs a Sartre to remind Christians that 'giving death is a matter of indifference to them, for they don't know what life is.' (*Les Mains Sales*).

16. Some argue from the fact that Jesus uses the word ἐχθρός (one who hates you) and not παλέμιος (the enemy in time of war) that he was referring to personal enemies not enemy soldiers. But πόλεμιος is never used in the New Testament, so ἐχθρός here clearly refers to both personal and national enemies.

17. Throughout the book this term is used to refer to all theories justifying war in certain circumstances and the Christian's participation in it.

18. Except for Gal. 2:11; but this is verbal, not physical resistance.

19. *Foi et Vie*, 1950, p. 329.

20. 'Every Christian community taken on its own is oecumenical (catholic) by definition, that is, united in solidarity with all the Christian communities which exist upon earth'. Barth, *Communauté*, 7.

21. *Refus*, 105.

22. R. Niehbuhr asserts that 'there is nothing in the gospels to justify non-violent resistance' (*An Interpretation of Ethics*, 196). Even if this were true, he would doubtless admit that there is also nothing in the Gospel justifying armed resistance. So allowing that the Christian must after all put up some resistance to injustice, should we not seek means as little as possible at variance with the Gospel? The fact that Jesus does not give explicit instructions on the manner of resisting evil-doers is no good reason for resisting them by criminal means. Abortion, sterilization, and genocide are not justified, either, by the sole fact that Jesus never spoke of eugenics!

23. *Guerre*, 50-52.

24. *New Testament Commentaries*, 2, 558.

25. Karl Barth gives this text a tendentious interpretation when he comments as follows: 'To take the sword means: to use for oneself one's power of killing, in an arbitrary and seditious manner.' He is drawing this subtle qualification from his own preconceived ideas, not from the text itself.

26. Because of Luke 9:3, where a scrip is referred to (for provisions), and from Matt. 10:10, I do not think the expression 'take a scrip' should be understood here in the sense, very common in Hebrew, of 'go into mourning.' But if this were so understood, in

the light of Matt. 11:21, it would be one argument the more for taking figuratively the word 'sword.'

27. This is the interpretation given by Calvin: 'In cryptic terms . . . taking the analogy of war, he warns them against unpleasant shocks and . . . the temptations they will have to pass through, and the fierce onslaughts in spiritual combats they will have to endure.' *Commentaries*, I, 660.

28. *Commentaries* I, 661.

29. *Guerre*, 62

30. This, in fact, is how Luther understands the episode: 'Jesus does not use his whip; the men retreat from their master before he strikes.' *Commentaries*, 29.

31. MacGregor, *Basis*, 19. See, for instance, Matt. 9:38: 'Pray ye . . . that he will send forth labourers into his harvest'; and compare Matt. 9:25.

32. The *Encyclopedic Dictionary* reveals that 200 men were needed every day simply to open and shut the doors.

33. Mark (11:18) states that 'the scribes and priests heard it, and sought how they might destroy him; for they feared him, because all the people was astonished at his doctrine.'

34. H. Bois (*Guerre*, 61) argues that Jesus, in 'whipping' the sheep and oxen, incontestably used violence. I wonder what our farmers would think of this; but in any case it is not even sure that Jesus actually struck these animals.

35. *Commentaries*, 2, 41.

36. *Commentaries*, 2, 41.

37. *Guerre*, 13.

38. *Commentaries*, 2, 518 and 685.

39. *Introduction to the New Testament*, Vol. 4, p. 10.

40. *Centenary Bible*.

41. Quoted in Strohl, *Substance* 353.

42. See Bainton, in Jones, *Church*, 75 ss.

43. *Foi et Vie*, April 1948, p. 222.

44. 3, 397.

45. 4, 281.

46. *Dieu nous parla*, 176.

47. *Institution Chrétienne*, Book 4.

48. It may be noted that I have deliberately chosen three episodes coming within the order of redemption, not of conservation.

49. Where, however, is the fulfilment of these Messianic prophecies? Modern Jews may say: you can see that Jesus was not the

Messiah because there are still wars. Traditionalist Christians may say: wars will only disappear in the Kingdom of God—and continue to take part in them; which is another way of denying that Jesus is the Messiah. The Christ has come, but His disciples still 'learn war,' as if the Messianic era had not yet begun. The early Fathers, however, claimed that in their time this prophecy had received its fulfilment, since Christians refused military service. Were they under an illusion?

50. I Sam. 1:14; Isa. 28:7; Ezek. 44:21; Dan. 1:8; Micah, 2:11.

51. II Kings 23:7; Jer. 2:20; 3:6-10; Ezek. 16:23; Hosea 1; 4:11-19; Micah 1:7.

52. II Kings 23:10; Isa. 57:5; Jer. 7:31; 19:5; Ezek. 16:15-19; 20:31; 23:37-39.

53. The so-called Apocryphal books of the Old Testament (Maccabees, etc.), which are almost contemporary with the New Testament, show even greater contrast: pitiless revenge and the massacre of enemies are the permanent *leit-motiv* here, without a trace of guilty conscience.

54. See my own study of David, which will clear me of any charge of succumbing to the Marcionite heresy.

55. See MacGregor, *Basis*, 126.

56. Translator's note: Cf. the lines in Blake's 'Jerusalem':
> 'I will not cease from mental fight,
> Nor shall the sword sleep in my hand . . .'

57. *Relevance*, 82.

58. See also: II Cor. 13:4; Gal. 2:20; 6:14; Col. 1:24.

59. Oldham, *Mission*, 236.

60. *Chrétien*, 413.

61. *Directives*, 13.

62. *Guerre*, 43-4.

63. *Réforme*, 3 February 1951.

64. *Commentaries*, II, 819.

65. *Commentaries*, IV, 201.

66. *Commentaries*, IV, 579.

67. Brutsch, *L'Apocalypse*, 160.

68. G. Dehn, *Anges*, 6.

69. See F. J. Leenhardt, *Servir*, 149.

70. In answer to those who deduce from Jesus' apparent silence on political problems that He was not interested in them, MacGregor gives a whole series of texts showing that 'without any doubt Jesus

foresaw the immense disaster for his compatriots which would result from their refusal to accept His own pacifist ethic' (Luke 13:1-9, 19, 41-44; 23:27-31). *Basis*, 64.

71. Using the word in its etymological sense: concerning the City.

72. G. Dehn, *Anges*, 2.

73. *Commentaries*, IV, 336 and 578.

74. *Commentaries*, IV, 581.

75. There were many former Jews in the primitive Christian communities. Through them the revolutionary spirit of the Zealots certainly penetrated into the Churches, some of whose members must have thrilled to this Jewish resistance. As we know, it was to be brutally crushed in A.D. 70 with the Roman destruction of Jerusalem. Most of the books in the New Testament were written in that period, and it would be very surprising if the Churches remained uninfluenced by the political obsessions of Israel.

76. G. Dehn, *Anges*, 3-5. In particular he quotes: Phil. 2:10; 3:20; Luke 22:25; Matt. 4:9; I Tim. 6:14-15; I Cor. 6:2 *et seq.*; I Peter 5:8-9 and 13.

77. *L'Etat*, 1.

78. *La Mission Historique de Jésus*, 65.

79. Loisy, *Mark's Gospel*, 348.

80. Dibelius, *Directives*, 19.

81. See Matt. 15:1; 19:5, 22:15-46; Luke 10:25; 20:4.

82. H. Roux, *L'Evangile du Royaume*, 223.

83. H. Roux, *L'Evangile du Royaume*, 247.

84. G. Dehn, *Le Fils de Dieu*, 191.

85. See also in Luke 22:25: '(they) *are called* benefactors.'

86. *Commentaries*, II, 373.

87. *Justice*, 10.

88. Matt. 7:29; Luke 6:36; Matt. 21:23; Luke 9:1; 10:19; John 10:18; Matt. 28:18.

89. *Servir*, 152.

90. *Commentaries*, III, 228.

91. *Justice*, 36.

92. *Communauté*, 22

93. See this witness in Eph. 3:10; 6:6-7; I. Tim. 6:1; Titus 2:10; I Peter 2:12:15; 3:1.

94. Goguel, *L'Eglise Primitive*, 589.

95. G. Dehn, *Anges*, 1.

96. M. Dibelius, *Etat*, 1-2.

97. M. Dibelius, *Etat*, 4 and 5.

98. *Directives*, 28.

99. Berdiaeff, *César*, 64.

100. G. Dehn, *Anges*, 16.

101. Cullmann explains very soundly the favourable judgment on the Roman State which Paul makes here: it was 'a State founded on Law. This is why the primitive Christian community does not protest against it until the disciple of Christ is summoned to recognise the Emperor as divine Lord and is forbidden to confess Jesus Christ as his only Lord. Otherwise the primitive Christian community exhibits extreme loyalty to the Roman State; for where it carries out the function proper to it, it is really a good State' (*Temps*, 145). But also there is no doubt that when Paul wrote this Epistle, 'he saw the State as a providential instrument thanks to which the Gospel could be preached: it was the Pax Romana which enabled him to make so many journeys. So Paul was proud of his status as "Roman citizen".' A. G. Knott, *State*, 7.

102. F. J. Leenhardt, *Servir*, 42.

103. *Institution*, IV, 237.

104. *Justice*, 38.

105. *Commentaries*, III, 230.

106. A. G. Knott, *State*, 10.

107. G. Dehn, *Anges*, 8.

108. M. Dibelius, *Etat*, 4.

109. *Servir*, 82.

110. Commentary on Romans 13:4.

111. 'It is a real paradox,' writes MacGregor, 'that our adversaries are so very anxious to see us imitate the transcendent God in His cosmic anger, and so dismayed to see us imitate the Cross of God incarnated in the man Jesus!' (*Basis*, 102).

112. *Temps*, 144. My italics.

113. The expression εἰς ὀργήν, in view of anger, confirms that the State is announcing the judgment it does not execute.

114. F. J. Leenhardt, *Servir*, 83.

115. Calvin, *Institution*, IV, 235.

116. See F. J. Leenhardt on this subject, *Servir*, 153.

117. *Servir*, 109.

118. *Justice*, 15.

119. See Cullmann, *Royauté*, 48.

120. 'The Christian of the first century,' writes M. Dibelius, 'lives as citizen of the Kingdom of God, and can thus renounce all the

rights of a citizen of this earth. Before this pagan State, which is alien to him, he can withdraw from his duties as citizen of this earth, when they are in contradiction with those of the Kingdom of God' (*Etat*, 25). This seems illuminating for the whole problem of war.

121. by Barth, Dehn, and others.

122. Barth, *Justice*, 15.

123. Cullmann, *Royauté*, 35.

124. 'The heavenly powers,' F. J. Leenhardt justly writes, 'are always for Paul more or less evil, in rebellion against God or his Christ; and Christ's work has had the effect of reducing them to impotence. It is hard to realise that these same powers preside over the destinies of the State which Romans 13 represents as conforming to God's will: a reconciliation with the State seems to have turned into a condemnation of it. These powers are nowhere seen playing a praiseworthy part. . . .' (*Servir*, 37-8).

125. O. Cullmann, *Royauté, passim*. 'By their submission to the Christ,' he writes, for example (in *Temps*, 141), 'the invisible powers have lost their evil character; they are now under Christ's rule and in His kingdom, *in so far* as they are subject to Him and do not try to withdraw from this subjection.' (My italics.)

126. *Servir*, 17-18.

127. *Justice*, 45.

128. *Anges*, 18, and see Oldham, *Mission*, 203: 'Under the form of authority over others, power bears in itself a demoniac element which tends always to pervert it. It would seem that one cannot trust sinful human nature with the use of power over others without its abusing that power. . . .'

129. What the scholastics called 'a just war' was by no means a war that was just in God's eyes, 'justified' in the Christian sense, but simply a war conforming to the rules of the feudal law of the time. Lentner has shown that the theory of the 'just war,' elaborated by Cicero as a puerile glorification of Rome's historic mission, was later, despite its pagan origin, 'adopted as deriving automatically from Christian moral theology' (*Juste*, 5).

130. It must nevertheless be acknowledged that some are at last rediscovering the Biblical perspective, and are using a firm, clear faithful language; this is a welcome change from the sickly flattery and worship of the State to which traditional theology had accustomed us. 'This kingdom of God we proclaim,' writes Martin Niemöller, 'is not superimposed on the powers governing the world

P

in order to let them exercise their power and use their force with impunity. The kingdom of God must expand, and that at the expense of the masters of this world. It challenges their authority and confronts them with the will of God which must be sovereign: it is the kingdom of the future, which is already coming nearer, while the kingdoms of this world are kingdoms destined to disappearance and already retiring. So it is not wise to advise Christians to adapt themselves to the existing powers, since they are in process of disappearing' (*Engagement*, 84). It is perhaps more than chance that the man showing such independence in face of the idol is the same man who has committed himself so fundamentally to opposing military service in Germany.

131. Cullmann, *Temps*, 143.

132. *Servir*, 7.

133. A fourth reason might be added. There are texts in the Old Testament which seem to justify the believer in disobeying the State in certain cases: e.g. Daniel (Ch. 1, 3 and 6) and Jeremiah (21:9; 27:12; 28:13; 36:31; 37:8, etc.); while the way in which David, driven from the court by Saul, 'went underground' without using his arms against his king, seems to have been one of the first manifestations of passive resistance to authority (I Sam. 21:27).

134. *Liberté des Cultes*, 1852, p. 363.

135. *Works*, 9, 702.

136. C. E. Raven, *Is War Obsolete?*, p. 65.

137. Strohl, *Substance*, 378. 'If you know with certainty,' Luther continues, 'that the prince is making an unjust war, you must obey God rather than men; you will not serve, and you will not make war; for you cannot have a good conscience before God. You will say, "But my Lord constrains me to it . . . I shall be condemned. . . ."' You must run this risk, and for God's sake let go all that shall be taken from you. God can return it you a hundredfold, as He says in the Gospel: "Whosoever shall leave house, wife, goods for my sake, shall receive it back a hundredfold." One is exposed to this danger equally in all the other situations in life where the authority would constrain us to commit injustice. But since God wills that we leave father and mother for His sake, we should *a fortiori* leave a prince . . .' *Ob Kriegsleute*). Unfortunately Luther does not explain when a war ceases to be just.

138. F. J. Leenhardt, *Servir*, 71-3.

139. My italics.

140. *Servir*, 79 and 80.

141. *Servir*, 15.

142. *Pourquoi*, 34.

143. *Royauté*, 26.

144. *Royauté*, 34.

145. Ibid., 42. One may wonder if that will have much effect on the State!

146. Barth, *Justice*, My italics.

147. 'The freedom left the Church for its preaching is the criterion of the State's fidelity to its function' (Ch. Westphal, *Responsabilité*, 332).

148. For instance, it might be maintained that calling up pastors for the army is such a hindrance.

149. *An interpretation of Ethics*, 171.

150. Strohl, *Substance*, 378.

151. Cullmann, *Temps*, 145-6.

152. Some recent events in Algeria, however, have shown how urgent it is to teach citizens to *disobey* the established authorities.

153. Articles 39 and 40.

154. Hagan, *Ethique*, 54.

155. Oxford, *Task*, 154.

156. These 5, *Foi et Vie*, July 1950, 357.

157. Institution, IV, 240.

158. Commentaries on Acts 4:19.

159. Commentaries on Acts 5:29.

160. *Liberté des Cultes*, 363-4.

161. 'The Church must judge the juridical system; and does so, obviously, according to the greater or less respect which the system shows towards the rights of man and the institutions created by God' (Ellul, *Droit*, 106). But Ellul does not specify how the Church, on a basis of the Revelation, will define these rights and institutions.

162. *Commentaries*, IV, 578.

163. Of course by 'God's order' I certainly do not mean what is commonly called a 'Christian social order,' a complete political and social system of which one could say it was Christian. But I do not believe that in the eyes of God the State is entitled to do everything. The error of a certain 'Christian socialism' does not excuse the still more serious error made by its adversaries.

164. Luther seems to have had something like this in mind: 'One must not resist the criminal abuse of power, one must endure it; but one must not approve it, nor support it' (Strohl, *Substance*, 363). And the Oxford Report: 'Taking account of the various historic

situations, the Church . . . will be called either to co-operate with the State, or to criticise it, or to oppose it' (*Task*, 151).

165. *Justice*, 29.

166. *Justice*, 211.

167. Oxford, *Task*, 122.

168. Luther, for instance, writes: 'The (prince's) hand which holds this sword, is no longer a man's hand, it is God's; and it is God, not a man, who hangs, quarters, beheads, strangles and makes war. . . . It is not I that bite and strike and kill, but God and my prince, of whom my hand and my life are the servants. . . .' (*Ob Kriegsleute*, 626).

169. This curious optimism is not avoided in Karl Barth's definition of the State, 'whatever the amount of human error and capriciousness manifested in it, not as a product of sin, but as a constant of God's providence and universal order, destined, for man's good, to be a counterweight to his sin: in a word, we are dealing with an instrument of divine Grace' (*Communauté*, 16).

170. 'The State's normal task,' says Barth, 'which it carries out also in wartime, consists internally as well as externally not in the destruction of human life but in its conservation and development. . . . Nor should anyone be in too much of a hurry to object that destruction as well belongs to its maintenance and development. As norm and rule, this biological wisdom has no place in ethics' (*Guerre*, 24).

171. The fate reserved in certain countries for 'enemies of the people' shows how important this point is.

172. 'Whenever man has claimed to be basing his rights on himself,' writes Ellul, 'it is on violence that those rights have rested. From then on there is no longer a distinction between violence and justice. Might is right' (*Droit*, 64).

173. 'The existence of the Christian community,' writes Barth, 'far from being a-political, is political in the highest degree' (*Communauté*, 7). 'It is impossible,' Oldham insists, 'to draw a perfectly neat dividing line between the Church's sphere and that of the modern State and its culture. By the sole fact of its existence the Church is a political factor of cardinal importance' (*Mission*, 205).

174. 'This ruinous distinction between public and private morals, which proclaims openly that Christ's teaching does not concern the conduct of States, has made modern Europe a Hell upon earth' (Dean Inge, *The Fall of the Idols*, 179).

175. 'A Christian', writes Luther, 'must be able to endure injustice,

not avenge himself, not appeal to Justice, for himself. But when his neighbour is concerned, he can and must ensure his neighbour's protection against all injustice *by all means*' (my italics). 'In a defensive war,' he says elsewhere, 'it is Christian, and consonant with the duty of loving one's neighbour, to kill enemies with a good conscience and do everything injurious to them in order to conquer them according to the usages of war' (Strohl, *Substance*, 336 and 378).

176. See H. Bois' prodigious effort (*Guerre*) to reconcile the Sermon on the Mount with the practice of war.

177. '. . . The same ecclesiastics who insist that the Church must take literally Jesus' words concerning divorce, refuse to accept anything but the "spirit" of His equally clear words on non-resistance to evil and loving one's enemies. . . . What is quaintly called the "spirit" of the Sermon on the Mount is very often its abrogation' (Mac-Gregor, *Pacifism*, 22).

178. A. Philip, *Le Semeur*, November 1927, 15.

179. R. Niebuhr, for instance, 'considers Jesus' morality as normative finally and in the last resort, but as inapplicable immediately for the ensuring of justice in a sinful world.'

180. H. Bois, *Guerre*, followed by Eberhard, *Pourquoi*.

181. Leuba, *L'Ordre de Dieu*, followed by La Gravière, Biéler, etc.

182. Romans 13 is referring to the *pagan* magistrate.

183. 'In the last analysis the evil to be put down by legislators and governments must be identical with the evil God condemns. Otherwise they would not be "servants of God" ' (Jean Héring, *Serviteurs*, 35).

184. Luke 7:6; Acts 10:23, etc.

185. F. J. Leenhardt, *Servir*, 81.

186. MacGregor, *Basis*, 98.

187. Voge, *Réalisme*, 335.

188. Visser t'Hooft, *Royauté*, 154.

189. The Hitlerian adventure shows where you get with the principle that the Scriptures leave the State a free hand in the political field.

190. Westphal, *Responsabilité*, 333.

191. Strohl, *Substance*, 346.

192. Barth, *Justice*, 31; see also pp. 38 and 47.

193. Cullmann, *Royauté*, 26.

194. Strohl, *Substance*, 372.

195. Oxford, *Task*, 133.

196. Oxford, *Task*, 151 and 154.

197. Ibid., 250.

198. Berdiaeff, *César*, 65-6.

199. Miéville, for instance, writes, following many others: 'The order of justice and law needs to be able to rest on force' (*Paix*, 34). But he seems to think force is never the negation of law, the destruction of justice. Pascal had more sense! (*Pensées*, Brunschwigg, 298).

200. e.g. H. Bois: 'The police are inseparable from the idea of constraint, legitimate, legal, regulated and organised. *The nature and degree of force used do not matter here, for that depends on the circumstances*' (*Guerre*, 25, see also p. 62).

201. Barth, *Justice*, 42.

202. F. J. Leenhardt, *Servir*, 87-88. It is striking the way the criterion of effectiveness is superimposed on his mind in the criterion of fidelity, while the crucial problem of means is left in the shade.

203. A great many Old Testament texts could be invoked here, severely condemning the excessive cruelty of certain kings and peoples: Exod. 3:7-10; I Chron. 12:8; Jer. 50 and 51; Ezek. 24; 25; 28:14-19; 31:11; 34:3; Joel 3:3-6; Amos 1; Mic. 2:1-2; 30:3; Nah. 3:19; 2:12-13, etc.

204. *Servir*, 62 and 64.

205. Matt. 28:19; Mark 16:15; Luke 24:47; Rev. 7:9, etc.

206. Barth, *Communauté*, 37-40.

207. *Communauté*, 52.

208. I have already refuted this idea when considering Rom. 13:4.

209. *Communauté*, 41.

210. Ibid., 54.

211. Luke 6:33-35; Mark 5:4; John 5:29; Rom. 2:7-10; II Cor. 5:10; Eph. 6:8; Gal. 6:9-10; I Thes. 5:15; II Thes. 3:13; Eph. 4:28; III John 1:1.

212. H. Roux, *L'Évangile du Royaume*, 240.

213. *Dictionnaire Encycl. Art. Noachiques.*

214. Christian advocates of military service seize on this text a little too hastily, I feel. If they use it to justify war, saying that God commanded the killing of those *responsible* for the war, I would remark that war ensures the massacre of the innocent, while the guilty usually escape. If they invoke the solidarity of peoples with their leaders to sanction the slaughter of peoples because of those who lead them, they are justifying mass exterminations of entire countries. In fact, those who try to apply this commandment to war are faced by a superhuman task: they must strike down the guilty

without the innocent, and also refuse absolutely to listen to this indiscreet question—aren't there some guilty on your side too?

215. Here is Pomeyrol's Thesis IV: 'The Church's message to the world is founded on all the Bible says about the life of human communities, notably in the Ten Commandments and the Biblical teaching on the State, its authority, its limits . . .' (*Foi et Vie*, 1950, 337). Article 39 of the Confession of La Rochelle is equally categorical.

216. Calvin, *Opera*, 9, 694.

217. Chenevière, *Calvin*, 84.

218. Calvin, *Opera*, 28, 107.

219. Calvin, *Constitution*, IV, 219.

220. Chenevière, *Calvin*, 104.

221. Ibid., 173.

222. Calvin, *Institution*, IV, 201.

223. Chenevière, *Calvin*, 242.

224. Ibid., 176.

225. *Dictionnaire*, *Encycl.*, *Art. Assyrie*, para. 8.

226. 'The commandments once given to the people of Israel, reaffirmed and reinterpreted by Jesus Christ, offer sufficient guidance (to those who live by the Scriptures) for them to be able to tell what is their real duty in a given situation, at least if they are personally obedient in their consciences to God's sovereignty' (Visser t'Hooft *Semeur*, January 1943, 86).

227. See in particular Exodus 20:5 and 12.

228. Jean Héring sees in Commandments 5 to 9 'the criterion whereby the State which is in accord with God's will can be distinguished from the State which is theologically unacceptable' (*Serviteurs*, 38). But we have to discriminate not only between different categories of State but also between the orders they all give which must or must not be obeyed.

229. Some Lutherans, it is true, are today returning to a more Calvinist position. 'No one, either child or adult, should be obliged to do anything whatever that would be against God's clear commandment' (Berggrav, *Staat*, 13).

230. Chenevière shows very aptly that the modern State's secularisation derives not from the Reformers but from St. Thomas.

231. Ellul justly condemns this error of Calvin's: 'To try to create a law valid for all starting from God's law, and still more from the Gospel, is undeniably a heresy, for it assumes that non-Christians can accept God's will and live like Christians' (*Droit*, 9). But Ellul

would certainly reject the opposite heresy as well, whereby Christians should resign themselves to obeying the actual law, without making any value judgment on it in the name of the Revelation. The truth is between these two errors. God's Law is neither the basis nor the content of the Law, but its criterion.

232. Quoted by Chenevière, *Calvin*, 241.

233. Ibid., 89.

234. On this subject see Peter Barth, *Contribution*, 45.

235. *Misère*, 79.

236. *Mission*, 232.

237. *Réforme*, 31/1/1953, p. 1.

238. 'The word used by John 18:40, to describe Barabbas the "robber" is very often used by Josephus to describe the revolutionary armed zealots' (*MacGregor*, Basis, 65).

239. A. Knott, *Times*, 11.

240. Notably Luther (in his small catechism), Calvin, Nyegaard, de Robert.

241. 'Of course it is always defensive! Holy simplicity'!

242. *La Voie Sainte*, 12. My italics.

243. *Cours de religion Chrétienne*. The second proposition is easier said than done.

244. *Vers Dieu*, 22.

245. *Je suis le Seigneur ton Dieu*, 2nd edition, 61.

246. Mark 2:4 confirms this extensive interpretation, as indeed does the whole New Testament.

247. in I Peter 2:13, the authorities are designated by the term κτίσις, creature. It can be seen from this that Peter is reacting against the tendency to idealise the Roman State on the authority of Romans 13, the very text which he is inspired by, and which he is here amending.

248. R. de Pury, *Catechism*, 8th edition, 74.

249. Ibid. Why should this not apply to the State as well?

250. 'All the political activities of the kingdoms of this world have in the last resort but one aim: to preserve men's lives, and thereby give them the chance of hearing the message of salvation' (Niemöller, *Engagement*, 86).

251. *Commentaries*, II, 247.

252. Quoted in *Christianisme social*, 1950, 355.

253. *Pensées*, Brunschwigg, 743.

254. *Connaître*, 19.

255. I doubt if those who would justify war in such a way would

argue from the death penalty as practised in totalitarian countries.

256. *Calvin*, 278.

257. *Instit. Chrét.*, IV.

258. In March 1545, Chenevière tells us, Calvin had an ordinance adopted by the small Counsel of Geneva obliging magistrates to attend divine service regularly 'to give the people a good example of going to the sermon' (*Calvin*, 288). So magistrates were exempt from the sixth commandment but not the fourth!

259. *Guerre*, 12.

260. Ibid., 35.

261. I do not claim to deal exhaustively with the subject of the death penalty, but only to refute the idea that it is legitimate in the view of the Scriptures.

262. In any case the second sentence cannot be turned into a juridical principle confirming the *lex talionis* without leaving out of account the first: 'Put up thy sword . . .' 'For it is just the defensive sword which comes here under Jesus' condemnation' (MacGregor, *Basis*, 30). The context (the legions of angels), suggests rather that Jesus' words are an echo of his own internal conflicts: He had refused to start a Messianic war, because He had learnt to consider war as fundamentally incompatible with His Gospel.

263. *De Idolatria*, 19.

264. *Commentaries*, III, 230.

265. For instance, Barth can write: 'That the State participates in the murderous nature of the present century appears very plainly in the fact that according to Romans 13 he beareth the sword' (*Justification*, 42). But is Barth speaking of the State as it is, or as God would permit it to be?

266. The word ἄρχων must be translated in this sense in two other New Testament texts where there is no possible ambiguity: Luke 12:58 and Acts 16:19. And it was the term used to designate the judges in Ancient Greece (Fustel de Coulanges, *La Cité Antique*, 210).

267. See Matt. 27:26; Acts 16:22 and 35:22-24.

268. Cf. Luke xviii, 6.

269. Cullmann acknowledges that 'these two texts should not be explained independently of each other' (*Temps*, 145).

270. See H. Monnier, *Objection*, 581.

271. I Cor. 6 illustrates what G. Dehn writes: 'The Christian community lived as far apart as possible from the State. The question of participating in a public service in the State, or even in military

service was wholly outside the horizon of the ancient community'
(*Anges*, 4).

272. F. J. Leenhardt admits the difficulty of pronouncing on this
problem (*Servir*, 75).

273. *Institut. Chrét.*, IV, 211.

274. It is doubtless in this perspective also that we must understand what might seem impertinence towards Pilate and his court in
Jesus' words to the second robber crucified with Him: 'Verily I say
unto thee, Today shalt thou be with me in Paradise' (Luke, 23:43).
If this statement does not expressly condemn the death penalty, it
does implicitly cast doubts on its legitimacy; for it emphasises the
relativity of human justice; after this Christians can only recoil in
horror at the idea of putting a man to death, even a criminal.

275. *Commentaries*, II, 170.

276. The constant confusion these prophets make between the two
orders of conservation and of redemption may be found most dis-
tressing by some modern theologians, who will perhaps even reproach
them for calling the kings and people of Israel to put their trust in
God for their protection by a genuine act of collective faith; but
then prophets are usually very bad theologians!

277. Barth is surely a little over-romantic when he says that it is
sometimes necessary to decide to go to war 'without regard for the
success or failure of the enterprise, or for the respective strengths of
the contestants' (*Guerre*, 33). 'For a living dog is better than a dead
lion' (Eccl. 9:4).

278. *Pensées*, Brunswick edition, 293.

279. Without even finding occasion to mention Christianity,
Pierre Boissier has stressed several times in a recent work *L'Épée et la
Balance*, that there is no common measure between war on the one
hand and morality, justice, and even law, on the other.

280. Niemöller, *Paix*, 345.

281. Quoted by Heering, *César*, 282.

282. Strohl, *Substance*, 363.

283. *Christianisme Social*, October 1950, 299.

284. In his *Open Letter to an Objector*, D. de Benoit describes the
Germans' massacre in 1944 of the village of Vassieux in Vercors,
and concludes that 'one must arm to drive out bandits, and so
avoid having other villages suffer the same tragic fate' (*Nouvelle
Revue de Lausanne*, December 1950). Unfortunately he forgets to ask
himself the only really important question: why did the Germans
massacre the villagers? Not having elucidated this vital point, he
cannot see that others with as much feeling and intelligence as

himself, and the same horror at an odious crime, can come to an exactly opposite conclusion; to try to drive out 'bandits' by arms is the best way of having other villages suffer the same tragic fate.

285. Even in 1943 Visser t'Hooft could write: 'I think of those who are fighting the masters of Europe, and many of whom, instead of resisting as much spiritually as politically, have let themselves be infected by the spirit of the jungle and use in their struggle the same methods as do their enemies' (*Misère*, 80).

286. *Défense*, 16.

287. Quoted by Goguel, Luther, 169.

288. *Guerre*, 112.

289. *Paix*, 45.

290. *Cahiers de la Réconciliation*, January 1952.

291. *Pourquoi*, 4.

292. *Paix*, 45.

293. Ibid., 46.

294. *Dagger*, 88.

295. A striking example of how hard it is to draw a line between lawful and unlawful war is to be found in Calvin's tergiversations on whether French Protestants might defend themselves by arms against their enemies, the Dukes of Guise. The day after the massacre of Vassy, he frankly encouraged and helped the Huguenots to organise their army, finding many fine pretexts, resting on great principles, to authorise such action. But quite soon afterwards, in April 1563, he wrote: 'I shall always recommend that arms be abandoned and that we should all perish rather than return to the confusions that have been experienced.' See on this subject, Chenevière, *Calvin*, 346, 349.

296. As it taught the German soldiers in June 1944 who were ordered to massacre the inhabitants of Oradour.

297. *Armée*, 38.

298. *Pourquoi*, 8.

299. The history of trade unions shows that in a fight to the death there are means more effective than murderous violence; in fact, every time in the last fifty years that the workers have resorted to violence, they have set back rather than advanced their emancipation.

300. *Guerre*, 17.

301. All the *real* advantages of military service, such as its being a school of discipline, civic spirit, self-sacrifice, and heroism, will be found again in the obligatory *civilian* service I should like to see;

as also in the general practice, organised by the State, of Gandhian non-violent resistance (Read: Corman, *Héroisme*).

302. Heering, *César*, 272.

303. 'The Christian's behaviour in the world will inevitably be considered as folly' (Niemöller, *Engagement*, 84).

BIBLIOGRAPHY

(The word in italics is used as abbreviated reference)

AMSTERDAM. Oecumenical Conference on the Church and International Disorder, 1948.

Karl BARTH. Justification divine et *Justice* humaine (Foi et Vie, Cahier Biblique, no. 5).

—— L'Evangile et la Loi, broch.

—— *Connaître* Dieu et le servir (Del. et Niestlé, 1945).

—— Les communautés chrétiennes dans la tourmente (Del. et Niestlé, 1943).

—— *Communauté* chrétienne et communauté civile (Roulet, 1947).

—— La *Guerre* et la Paix (Labor et Fides, 1951).

Peter BARTH. *Contribution* à l'éthique social du Calvinisme (Christ. Social, July, 1935).

Nicolas BERDIAEFF. Royaume de l'Ésprit et Royaume de *César* (Del. et Niestlé, 1951).

Eivind BERGGRAV. Le témoignage chrétien dans la vie internationale (Foi et Vie, August 1948).

—— *Staat* und Kirche in Lutherischer Sicht, Hanover, 1952.

La Bible Annotée. (Sandoz et Thuiller, Paris.)

S. BIDGRAIN. L'Eglise universelle en temps de guerre (Semeur, April 1940).

Marc BOEGNER. L'Eglise et les questions du temps présent (Je Sers, 1932).

—— La liberté de l'Eglise (Foi et Vie, 1938).

Henri BOIS. Jésus et la *guerre*, 1917.

Jacques BOIS. Le Christianisme et la guerre (Christ. Social, June 1932).

—— Politique et religion (Christ. Social, September, 1935).

—— Christianisme, Eglise et Etat (Semeur, May 1936).

Pierre BOISSIER. L'Epée et la *Balance* (Labor et Fides, 1953).

Ch. BONNAMAUX. Non, à l'objection de conscience (Le Guide).

BONNARD, Guisan, Girard, Biéler. L'Eglise, l'*Armée* et l'objection de conscience (Labor et Fides, 1951).

Jean BOSC. Le protestantisme dans le siècle (in Protestantisme français, Plon, 1945).

Jean Bosc. *L'Eglise* et la vie politique (Les Deux Cités, 1946, 1).

Jean Bresch. Le chrétien et l'Etat (Christ. Social, July 1928).

Emil Brunner. Les fondements d'une morale chrétienne (Oxford, 1927).

Ch. Brutsch. L'Apocalypse (Labor, 1941).

Jean Calvin, *Commentaires* sur le Nouveau Testament (Meyrueis, 1854).

—— *Institution* de la religion chrétienne (Ed. Budé, 1936).

Albert Camus. L'Homme Revolté (N.R.F.).

Bern. Charbonneau. Rendez à César . . . (Foi et Vie, March 1951).

Mad. Chasles. La Guerre et la Bible.

Marc. Chenevière. La pensée *politique* de Calvin (Je Sers).

Eug. Choisy. Calvin, éducateur des consciences (La Cause, 1925).

Henri Clavier. De quelques traits et *postulats* sociaux du calvinisme (Christ. Social, May 1936).

Communauté. Divers auteurs (Je Sers, 1942).

Paul Conord. Le *chrétien* et la societé d'après le néo-calvinisme (Christ. Social, May 1936).

—— Principes d'une *sociologie* chrétienne (Je Sers, 1936).

—— Le problème de l'Ethique chrétienne (Conseil Oecumenique, Geneva 1945).

Consultation théologique à-propos de l'objection de conscience (Christ. Social., April 1935).

Dr. Corman. Une école d'*héroïsme*: les campagnes non-violentes de Gandhi (Stock, 1951).

Oscar Cullmann. La *royauté* du Christ et l'Eglise (Foi et Vie, Christmas 1941).

—— Le Christ et le *temps* (Del. et Niestlé).

Gunther Dehn. Anges et autorités.

—— Le Fils de Dieu (Marc, Je Sers, 1936).

G. Deluz. La justice de Dieu (Romains, Del. et Niestlé).

Martin Dibelius. Les *directives* sociales dans le Nouveau Testament (Christ. Social, July 1935).

—— L'Eglise en face de *l'Etat* au premier siècle.

Dictionnaire Encyclopédique de la Bible (Imprimeries Réunies).

Suz. de Dietrich. Le Dessein de Dieu (Del. et Niestlé, 1945).

La Documentation catholique. (Bonne Presse.) Special number on conscientious objection (23 April 1950).

Donnedieu de Vabres. Introduction au problème de l'Eglise et de l'Etat (Semeur, February 1936).

—— L'ésprit protestant et les relations internationales (Christ. Social, May 1936).

André DUMAS. Abordons les questions économiques en chrétiens (Semeur, November 1943).

H. EBERHARD. *Pourquoi* je ne suis pas objecteur de conscience.

Jacques ELLUL. Le fondement théologique du *Droit*.

—— Le réalisme politique (Foi et Vie, December 1947).

ESPRIT. Révision du pacifisme (February 1949).

M. GANDHI. Autobiography (Ahmedabad, 1927).

—— La Jeune Inde (Stock).

Jean GASTAMBIDE. Notes sur la Guerre Sainte (Semeur, January 1940).

Grillot de GIVRY. Le Christ et la *Patrie* (Paris, 1924).

Maurice GOGUEL. Les premiers *temps* de l'Eglise.

—— L'Eglise primitive.

—— Vie de Jésus (Payot, 1932).

Elie GOUNELLE. La défense du *Droit* (Christ. Social, October 1930).

—— A propos de la consultation des théologiens (ibid., April 1935).

—— Le Chrétien et l'Etat (ibid., January 1940).

GRAHAM. Conscription et conscience (Fischbacher, 1935).

J. M. H. Des ordres de la Création chez Brunner (Christ. Social, April 1951).

E. J. HAGAN. *L'Ethique* social du calvinisme écossais (Christ. Social, 1935).

Adolphe HARNACK. L'essence du christianisme (Fischbacher, 1907).

Percy HARTILL. Into the Way of Peace (London).

G. J. HEERING. Dieu et *César* (1933).

—— Le christianisme et la guerre (Réconciliation).

—— K. Barth et le problème de la guerre (Réconciliation, March 1952).

Jean HÉRING. *Serviteurs* de Dieu (Revue d'Historie et de philosophie religieuse, Strasbourg, 1950, I).

H. J. IWAND. Du sollst nicht töten! (Bekennende Kirche, December 1950).

André JACQUES. Refus de légitimer le meurtre (Réconciliation, February 1947).

—— Eglise et désordre international (Christ. Social, October 1949).

J. S. JAVET. Dieu nous parla (Hébreux) (Je Sers, 1941).

J. JEZEQUEL. Les Eglises devant la conférence du désarmement (Christ. Social, January 1932).

Rufus M. Jones, etc. The *Church*, the Gospel and War (Harper, 1948).

André Jundt. Le Christianisme et la vie nationale d'après Luther (Bull. Fac. Theol. Paris, May 1940).

A. G. Knott. The Christian in the *State* (London, 1942).

—— The *Times* of Jesus (London, 1948).

E. La Graviere. La conscience chrétienne et la guerre (Terre humaine, 1951).

Jean Lasserre. Service militaire (Semeur, March 1932).

—— David, prophète de Christ (La Bible jour par jour, February 1949).

—— Le Chrétien et la politique (Société Centrale).

—— Tu ne *tueras* point (Réconciliation, January 1950).

Elie Lauriol. La jeunesse et la guerre (Christ. Social, January 1932).

—— La fabrication et le *commerce* privé des armes (ibid., March 1933).

—— Nos Eglises contre la guerre (ibid., August 1950).

F. J. Leenhardt. Le christianisme primitif et la guerre (ibid., October 1930).

—— Le chrétien peut-il *servir* l'Etat ?

Lentner. La "guerre *juste*" et la politique de paix de l'empire romain (Réconciliation, May 1953).

J. L. Leuba. Tu ne tueras point, dans: L'Ordre de Dieu (Del. et Niestlé).

Marc Lods. L'Eglise du IIIme siècle devant le service de l'Etat (Bulletin Faculté Théologie Paris, December 1950).

R. P. Lorson. Un chrétien peut-il être *objecteur* de conscience ? (Le Seuil, 1950).

—— Défense de tuer (Centurion, 1953).

—— Le Catholicisme devant les problèmes modernes de la guerre et de la paix (Routes de la Paix, December 1952).

Martin Luther. Propos de table (Ed. Sauzin, Montaigne, 1932).

Walter Luthi. L'Evangile de Jean (*Comm.*) (Del. et Niestlé, 1942).

G. H. C. Macgregor. The *relevance* of the impossible (London, 1941).

—— The New Testament *Basis* of pacifism (Clarke, 1940).

—— The bases of Christian pacifism (with Dodd).

Jacques Martin. Comptes rendus de ses procès (Réconciliation, 1932 and 1935).

Pierre Maury, L'Eglise et le Monde (Conf. Oecumen., Oxford, 1937).

—— Les Autorités et l'Autorité (Les Deux Cités, 1946, 2).

Roger MEHL. Le message politique de l'Eglise (Christ. Social, April 1946).

—— Valeurs chrétiennes et valeurs humaines (Semeur, November 1940).

—— Communauté, histoire, *Droit* (Semeur, April 1943).

H. L. MIÉVILLE. Autour du problème de la *paix* (Lausanne, 1950).

Arnold MOBBS. Enquête sénatoriale américaine sur les marchands de *canons* (Christ. Social, September 1935).

Henri MONNIER. A propos de l'objection de conscience (Semeur, July 1934).

Wilfred MONOD. Désarmement et opinion publique (Christ. Social, October 1931).

—— L'Eglise et l'objection au service militaire (Christ. Social, August 1933).

V. MOUCHON. La Nation et l'Etat dans la Bible (Christ au XXme siècle, 18 February 1943).

Reinhold NIEBUHR. Christianity and Power *Politics* (Scribners 1948).

—— L'Ordre de Dieu et le désordre actual (Christ. Social, January 1948).

Martin NIEMÖLLER. Que peut l'Eglise pour la *Paix*? (Christ. Social, August 1950).

—— L'*Engagement* du chrétien dans le monde présent (Cahier du Renouveau, 1953).

OLDHAM et VISSER T'HOOFT. La *mission* de l'Eglise dans le monde (Je Sers, 1937).

OXFORD. Les Eglises devant leur *tâche* actuelle (Je Sers, 1937).

Daniel PARKER. *Refus* de la guerre (Le Chambon, 1949).

Jacques PASCAL. Les exigences de Dieu à l'égard des nations (Christ. Social, April 1939).

Hubert PERNOT. Pages choisies de l'Evangile (Belles lettres, 1925).

André PHILIP. Le christianisme et la *Paix* (Je Sers, 1931).

—— Le christianisme et la guerre (Christ. Social., June, 1932).

—— Dieu et César (Christ. Social, May 1936).

Roland de PURY. La fin et les *moyens* (Foi et Vie, April 1948).

Leonard RAGAZ. La communauté nouvelle (Réconciliation, March 1934).

—— Cieux nouveaux, terre nouvelle (Réconciliation).

—— Le message révolutionnaire (Del. et Niestlé, 1945).

H. ROHRBACH. The Problem of Christian Illegal Resistance (Union Seminary Quarterly, June 1952).

Cam. ROMBAUT. Compte rendu de son procès (Réconciliation, 1932).

Henri ROSER. L'objection de conscience, affirmation de l'Esprit (Christ. Social., October 1930).

—— Servir, comment? (Réconciliation, February 1935).

—— L'objection de conscience à l'heure actuelle (Christ. Social, December 1949).

—— Responsabilité politique du chrétien (Foi et Vie, March 1951).

—— Le chrétien devant la guerre (Labor et Fides, 1953).

Hebert ROUX. L'Evangile du Royaume (*Matthieu*; Je Sers, 1942).

C. G. RUTENBER. The *Dagger* and the Cross. (Fellowship of Reconciliation, 1950).

Ch. RUYSSEN. Encore l'objection de conscience (Christ. Social, December 1930).

J. W. STEVENSON. Pour une chrétienté désarmée au sein d'un monde en armes (Réconciliation, September 1935).

R. P. F. STRATMANN. Jésus-Christ et l'Etat (Castermann, 1952).

H. STROHL. La *substance* de l'Evangile selon Luther (La Cause, 1934).

E. THURNEYSSEN. Le Sermon sur la Montagne (Foi et Vie, cahier 3).

André TROCMÈ. La résistance du chrétien (Réconciliation, November 1946).

—— L'Europe se prépare-t-elle à une guerre sainte? (Christ. Social, March 1947).

—— Les tâches actuelles de L'Eglise pour la paix (ibid., April 1947).

—— Le service de l'Eglise au sein du désordre international (Christ Social, December 1949).

—— Conditions d'une résistance française à la guerre (ibid., March 1951).

Jean VAN LIERDE. *Pourquoi* je refuse d'être soldat.

Philippe VERNIER. Comptes rendus de ses procès (Réconciliation, 1933 et 1934).

Alexandre VINET. La persécution et le Droit (Nouvelles études evangéliques, Paris, 1862).

— Le devoir de la soumission mutuelle (Nouveaux discours, Lausanne 1913).

—— Liberté religieuse et questions ecclésiastiques (Paris, 1854).

VISSER t'HOOFT. *Misère* et Grandeur de l'Eglise (Labor, 1943).

—— *Défense* de l'Europe (Cahier du Renouveau, 1953).

—— *Droit* naturel ou droit divin (Semeur, January 1943).

—— La *Royauté* de Jésus-Christ (Roulet, 1948).

Maurice VOGE. Le *réalisme* politique (Christ. Social, August 1946).

—— Le sacre de la guerre (ibid., January 1952).

Charles WESTPHAL. Responsabilité politique de l'Etat (Foi et Vie, July 1950).

E. WOLF. De l'*éthique* social du lutheranisme (Christ. Social, July 1935).

BIBLICAL INDEX